Reforming the Higher Education Curriculum

Internationalizing the Campus

Edited by
Josef A. Mestenhauser
and
Brenda J. Ellingboe

AMERICAN COUNCIL ON EDUCATION ★
ORYX PRESS ★
Series on Higher Education
1998

The rare Arabian Oryx is believed to have inspired the myth of the unicorn. This desert antelope became virtually extinct in the early 1960s. At that time several groups of international conservationists arranged to have 9 animals sent to the Phoenix Zoo to be the nucleus of a captive breeding herd. Today the Oryx population is over 1,000 and over 500 have been returned to the Middle East.

© 1998 by The American Council on Education and The Oryx Press
Published by The Oryx Press
4041 North Central at Indian School Road
Phoenix, Arizona 85012-3397

Published simultaneously in Canada
Printed and Bound in the United States of America

∞ The paper used in this publication meets the minimum requirements of American National Standard for Information Science—Permanence of Paper for Printed Library Materials, ANSI Z39.48, 1984.

Library of Congress Cataloging-in-Publication Data

Reforming the higher education curriculum: internationalizing the
   campus / edited by Josef A. Mestenhauser and Brenda J. Ellingboe.
      p. cm.—(American Council on Education/Oryx Press series on
   higher education)
   Based on papers presented during a faculty/student seminar held at
   the University of Minnesota in spring 1996.
   Includes bibliographical references and index.
   ISBN 1-57356-173-8 (alk. paper)
   1. Education, Higher—United States—Curricula—Congresses.
   2. International education—United States—Congresses.
   3. Curriculum change—United States—Congresses.   I. Mestenhauser,
   Josef A.   II. Ellingboe, Brenda J.   III. Series.
   LB2361.5.R43   1998
   378.1'99'0973—dc21
                                                       98-22654
                                                          CIP

CONTENTS

CONTRIBUTOR
BIOGRAPHIES

EDITORS

Josef A. Mestenhauser has devoted his entire career to international education as a teacher, researcher, administrator, office director, international student counselor, and consultant. He has published more than 80 documents, including books, monographs, articles, and book chapters on educational exchanges, international studies, transfer of knowledge, cross-cultural relations, leadership development, cultural change, educational reform, and professionalism. He is a three-time holder of senior Fulbright grants in the Philippines, Japan, and Czechoslovakia. He was president of NAFSA (the Association of International Educators) and ISECSI (the International Society of Educational Cultural and Scientific Interchanges). Presently, he is at the University of Minnesota, Twin Cities Campus, where he teaches international education courses in the Department of Educational Policy and Administration, and coordinates international education programs for the College of Education and Human Development. His honors include the Marita Houlihan Award for Excellence in International Education. He holds a doctorate from Charles University in Prague and a doctorate in political science from the University of Minnesota.

Brenda J. Ellingboe is a Ph.D. candidate in higher education at the University of Minnesota, Twin Cities Campus, and a teaching assistant for Dr. Josef Mestenhauser in the Educational Policy and Administration Department's comparative and international development education concentration. At the University of Minnesota, she completed an M.A. in educational policy and administration with graduate minors in public affairs and educational psychology. She also earned an M.A. in Latin American studies (with a concentration in international education) from U.C.L.A. Her research interests include the internationalization of colleges and universities, career planning for college students, strategic planning and leadership models in higher education, faculty development issues, organizational communication, and intercultural communication. Her work experience includes both academic and student affairs positions at two universities, three private colleges, and one community college.

CONTRIBUTORS

John J. Cogan is a professor in the Departments of Curriculum and Instruction and Educational Policy and Administration at the University of Minnesota, Twin Cities Campus. He earned Master's and Ph.D. degrees from The Ohio State University. He is a specialist in comparative and international development education and in social education. He was a senior Fulbright researcher at Hiroshima University in Japan during 1982-83, and he has lived, studied, and researched in Asia, Europe, and the Caribbean. He consults internationally on issues of educational policy and reform and has published widely in these areas.

Susan Lewis English has worked with minority and international students and scholars in the U.S., China, Europe, and West Africa. She received her Ph.D. in higher education from the University of Michigan, Ann Arbor, looking at college influence on international competence. Her administrative experience includes leadership of English language programs and coordination of research projects. She is author of the textbook *Say It Clearly*. As a consultant, she has conducted training for Peace Corps volunteers and AID scholars, as well as evaluation of educational and social programs. She was a senior Fulbright scholar and remains an active member of the Fulbright Association.

Kerry Freedman is an associate professor in the Department of Curriculum and Instruction at the University of Minnesota, Twin Cities Campus. She received her Ph.D. from the University of Wisconsin in Madison. Her research focuses on questions concerning the relationship of curriculum to art, technology, and culture. Professor Freedman has published widely, including in the *Journal of Curriculum Studies, Studies in Art Education, Educational Technology Research and Development,* and *Journal of Art and Design Education.* Her most recent book, coedited with Fernando Hernández, is on international art education.

C.Victor Fung is an assistant professor in the Music Education Department, College of Musical Arts, Bowling Green State University, Ohio. After receiving a Ph.D. in music education from Indiana University in Bloomington, he has taught at the University of Minnesota, Twin Cities, and Hong Kong Baptist University in Hong Kong, China. His research interests include multicultural music education, psychology of music, and philosophies of music education in the East and the West. He has presented his research at professional meetings in Asia, Europe, and North America.

Peter H. Graham is a professor in the Department of Soil, Water, and Climate at the University of Minnesota, Twin Cities Campus. He received his Ph.D. in soil microbiology from the University of Western Australia in Perth. His research interests build on experience in India and Colombia and emphasize biological nitrogen fixation and the sustainability of crop and pasture production. Topics covered include plant selection for enhanced N_2 fixation in beans and soybeans, soil acidity constraints to nodulation and nitrogen fixation, and the microbial biodiversity of prairie soils. His research has a focus toward Latin America, and many of the students involved are from Colombia, Ecuador, and Mexico.

Arthur M. Harkins is a professor in the Department of Educational Policy and Administration at the University of Minnesota, Twin Cities Campus. His interests are in future studies. He is the recipient of multiple research grants for his Story-Tech projects. His latest articles examine knowledge-based learning and the emergence of cross-national knowledge-based workforces. Two of his latest books are *Education: A Time for Decisions* and *Cultures of the Future*. His research and development work is based on techniques associated with Japanese Shinto. He was awarded a Fulbright grant to lecture in Brazil and Central America, and is a frequent radio and television commentator on change and the future, preparing the strategic workforce, and the future of human capital development. He holds a Ph.D. in sociology from the University of Kansas.

Marion L. Lundy Dobbert is a professor at the University of Minnesota, Twin Cities Campus in educational policy and administration. She received her Ph.D. in anthropology and educational policy studies from the University of Wisconsin. She teaches courses in the anthropology of human learning, which focuses on non-Western cultures, general systems theory, ethnographic methods, and North American young people of different cultural backgrounds. Her recent research focuses on multi-ethnic initiatives in inner city schools; the folklore of U.S. small towns; the application of mammalian and nonhuman primate learning, cognition, and play to human learning; and the application of dimensional analysis to the study of patterned human behavior.

Michael F. Metcalf is professor of history and executive director of the Croft Institute for International Studies at The University of Mississippi. He received his A.B. from Harvard and his M.A. and Ph.D. from Stockholms Universitet. A specialist on early modern Scandinavian political institutions and eighteenth-century Swedish political parties, he served as professor of Scandinavian history (1977–1998) and as assistant vice president for international education and director of the Institute of International Studies and Programs (1993–1998) at the University of Minnesota. Previously, he served as director of the University of Minnesota's title VI National Resource Centers in Western European Studies (1981–1986) and in International Studies (1988–1997).

R. Michael Philson has extensive experience in international education, having taught at universities in Fiji, Thailand, Taiwan, Korea, and Japan. He presently serves as executive director of Foreign Language and Culture Exchange, a nonprofit organization based in Ann Arbor, Michigan, that is involved with teacher training and assisting colleges and universities to initiate Chinese language programs. His current research interests include the role of technology in higher education, international faculty collaboration, and international exchange. He has received degrees from Washington University, the University of Wisconsin in Madison, and the University of Hawaii. He is currently a doctoral candidate in higher education at the University of Michigan, Ann Arbor.

Herbert L. Pick, Jr., completed both his undergraduate degree in sociology and his Ph.D. in experimental psychology at Cornell University. He is currently a professor in developmental psychology at the Institute of Child Development at the University of Minnesota, Twin Cities Campus. His primary interests are in perception and perceptual development and in cognitive development. He has a long-standing ancillary interest in Soviet and Russian psychology and has spent sabbatical leaves teaching and doing research in Holland and Uganda.

Harvey B. Sarles is professor of cultural studies and comparative literature at the University of Minnesota, Twin Cities Campus. He works in the context of American Pragmatism following G. H. Meade. His research interests include the study of human nature, language and the body, meaning and identity, and teaching as a dialogue. He received a Ph.D. in anthropology from the University of Chicago.

Barbara Turlington is director of international education at the American Council on Education (ACE) in Washington, D.C. Before coming to ACE, Ms. Turlington taught international relations and comparative politics at Connecticut College and Mount Holyoke College and was dean at Hampshire

College. She did undergraduate work at Swarthmore College and the American University of Beirut and graduate work at Columbia University. She serves on the Board of Directors of the Alliance for International Educational and Cultural Exchange, the Association for Consortium Leadership, and the National Council for Evaluation of Foreign Educational Credentials. Her publications include *Internationalizing the Undergraduate Curriculum: A Handbook for Campus Leaders*, with Sarah Pickert, and *Spreading the Word: Improving the Way We Teach Foreign Languages*, with Robert Shoenberg.

FOREWORD

by Barbara Turlington
Director of International Education,
American Council on Education

B usiness, political, and education leaders throughout the world agree that the events of the past decade require us to change the way we approach our work, our relationships with other nations, and our teaching and research. Higher education leaders recognize that the changing international environment, the global economy, and such worldwide issues as environmental degradation and public health call for changes in curricula and teaching methods. Judging by the increasing number of conferences, workshops, policy statements, and studies, the internationalization of American higher education is a major issue in higher education today. Yet, few would claim that our colleges and universities are very far along in providing an adequate international and intercultural background for all their students.

"If our nation and its people are to prosper in the new environment of the 21st century, our colleges and universities must truly become institutions without boundaries," according to a statement by the American Council of Education's Commission on International Education (American Council on Education, 1995). "Unless today's students develop the competence to function effectively in a global environment," the Commission noted, "they are unlikely to succeed in the 21st century." The Commission also insisted that international education must be made "more democratic and universal," not just the province of specialized language and area studies programs. "*All* undergraduates need exposure to other peoples, languages, and cultures. . . . Parochial and provincial outlooks are not options for today's undergraduates." Higher education leaders "must rethink what is taught, how it is taught, where it is taught, and who teaches it."

The University of Minnesota is one of a small number of higher education institutions that has taken a systematic look at ways in which the university can become truly international—through curriculum, study and internship abroad, participation in development projects, and linkages with institutions in other countries. The essays presented in this volume, which are based on a faculty/student seminar, focus on ways to internationalize the curriculum across the diverse programs and instructional units of a major university.

The essays analyze what is missing in the university's commitment and ability to provide every student with competence in cross-cultural communication and the international knowledge and skills required for jobs and professions in the twenty-first century. They examine issues of effective teaching, including the use of new technologies. They analyze the problems associated with promoting meaningful interdisciplinary approaches within a structure dominated by disciplinary departments. They argue the strengths and weaknesses of the "infusion" approach to internationalizing the curriculum. Several essays challenge the assumptions often made about what students need to know and how they can acquire that knowledge.

The essays also offer practical descriptions of what can be done to inject an international focus into certain disciplines—ranging from the study of cognitive development to agriculture, language, and music. They make a strong case for ensuring that every student, in every major, achieves an international perspective. Moreover, they tackle the difficult—and crucial—issue of how to evaluate the effectiveness of various approaches and programs. A final chapter demonstrates a method for assessing the degree of internationalization within units of the university and the factors that encourage or discourage that process.

Taken together, the essays provide both a theoretical framework for considering what makes internationalization succeed and several working models of effective approaches. These essays are designed to provoke discussion among faculty and administrators in all sectors and at all levels of higher education. They will provide useful guideposts for any college or university attempting to incorporate this important dimension into its curriculum and its culture.

REFERENCE

American Council on Education. (1995). *Educating Americans for a World in Flux: Ten Ground Rules for Internationalizing Higher Education.* Washington, DC: American Council on Education.

ACKNOWLEDGMENTS

This book is a tribute to the cooperation that made it possible. That cooperation occurred within the six departments of the University of Minnesota's College of Education and Human Development, across collegiate lines, through interdisciplinary domains, and with central administration as represented by the office of the vice president for international education. This book is based on papers presented during a faculty/student seminar on the subject of internationalization of the curriculum. Robert Bruininks, former dean of the College of Education and Human Development and presently the executive vice president of the University of Minnesota, and Michael Metcalf, assistant vice president for international education and director of the Institute of International Studies and Programs, deserve the first credit for their visions, for their support of a university-wide discourse on a faculty-student seminar on internationalization of the curriculum, for their recognition of the need for interdisciplinary perspectives, for their respect for the somewhat unorthodox learning environment, for their confidence in the outcome, for their interest in bringing international education to a higher level, and, indeed, for the international ambiance itself.

Whatever contribution this publication will make to the field of international education is due to Susan Slesinger, senior vice president, and John Wagner, senior editor of The Oryx Press, and to the reviewers of the early draft at the American Council on Education, whose unfailing confidence in seeing these papers published will hopefully spark another round of interest in higher educational reform toward internationalization. Special thanks must go to Barbara Turlington, director of international education at ACE, for contributing the foreword. An intellectual debt is owed to Sven Groennings,

Richard Lambert, Humphrey Tonkin, Maurice Harari, and Barbara Burn, whose pioneering works have inspired many papers in this volume.

To list the names of everybody who made this publication possible would marginalize everybody. To mention only a few would neglect the wisdom and contributions of the many. I want to err on the side of inclusiveness. It may be best to describe how the book came to be because more than a collection of individuals were involved in its making.

It started with a few faculty who met in an informal and totally unstructured "seminar" to discuss only one agenda—how to make the curriculum more intentionally relevant for students. Given the turmoil in many disciplines and given the decline of public support and confidence in higher education, this seminar was welcome evidence of the willingness of individuals to come together to seek improvements in this troubled field of human activity. We soon discovered how much we had to share, and how seldom such occasions arise. We also had fun debating, arguing, and clarifying assumptions; the traditional lightbulbs were being turned on everywhere for the cost of a few refreshments and the audiotapes needed to save these discussions for future use. The outcome was a spontaneous recommendation to do it again, only this time more formally, over a longer period of time, and with written papers.

We were just then beginning to prepare for a major change from a quarter to a semester system during which all courses had to be redesigned. Why not use these papers as a guide for this process and why not aim to include international dimensions in the new courses? Then one idea led to another. With such a distinguished assemblage of faculty, why not open this faculty seminar to a few graduate students across several colleges in the university and enroll them in a companion seminar for credit, using the papers as texts? And why not encourage faculty to present papers of publishable quality? This kind of structure is also symbolic of what an international education curriculum should be: striving toward learning synergy.

The next acknowledgment goes to those faculty members who took time out of their busy schedules to spend eight Friday afternoons attending this joint faculty/graduate student seminar: Kerry Freedman, Marion L. Lundy Dobbert, Arthur M. Harkins, Michael F. Metcalf, Herbert L. Pick, John Cogan, C. Victor Fung, Peter Graham, Earl W. Morris, Harvey B. Sarles, Kay Thomas, and R. Michael Paige.

The graduate students who attended the seminar in the spring of 1996 were all M.A. or Ph.D. students and, like the rest of the faculty, came from several disciplines, colleges, and countries. Three additional international visiting scholars also attended this experimental seminar, thus contributing further to its synergy. In addition to attending and participating in the seminar, listening to the faculty presenters, and providing high level discourse, the graduate students also wrote a collaborative paper based on their own perspectives on curricular internationalization. I want to acknowledge them individually: Mohammed Almosa, Margaret Dexheimer-Pharris, Brenda J. Ellingboe, Elina Erdavletova, Soaring Hawk, Miki Horie, Myrza Karimov, Vera Kovacovic, Imed Labidi, J.P. Maier, Lyudmila Oreshkina, Jessica Voigts, Yelena Yershova, and John Zuber.

The individual papers were forwarded to 85 administrators, deans, and faculty members chairing semester conversion committees for their consideration. The following staff members helped to coordinate the efforts within the Institute of International Studies and Programs and produced the final papers that comprise 10 of the chapters in this book. Thanks go to Kathy Allen, Natalie Griffith, Gayla Marty, Kathleen Sellew, and Kristin Zibell.

Four additional authors were invited to complement these original seminar papers. Two colleagues from the University of Michigan contributed chapters on evaluating outcomes of internationalization (Susan Lewis English) and on using technology to enhance internationalization (R. Michael Philson). The chapter on internationalization of the curriculum through foreign languages was contributed by Michael Metcalf, assistant vice president for international education and professor of history in the College of Liberal Arts. Finally, Brenda J. Ellingboe, the coeditor of this book, was invited to summarize her own comprehensive master of arts thesis on a five-college case study at the University of Minnesota. The response of these individuals to a belated request to write chapters and their quick entry into the conceptual framework of the theme are very much appreciated.

Within the College of Education and Human Development, the program was endorsed, supported, and monitored by a very active Committee on International Education for which this seminar was the most important part of its charge, namely, to internationalize the curriculum.

Finally, much appreciation and credit is extended to two associates who are also full-time Ph.D. students in Educational Policy and Administration and who participated in the graduate seminar. Jessica C. Voigts provided administrative assistance for the Committee on International Education and edited a collaboratively written student paper from that seminar. Brenda J. Ellingboe led discussion during the student seminar, coordinated this book project, and prepared the book prospectus for the publisher. Without their help, support, enthusiasm, and attention to both the trees and the forest, this project could not have been undertaken and completed.

Josef A. Mestenhauser

I also wish to acknowledge several individuals who have inspired me and without whom I could not have completed my master's thesis or the chapter in this volume that is based upon it. I want to thank three professors at the

University of Minnesota for teaching and designing several comparative and international education courses: Josef A. Mestenhauser, John J. Cogan, and R. Michael Paige. The knowledge that I gained in their courses and seminars, the interest I have in global issues, and the commitment I hold for this field were greatly strengthened after enrolling in Comparative and International Development Education courses at the University of Minnesota in 1994 and being a teaching assistant.

I would like to recognize Josef Mestenhauser's own lifetime commitment to internationalization efforts for colleges and universities throughout the world and his indefatigable efforts here at the University of Minnesota as the former director of the Office of International Education and presently as professor of Educational Policy and Administration and coordinator of international education activities in the College of Education and Human Development. Josef Mestenhauser was the visionary catalyst and the initiator for the spring 1996 faculty/student seminar on internationalization of the curriculum. Because of his belief in this book, which is indeed a symphony of synthesis, this work can be shared with others to inform higher education institutions worldwide about the campus portraits of international education.

I would like to acknowledge three other people who guided my educational process during the research and writing stages for my master's thesis. Thanks to Caroline Sotello Viernes Turner, associate professor in Educational Policy and Administration, whose creatively designed Case Study for Policy Research course served as the basis for my choosing the case study research method and enabled me to develop an interview schedule, a timetable for my fieldwork, and a thorough outline for my case study. Thanks to Mark A. Holman, a Ph.D. candidate in higher education policy at the University of California at Berkeley, for critical feedback on an early draft. Finally, I want to acknowledge Assistant Vice President Michael F. Metcalf for giving me helpful feedback on the original thesis and for being interested in implementing many of the findings.

Brenda J. Ellingboe

INTRODUCTION

by Josef A. Mestenhauser

Most research universities like to think of themselves as "world class" institutions. What makes them world class, however, remains to be revealed. Instead of addressing that question, this volume is devoted to one aspect of global education, the curriculum, the formal instruction from which students graduate and attain qualifications needed for employment.

Although "international education" has been the subject of legitimate scholarly interest since the end of World War I, its focus has been generally subsumed under an undergraduate major in international studies or foreign languages, or under a few courses within the liberal studies requirements. Occasionally, one would find "international education" in educational exchange programs, or in some disciplinary concentrations, such as international business, where it might be a sub-specialty of a sub-specialty. Although several attempts to raise international education to higher levels have been made since the late 1940s, its popularity has experienced a roller coaster ride of rapid rise and fall, driven by the Cold War; by various international crises, such as the hostage or oil crisis; or by the laissez-faire forces of demand and supply. When rapid growth seemed just around the corner, other educational or political priorities have pushed international education aside, as happened when the International Education Act of 1966 failed to be funded, a failure that had devastating effects on academia. When we were considering a suitable title for this book, we quipped half seriously that it should be "International Education on the Verge." Indeed, during the past 50 years, it was on the verge of becoming the mega-trend, but never quite made it. We hope to contribute to turning the corner and crossing that "verge." The chapters in this book challenge past practices and assumptions: that international education is for a few specialists, that one or two courses taken during the first two years of college in liberal studies requirements suffice for the rest of the students, that a few international materials taken usually from one country in the same disciplinary domain are adequate to provide upper class "majors" with global perspectives, that technical competence is all that is needed by students in sciences and technology, and that students pick up international sophistication from daily exposure to mass media.

PURPOSE AND SCOPE

These chapters also challenge the three principal assumptions that have caused this field to be undervalued, underappreciated, and conceptually confusing: (1) that knowledge is universal and "portable" from anywhere to anywhere; (2) that academic freedom determines what faculty teach and how they teach it; and (3) that students as consumers have choices that excuse universities from changing their cafeteria approach to the curriculum. If we really mean what we say about our graduates being able to practice their professions in any country of the world, then we need to send a different message than the one we have sent so far. A substantial number of required courses should be internationalized, and institutions of higher learning should develop a motivational policy designed to encourage students to enroll in specialized elective courses devoted to international and intercultural education, supplemented with study abroad, study of foreign languages beyond the required course seat time, and the cultivation of intellectual, professional, and personal associations with people from other cultures. We also need to tell them that working with other people, understanding them, and perhaps even having empathy for them does not mean losing our own identity because the very concept of identity itself has a global dimension. The supermarket approach to the curriculum does not tell students what we as educators expect of them at the conclusion of their studies.

Since the Cold War ended, international education has experienced a revival. But literature about the field—though rich and plentiful—remains, as one scholar puts it, accidental, occasional, and random. The literature of international education is programmatically unintegrated with the rest of the curriculum, is out of touch with the unprecedented change toward globalization of knowledge and of professions, and appears to be dominated not by solid theoretical foundations, but by pragmatic concern with international competitiveness. Whatever conceptualization is evident, it is often based on a variety of assumptions that are generally neither questioned nor explicit. Such assumptions include the belief that we are already "doing it," that what we do not know does not exist, and that selected information about other countries is adequate. Moreover, our assumptions continue to target the few under-graduate students who think they want to enter international (as opposed to domestic) careers and who do not know enough about either to recognize that these lines have been blurred beyond recognition.

The contributors to this book address such major issues as the nature of knowledge (who produces it, how it is taught and applied), whether adding international dimensions requires higher levels of analyses and some new intellectual skills, whether there are different levels of knowledge ranging from basic to intermediate to advanced, how these levels are to be integrated and "mainstreamed" in the disciplinary and degree programs, and, depending on how these issues are resolved, what major changes and reforms may be necessary to graduate our students with global skills and perspectives. The basis of educational reform is usually a recognized "knowledge gap" between what is and what we would like to have in the future. Recognition of what is requires much self-reflection and meta knowledge of how and why we are where we are. A look at the future from which our goals are formulated depends on how we see the continuity between the present and the future. If the "gap" is simply random content- oriented knowledge about other countries from the same discipline, the corresponding reform is merely an addition of that information from within the same paradigm. That appears to be the solution that most of our colleges and universities selected. If, on the other hand, the "gap" is a way of thinking, knowing, and reasoning, then the gap is enormous; it transcends several paradigms and requires major change in the curriculum

The chapters in this book illuminate these and other issues; they invite a public discussion that will begin to make the many tacit assumptions about international education explicit, they demonstrate faculty experiences with efforts to internationalize courses, and they provide a practical guide for others who wish to follow suit. Above all, this volume urges its users to consider international education for the majority of graduates and to view it as func-tioning at various levels of sophistication. Consistent with the field itself, the authors address all ranges of the gap, and recommend several levels of depth from elementary to intermediate to advanced.

These chapters are more than a collection of insights. They are a challenge to universities and their faculties and students to discard naive assumptions and practices, to finally recognize the urgency of curricular changes, to accept the complexity of international and global education, and to raise the field to its cutting edge.

The University of Minnesota faculty/student seminar, on which the chap-ters of this book are based, was an invitational affair that sought papers from experienced faculty in any of seven areas: (1) utilization of foreign study, research, and teaching; (2) initiation of international courses; (3) collaboration with foreign scholars; (4) participation in educational reform in this country and elsewhere; (5) utilization of international students or U.S. students with study abroad experiences; (6) planning and implementation of degree programs or concentrations with international emphases; and (7) experiences with teaching courses that may be presumed by definition to be "international." This book differs from others by being less focused, more expansive, and somewhat eclectic. Unlike many other publications that are focused and directed toward the same theme, this one reflects the broad and multidimensional nature of international education. Contributors could select any one of seven broad areas to write on and still remain in international education. In other words, this book is evidence that international education can be approached from several perspectives, depending on where one stands, how long one stands there, and what equipment one uses to observe the field.

The same diversity of views prevails when we consider the goals of international education. When inviting faculty to present papers to the seminar, we identified seven objectives: (1) to facilitate discussion about the internationalization of the curriculum; (2) to influence the semester conversion process; (3) to lay the foundation for a book-length manuscript for possible publication; (4) to promote interdisciplinary, intercollegiate, and multidimensional cooperation among faculty; (5) to integrate study abroad and international student and scholar programs into the process of internationalizing the curriculum; (6) to use international knowledge and experiences of faculty; and (7) to strengthen all international programs at the University of Minnesota. These goals also reflect the multidimensional nature of international education. Consequently, the focus of this book is internationalization of the curriculum—about which faculty responded within their own experiences, disciplinary orientations, and international perspectives.

Consistent with the complex nature of international education, the chapters address multiple topics, such as internationalization of selected disciplines, organizational arrangements, social psychological and learning perspectives, curricular theories, epistemology of internationalized programs, and conceptualization of "international" knowledge. Similarly, they represent ranges of views from, for example, an argument about the impossibility of internationalization, to a view that internationalization is already outdated and has been replaced by a new framework of the technological future.

This book is not comprehensive. A number of significant topics remain to be covered in future publications, especially the economic factors, the administrative leadership, and the politics of internationalizing the curriculum. However, the individual chapters are relevant, provocative, controversial, and insightful because they address the question that every college and university must eventually confront: Are we preparing our students to live and work in the global setting of the future? We can no longer hide behind simplistic and undocumented assumptions about what constitutes a "world class" university and do more of the same without a sophisticated debate about the nature of knowledge. This book is thus a timely publication for universities, transnational institutions in their own right, that are now entering into a new era of post-Cold War international cooperation based on knowledge.

This book stems from a thorough reassessment of the literature written on internationalization in a wide variety of disciplines, viewpoints, and geographic perspectives. While many books, articles, and conference papers address university attempts to internationalize, the curriculum has remained hidden from public discourse and untouched by faculty and students.

AUDIENCE

This book targets a large and varied audience. First, it will be of great interest to most faculty members in social science and the humanities because the concepts defining studies of societies and cultures concentrate in these areas. Among teachers of the defining disciplines—anthropology, psychology, communication, political science, and education, to mention a few—the book seeks to initiate a broad discourse about the international and intercultural dimensions of these fields and about the interdisciplinary contributions these teachers can make to international education of their students. Second, the book will appeal to university administrators—from department heads to deans and central administrators—who are called upon to make difficult decisions about curricular matters in international education without necessarily having any academic preparation or intercultural experiences themselves. Third, the many people associated with international educational programs will also find this book useful. Occupying supportive roles as advisers, counselors, directors of programs, employees of nongovernmental organizations, administrators of government international programs, and foundation executives, these international education professionals make international educational exchanges work. Through their activities, knowledge, and experiences, they contribute toward formal and nonformal instructional programs. Fourth, the book will assist the directors of various international programs in universities and colleges to better manage and supervise their programs. Since international education is about knowledge, these professionals, who are often members of faculties, should see their roles less as administrators and more as knowledge brokers and knowledge managers. This book addresses these potential and prospective roles. Fifth, the book will also interest the domestic and international students for whom international education is intended. It asks them to stop being passive recipients of what they are being offered and to make an equal contribution of their own as partners in their learning with each other and with their faculty. Finally, since international education is a global affair, the book addresses not only American educators and academic professionals, but the same categories of people anywhere in the world where international education is found—and that is around the globe.

The creation of the European Union has given new impetus to this field internationally, and the Organization of Economic Cooperation and Development (OECD) has endorsed several studies on how different countries respond to internationalization. This book will make a contribution to this growing global discourse in areas that have not been addressed by existing literature.

CHAPTER SUMMARIES

The papers submitted and additionally requested for this compendium fall into three parts. Part 1 contains four conceptual papers about the nature of international education and its curriculum. Part 2 offers seven chapters that address specific fields of study, including the integration of foreign languages across the curriculum and the use of technology in professional development of faculty. Part 3 comprises two chapters devoted to evaluation of international competencies and programs.

Part 1, "Internationalization for the Twenty-First Century"

Josef Mestenhauser's provocative opening chapter seeks to place the curriculum of international education into its systemic perspective. By walking the reader through the relatively brief history of international education, he shows that the field has not yet been taken seriously and he challenges the assumption that the main focus of the field should be on training a few students in international and area studies and foreign languages as future international affairs specialists. For all other students, the antecedent of international education is presumed to be limited knowledge about other countries; most universities offer students only one or two international or multicultural courses as part of their liberal studies requirements. The complacency of universities in addressing the larger issues ignores the fact that all our graduates will work in a global setting, that professional people will have to be prepared to practice their professions in any country of the world, and that the main involvement in international affairs will not be by "international affairs specialists" but by scientists, engineers, agriculturists, network builders, and information experts. Mestenhauser's "uncommon" perspective challenges current university education, its content, its knowledge acquisition process, its expected outcome, its process of application, and, indeed, the nature of knowledge itself.

Chapter 2 by Kerry Freedman focuses entirely on the curriculum and its change from traditional to international. Freedman's conditions of a curriculum based on perspectives design, conception about learning, and selection of content, reflect underlying assumptions about the appropriate purposes and practices of education. The chapter has three parts. The first part is a brief summary of four influential theoretical approaches to curriculum. The second part discusses a common model of learning in higher education and its limitations for an international curriculum. The third part concentrates on two types of content that could be used in conjunction with a recommended approach to design and conceptualization of learning to promote internationalization of the curriculum. Work currently being done could be improved and could lead toward the transformation that would prepare our graduates to better deal with conditions of interdependence.

Chapter 3 by Marion L. Lundy Dobbert will jolt the minds of those who believe that an infusion of some international materials across the curriculum can produce more internationally and globally educated graduates. Using the analytic point of view of modern structural anthropology, Lundy Dobbert demonstrates the impossibility of such internationalization, which she calls a form of academic shorthand and cultural reductionism. Her argument centers on two structural factors that militate against such a format of internationalization: (1) a discipline-based curricular organization and (2) the need for more time to teach new content. Using her anthropological concepts, she explains that internationalization can occur only by changing the interaction patterns within the university. This, she claims, could be done primarily by having large numbers of students and faculty involved in long-term and significant immersion experiences that include an intense study of foreign languages and detachment from one's own culture for extended periods of time. Her proposals might be shocking to the "traditionalists," but a delight to international exchange professionals, language teachers, and some funding sources.

Chapter 4, by the well-known anticipatory sociologist Arthur M. Harkins, is even more provocative than the preceding chapters. Harkins believes that internationalization has already been outlived by post-internationalism and post-culturalism. He discusses these concepts within a large conceptual framework that offers different technologically driven organizing principles for human system designs, development, and operations. These new systems will be largely self-regulated by the desire of the clients for knowledge and information. He sees current academic practices as being one or two steps behind changes already occurring in industry and government, and suggests that academics risk becoming redundant when they seek to satisfy educational need on the basis of doing more of the same. He calls for a shift from teaching, research, and service to research, demonstration, and assessment. The result would be self-evolving learning organizations. Based on this analysis, Harkins describes a possible curriculum of the future that looks nothing like present curricular practices. Future learning opportunities will be, according to Harkins, independent of time and distance, and will also become increasingly accessible to large masses of people presently excluded from such opportunities because the new education will also be independent of the costs associated with the privileges of the well-to-do.

Part 2, "Multidisciplinary Perspectives on Curricular Change"

Part 2 contains seven chapters that address internationalization of the curriculum in specific disciplines or areas of study. The first section of Chapter 5 by Michael F. Metcalf is intended for policymakers at colleges and universities, foundations, and government agencies whose attention over the past several years has been called to the expansion of the role of foreign languages in the undergraduate curriculum. The second section follows from the first and presents the movement toward content-based curricula in language instruction, as well as the languages across the curriculum movement (LAC) and instruction in languages for special purposes. The third section concerns itself with the resources that administrators need to implement content-based courses and LAC on their campuses.

Chapter 6, by Herbert L. Pick, Jr., is devoted to teaching about cognition, and includes a discussion of the development of such cognitive processes as how we think, reason, perceive, remember, and solve problems. Since the study of cognition is essentially thinking about thinking, it is difficult to transcend the boundaries of one's own thinking to gain objectivity and perspective. Pick's examination of how thinking goes on in people from different social and cultural milieu offers a possibility to discover ways of thinking and reasoning that we may not have imagined from our own limited cultural perspective. Pick divides his chapter into two sections. The first provides examples of how cultural practices influence cognitive processes. The second section provides a theoretical view of thinking that was developed by Russian psychologist Lev Vygotsky in the late 1930s. Pick spells out several implications of this theory for the curriculum.

Chapter 7 by John J. Cogan is a strong defense of the concept of infusion of international materials into the curriculum, as compared to developing new courses. This chapter is based on the personal experiences of a well-known curricular scholar who has made several partially successful efforts to internationalize the curriculum. These experiences have led Cogan to become a strong advocate/curricular activist in the area of infusion, which he defines as integration of examples of research and other scholarly works into assigned readings, lecture illustrations, actively collected ancillary course materials, and student assignments. He believes that students and faculty must see themselves connected both personally and professionally to the wider world if they are to be active players in it in the next century. By highlighting his own experiences, Professor Cogan challenges students and faculty to become involved in the world.

Chapter 8 by C. Victor Fung provides a refreshing approach to music as a mind-opening experience. By linking music education with the psychological concept of open-mindedness, Fung suggests that music has both universal and nonuniversal qualities. The universals are the worldwide use of music and its positive affect on people. The nonuniversal aspects are various musical systems, elements, and philosophies that are based on the various cultures and the behavior of people in them. With reference to the curriculum, Fung discusses three approaches to organizing an international music curriculum: cultural-geographic, musical, and topical.

Chapter 9 by Peter Graham covers the field of agriculture, which has always claimed to be substantially internationalized. Graham presents another challenge to those involved in the curriculum in soil sciences and agronomy. Drawing on his extensive experiences primarily in Latin America, Professor Graham suggests that population changes and already accomplished internationalization of agriculture will necessitate further changes in the nature and content of these two fields as they are now taught. Some of his examples complement Cogan's infusion approaches in Chapter 7. Graham also sees many possibilities for long distance education.

Chapter 10 by Harvey B. Sarles adds another distinguishing feature to the kaleidoscope of curricular approaches: study about how others see us. Professor Sarles proposes a practical way of introducing American students to global thinking by rethinking the notion of America with newly arrived international students in a brief mini course. Sarles' chapter is both a specific course proposal and a conceptual framework for teaching American Studies with a comparative and cross-cultural perspective. His proposal is not one-sided. While international students have a need to understand this country in a variety of ways, American students, studying together with the internationals, will learn to see their own experiences through new and expanded lenses.

Chapter 11 by R. Michael Philson discusses the use of technology to enhance international education. The chapter begins with three important points that have often been neglected in today's fascination with the rapid development of electronic technologies: (1) dramatic changes are not limited to the past five years; (2) predictions for the future are difficult to make accurately; and (3) traditional educational institutions are slow in responding and adapting to changes that are already here. As a consequence, much of the electronic development is taking place in the private sector, and tends to be dominated by the hard sciences and business. Philson's chapter discusses, in three sections, the interface between campus efforts at internationalization, and the use of information technologies in higher education. Philson concludes with recommendations for faculty and administrators interested in using the new tools for furthering faculty international competencies.

New technologies can be used to develop virtual universities, teach entire courses and degree programs electronically, and allow access to education to those presently excluded. As one user quoted by the author stated, these technologies provide the user with a dramatic affective and motivational implication for learning, and a seductive sense of being in a global community.

Part 3, "Evidence, Evaluation, and Outcomes of Internationalization"

The two chapters of Part 3 of this book deal with the questions of when and how we know that the goals of internationalization are accomplished. The demand for outcome-oriented learning is making its way to universities and colleges, where current assumptions about outcome have been dominated by enrollments in major and minor fields, the number of courses with titles implying that something international was taught, and the grades received in all of them. In Chapter 12, Susan Lewis English challenges these assumptions by presenting evaluation as an appropriate means to understanding and guiding the internationalization of higher education. She asks readers to refocus their view of internationalization through at least three types of evaluation lenses: (1) outcome assessment, (2) process evaluation, and (3) program review. She distinguishes between "research" and "evaluation." Because research is no longer being supported by foundations and government agencies, evaluation studies are that much more needed in higher education at a time when virtually everything is being questioned, outcomes are being doubted, and contradictory assumptions are being made. In addition to citing her own research on internationalization, English illustrates the link between theory and practice by using the 1995 research agenda for the internationalization of higher education that was produced by the Association of International Education Administrators.

Chapter 13, written by this book's coeditor, Brenda J. Ellingboe, paints a portrait of one university's divisional strategies to internationalize its curriculum, leadership, and personnel. The chapter summarizes Ellingboe's Master's thesis, which was a case study of five colleges within one large public research university. Ellingboe devotes most of the chapter to describing results based on interviews with faculty, deans, directors, and central administrators. Her study reached five major conclusions: (1) it identified the rationales used to explain the internationalization; (2) it found nine distinct sources of resistance to internationalization; (3) it discovered several encouragement factors; (4) it pioneered a six-stage attitudinal assessment scale for measuring readiness for internationalization; and (5) it provided explanations of differences in intercollegiate and intracollegiate attempts to internationalize colleges. Ellingboe also conceptualized lessons learned from this case study, and made key recommendations that may be helpful to other colleges and universities facing similar obstacles and wide variations of stakeholders' interests.

CONCLUSION

Interest in internationalization, its defense and advocacy, and concentration on the curriculum are the common threads of this book. This volume focuses on the importance of culture as a major variable, the significance of communication in the classroom, the use of electronic media in the future of international education, the need to use a variety of conceptual and cognitive frames, the importance of disciplinary knowledge as a basis for internationalization as well as for interdisciplinary approaches to international education, and the need to involve and connect faculty in international activities. The fact that international educators need to keep justifying their activities—continuously for about 50 years now—is evidence of the failure of our universities to recognize international education as a major goal and to mainstream it throughout the disciplines and academic programs. During these decades, universities depended on soft funds, and when they ran out, the programs were seriously affected. Privately run educational institutions are now providing formidable competition to established institutions. As Arthur Harkins indicates in Chapter 4, only those who can adjust to the global changes will survive. But for this to happen, there has to be a serious discourse about the nature, character, role, and importance of the curriculum in international education as a multifaceted, multidimensional, and interdisciplinary field. This book is both evidence that such a broad discourse has not yet occurred, despite many valiant efforts, and incentive to help it take place.

PART 1

· · · · · · · · · · · ·

Internationalization for the Twenty-First Century

CHAPTER 1

Portraits of an International Curriculum

An Uncommon Multidimensional Perspective

by Josef A. Mestenhauser

INTERNATIONAL EDUCATION AS METAPHOR

Over the past 50 years, international education has enjoyed varying degrees of prominence on the agenda of higher education. It has been defined as a mega-goal that drives other educational goals, as a scattering of international programs and projects, and as a simple addition of international content courses already in existence. While the literature on international education is voluminous, it tends to focus on programs and projects. Internationalization of the curriculum has received relatively minor attention, and then primarily in connection with the three areas that have defined international education since its inception in the late 1940s: foreign languages, international studies, and the so-called liberal/general education requirements of undergraduate degree programs.

This chapter will focus instead on international academic programs and courses—which are, after all, the primary reason why domestic and international students pursue disciplinary majors to prepare themselves for careers that will span beyond the millennium. Universities make lofty pronouncements intended to assure students and other clients that they are indeed "world-class institutions," that they enroll many international students, that they send students abroad to study, and that they encourage faculty involvement in global intellectual cooperation. Their lists of international accomplishments are often long and impressive. Yet their claims frequently lack conceptual and theoretical foundations and hide the fact that international and minority students are not well-integrated and that only a few students and faculty actually study or conduct research abroad. My own experience, as well as empirical evidence, highlights the gap between what is being said and what is actually happening. I believe that this gap is perceptual. Resistance to internationalization is often a result of conceptual confusion about what international education means—a lack of answers to such questions as: For whom is international education intended? How is it to be taught? Who is to teach it? How can it be integrated with other educational programs? Whose responsibility is it? What balance should there be between "international," "disciplinary," and "domestic," and what educational outcomes are expected from that education?

Associated with these questions are three other troublesome issues. First, there does not appear to be any significant, self-reflective discourse about international education and its role in higher education. Second, there seems to be an implicit understanding that international education is for a few international specialists, while the average student receives only a small dose—one or two courses in the lower division of undergraduate education. Third, the literature on international education is either timid or silent about the field's complexity; international education is multidimensional and multidisciplinary because its concepts and theories come from many disciplines and cultures and because it has several levels of analysis. Furthermore, its variables come in elementary, intermediate, and advanced levels of conceptualization. This chapter is not, then, a critique of what is being or is not being done, but a call for a larger debate. It argues that international education deserves consideration as an important educational mega-goal that should permeate the entire educational system and that should be accorded much more conceptual and theoretical complexity than it has been.

The major theme of this chapter, analyzing international curriculum as metaphor, was inspired by one of the best books available on internationalization of the curriculum, *Group Portrait* by Groennings and Wiley (1990). Actually, it was not much of a group portrait. Of the 36 academic disciplinary associations that were invited to contribute chapters, only eight did so. Of these eight, one, geography, came not to be internationalized, but to internationalize others. Most of those who did come were "alternates." Those originally invited were the disciplinary professional societies, who were asked to contribute chapters to *Group Portrait* from the mainstream of established "traditional" scholarship. Completely missing the point, the societies delegated the task to international specialists within their disciplines, who were, for the most part, already converted internationalists. In real life, this is the general pattern of internationalization; rather than being addressed as a whole, only the discipline's "international specialization," which often turns out to be a subspecialty of a subspecialty and whose courses are mostly electives, is addressed. The quality of the portraits was also uneven, ranging from exceptionally clear to blurred. Because the book was interdisciplinary, it was, to our knowledge, not reviewed by disciplinary journals, and it did not sell well either. While most professional associations did not respond, two, economists and anthropologists, declined the invitation on the grounds that they were already international and thus their attendance would be redundant.

The use of metaphor is a method of explanation (Morgan, 1986) particularly interesting to international educators because virtually every international or cross-cultural explanation implies an analogy as its principal method of analysis. An analogy explains one phenomenon by another and is explicit or implied whenever we include another country or culture in our thinking, even though we may be unaware of making comparative judgments. Comparative analysis and comparative thinking are the heart of the field, and yet the literature on internationalization of the curriculum seems to confuse comparative research methodology and comparative thinking as an intellectual competence (Asia Society, 1976; Bogner, 1994; Bond, 1988; Bornstren and Pittman, 1992; Gerlach, 1990; Oyen, 1990; Schriewer and Holmes, 1990; and Sarles, unpublished paper, n.d.). As a result, the dominant concern is with the number of countries to be included in comparative analysis and with the use of a traditional research methodology that is suitable to the way we study a particular phenomenon. The "other culture" is usually a context in which the disciplinary methodology functions. Comparison is more than research methodology; it is an intellectual skill, like critical or creative thinking, that is yet to be understood as a significant tool for analysis and an essential outcome of international education. Gardner (1993) addressed this concern when he described comparative thinking as the capacity for analogical/metaphorical thinking. He regards analogical thinking as an important intellectual skill of the second order, not as important as his seven "intelligences," but much more important than other intellectual skills. On the other hand, Ennis (1996) does not mention comparative thinking in any relationship to critical thinking. The closest to an analogy is his concept of analogical argumentation, in which the "arguer offers another case on which it is assumed there is an agreement on conclusion" (p. 306). The value of such argumentation rests on assumed *similarity* regarding either facts or values.

I'll return to that subject later; now let me use the portrait metaphor as a way to explain international education itself, specifically, internationalization of the curriculum. Of the many issues associated with comparative thinking, three stand out. First, a well-chosen metaphor can not only be "seen" in writing or "heard" in lectures, it also has a visual effect. When we use "portrait" as metaphor, people can visually imagine somebody with a camera taking a picture or a series of pictures of a group of people, manipulating equipment and people. We know from research on learning that visual learning is extremely important. Most of us still remember the powerful imagery of the domino theory during the Cold War: we can visualize the falling dominoes. Second, a metaphor can explain some things vividly while leaving others obscured. Thus, the use of simple or single metaphors can actually be misleading or inhibit the understanding of a phenomenon unless more than one metaphor or more than one method of explanation is used (Morgan, 1986). In addition, as Ennis (1996) points out, all components can be contested: the presumed similarity, the facts of the cases, and the values involved in them. When more than one culture is involved in comparisons, these components grow and intensify. Yet many disciplinary writers often use simple metaphors in lieu of more sophisticated explanations involving other cultures, thus revealing gross misunderstanding and outright ignorance of both our own and other cultures. Many stereotypes are based on such simple metaphors; much of popular cross-cultural training is designed to remove and eliminate such stereotypical thinking. Third, any given metaphor can be viewed on at least three levels of abstraction. The "meso level" is the general category of objects the picture intends to portray. The "micro level" is the specific circumstance under which individual pieces have been assembled for the picture. Finally, the "macro level" is the context that may not be shown in the picture, but of which it is a part. Theoretically, these levels of abstraction require corresponding levels of analysis. Without these differing analytical levels, metaphorical explanations are only partially effective because they fail to take variables operating on various levels of abstraction into account.

To apply the portrait metaphor to the curriculum, we can say that the portrait of the curriculum also depends on the disciplinary lens (paradigm) used, the number of faculty or students involved in it, their prior education and experience, the priority given to international content, the focus from which the explanation is taken, and the depth of the field or the context in which it is placed. Conversely, these variables, e.g., the metaphorical choice of film, distance, and lens, then determine the outcome. The knowledge we gain depends upon the questions we ask, and often the questions we ask are programmed by our culture. Reporting on a study about U.S. attitudes toward foreign aid, Joy (1990) concluded that people saw what they believed, rather than believed what they saw. Jervis (1976) has devoted an entire book to the role of perceptions in foreign policy. Koester (1987) has provided a different and equally interesting example of how perceptions influence decision making, in this case students' decisions to study abroad. Her data show that studying abroad for three months or less did not produce appreciable educational results. She concluded that students who chose short-term programs (three months or less) also inadvertently chose the outcome. Conversely, faculty members who choose the minimalist approach to internationalization have also chosen the outcome of international learning for their students.

One could extend the metaphor further to include additional levels of analysis. Most group portraits are static. To show action, we need either rapidly moving objects or video equipment that can capture motion, speed, and direction. Still, the portrait can only be two-dimensional, unless we use special equipment for three-dimensional pictures or X-ray machines for an inside view. Even then, the picture is framed and does not show the context that goes beyond the portrait—unless we use holography. Then we will see for each picture both the whole and its parts. That is the kind of picture taking that appeals to me most, and that I consider the "maximalist" approach to internationalization of the curriculum. Much of what I see in international education in the United States is minimalist, instrumental, introductory, conceptually simple, disciplinary-reductionist, and static. There is an urgent need to study international education on the highest level of sophistication as a multidimensional, multiplex, interdisciplinary, intercultural, research, and policy-driven system of global scope at all levels of education.

This extended metaphor suggests that there is not one but several international educations, depending on the frame, the content, the context, the skill, the equipment, the dimensions, and the sophistication involved in the portrait taking. The literature about internationalization of universities suggests that, although increasingly larger and larger numbers of people are involved in the world, they are psychologically detached from it. The picture is taken with an old brownie camera, using black-and-white film.

Let's pursue the portrait metaphor one step further. Most professional photographers have tremendous knowledge of the interplay between technology and natural conditions; they select the distance and the light, lens, aperture, or double exposure deliberately to create the desired effects. In other words, they have a meta-knowledge of photography that helps them explain what they have done and why. Those who have these meta-skills and combine them with teaching skills have successful careers as both outstanding photographers and teachers of photography to others. Such meta-knowledge is largely missing from the internationalized curriculum. Explanations about expected outcomes, complexity of materials, sequencing, and integration with other disciplinary concepts are superficial, untested, and, often, simplistic. Many course syllabi I have examined make extravagant claims about the competencies and skills they teach students, but the only evidence of such learning is the seat time and the grades. Because most literature treats international education as an undergraduate enterprise directed at lower division students, a holographic and interdisciplinary approach is hard to find in the curriculum.

That is what this chapter hopes to accomplish by treating the curriculum as a system. Most references to internationalized curriculum are fragmented by disciplinary thinking. Faculty members are responsible for only their courses, and thus tend to treat the international dimension as an add-on to the traditional content for which they are accountable to their departmental and collegiate curriculum committees and to their professional and disciplinary associations. University officials who attempt to internationalize the curriculum are faced with having to negotiate with each member of the faculty. Setting up international projects and centers is preferable to internationalizing the curriculum because potential confrontation with resistant individual faculty members is avoided. Virtually every study on this subject bypasses the problems of the curriculum and dwells on specific programs. In a rare recent compendium on this subject, university presidents listed internationalization of the curriculum as the most difficult component of international education (Hanson and Meyerson, 1995).

Each college and university has its own procedure for approving courses and degree programs, and these differing procedures are difficult to compare across the institutional spectrum of U.S. higher education. When Lambert (1989) painstakingly examined the transcripts of many thousands of students across the country to see what international courses they had taken, his research provided previously unknown data showing that only a small number of students enrolled in these courses. Although helpful and important, these data cannot explain other major concerns: how well students performed in these courses; what content was taught; what texts were used; what dominant paradigms the texts represented; and what intellectual skills, if any, were actually learned. These data cannot explain why these students enrolled in these courses and why the majority of students in our higher education system did not enroll in them.

INTERNATIONAL EDUCATION AS SEVERAL KNOWLEDGE SYSTEMS

One of the reasons I subscribe to the systems approach in international education is that I have performed many functions normally classified separately. I was a foreign student adviser; managed international offices; taught courses in international relations, communication, and now in education; and consulted and lectured in many countries. I worked on development projects, held leadership positions in international professional associations, raised money for international projects and scholarships, lobbied for international legislation, organized conferences and symposia, and published articles and books on international education issues. No matter how fragmented, unintegrated, and enclosed these functions were inside the educational institution, the people I dealt with outside of them understood that international education was one system.

Of all these activities, the most defining was my work with international students and scholars. Working with them was extremely interesting, and I learned so much from them—every day brought some new knowledge or perspective. I became highly motivated to make these learning opportunities available to larger numbers of U.S. students and, vice versa, to make the same learning opportunities possible for international students and scholars. My research sought answers as to why the majority of both U.S. and international students could not see the relevance of exchange programs to the wider system of international education and why international offices were enclosed and encapsulated into narrowly defined "service agencies."

Even more surprising was the fact that study abroad programs for U.S. students were equally divorced from other international programs. Most faculty members neglected the enormous learning potential of this field. International student and scholar programs are not only necessary services, provided largely due to the educational system's inability to deal with the complex issues of cultural differences; they are also repositories of knowledge and experience with political relationships across the globe, with intercultural communication, with transfer of learning, with the role of culture as either dependent or independent variable, with the process of adjustment and cross-cultural effectiveness, with the role of education in development of countries, and with the education needed for providing a hospitable reception for people from other countries. We need constantly to explain ourselves to the international students, to explain them to Americans, and to help them explain themselves. When the international student program is made up of people from many countries, the concepts of interdependence, globalism, cultural diplomacy, international cooperation, competition, acceptance, respect, trust, and confidence are more likely to be understood. In short, the international student program is a giant laboratory, recreating real-world conditions of interdependence and competitiveness.

Central to these functions is an understanding of the sophisticated concepts that originate in complex cultural contexts. They need translation and de-coding to fit into understandings of meanings that are often subconsciously learned. The holistic field of international education has its own social psychology that places international student and scholar programs in the minority of educational concerns. The learning from them does not transfer to the curriculum, whose disciplinary borders extend only to a formal classroom, and whose rules regulate the status of insiders and outsiders. Yet virtually every study of international education lists the presence of international students and programs as a centerpiece of the institutional commitment to international education and as evidence of an international ambiance. It appears that the social psychology of international students places them into the category of those who learn from us. In addition, the paradigm of global competitiveness appreciates international students and scholars as an educational export commodity, one the U.S. Department of Commerce has begun to classify as a significant factor in international trade and commerce.

Extending the kind of learning described above to the general curriculum eventually confronted the very nature of knowledge we teach in various key disciplines. Troublesome issues emerged: are significant parts of what we teach international students irrelevant to their countries (1ee et al., 1981; Baron, 1979)? Conversely, might we then not be teaching our own students what they need to know for their professional futures? Unfortunately, these issues are not being addressed. Before I do so, it might be useful to provide a brief history of how the field of international education came to be.

ANTECEDENTS OF INTERNATIONAL EDUCATION: THREE PHASES

Although the term "international education" has existed since the end of World War I, its comprehensiveness was coined by the drafters of the International Education Act, in which a variety of fragmented disciplines and programs were lumped together under "international education." The term was defined by outsiders who put all players, regardless of their varied interests, together on the same field. International education as a system was born, but it was a system whose parts were largely unintegrated and fragmented. The partners brought uneven conceptual strengths, resources, and relationships to each other and to the outside, as well as unintegrated and fragmented constituencies and client groups into the partnership. For many years, they preferred it this way, on the grounds that separately they could better raise funds for their discrete causes. For these reasons, one, overarching definition of international education is difficult to formulate. On an institutional scale, this problem resembles efforts to draft university mission statements that include international education as a goal.

The historical antecedents of international education have not been fully established. Depending on one's frame of reference, its beginnings go back to the Middle Ages when wandering scholars traveled freely from university to university, or, as this chapter argues, are of very recent origin. Since the late 1940s, three distinct phases of international education can be discerned, with a fourth one emerging in the 1990s.

The first phase, which can be called "euphoria," lasted roughly from the passage of the Fulbright legislation in 1946 to the Vietnam war and oil crisis in the 1960s and 1970s. Foundations and governments supported international education liberally; faculty traveled abroad; research and publications abounded. The components of the field were defined and still exist today: international relations and area studies, foreign languages, internationalization of the liberal arts and professional education, foreign students, study abroad, faculty exchanges, development contracts, university-to-university exchange agreements, administration of international programs, research, and policy. Then, as now, the defining publications of this phase were not widely read or reviewed, and, judging by the lack of citations in contemporary works, are still largely unfamiliar to present-day writers and educators. Amazingly little institutional memory exists about the following publications, which should be regarded as true classics: (Amir, 1969; Beals, and Humphrey, 1957; Bennett, Passin, and McKnight, 1954; Butts, 1963; Cleveland, Mangone, and Adams, 1960; Coelho, 1958; Cole, 1958; Coombs, 1964; DuBois, 1956; Education and World Affairs, 1964, 1965, 1967; Ford Foundation, 1960; Frankel, 1965; Fraser and Brickman, 1968; Fuller, 1957; Gange, 1958; Garrity and Adams, 1959; Houle and Nelson, 1956; Lambert, 1954; Lambert and Bressler, 1956; Morris, 1960; Sanders and Ward, 1963; Scott, 1956; Selltiz, Cook, and Christ, 1963; Sewell and Davidson, 1961; Swift, 1959; Taba, 1953; Useem and Useem, 1955; Weidner, 1962; Wilson, 1951, 1956).

The next phase, which can be termed "darkening clouds," began with the International Education Act of 1966, a fiasco that has never been funded and that became a bad omen for subsequent efforts to resuscitate interest in international education. The initial euphoria created false expectations of large and permanent resources, and the subsequent failure to fund this act devastated the international programs of universities, which expected federal funding to replace grants from foundations. The most significant failure, however, was that of universities to "mainstream" international education into "hard item" regular academic programs, which the foundations expected to happen. Universities preferred to sustain programs through unbudgeted "soft" funding and grants. The failure of universities to provide hard funds to implement their international missions was caused, paradoxically, by one of international education's dominant paradigms: international relations theory. This theory drew a sharp distinction between domestic and foreign relations. If the national government was to be the primary beneficiary of international education by being provided with international affairs specialists, state legislatures perceived the need to shift responsibility for funding such programs to the federal government and other agencies.

We are still suffering today from at least five consequences of this situation.

1. International relations are the functions of Washington and a few specialists there associated with foreign policy.
2. Educational institutions surrendered leadership to various national professional associations, which assumed or continued to conduct advocacy for the field. Major initiatives come from outside institutions of learning.

3. These associations were generally oriented to the administration and management of various exchange programs, leaving the disciplines and their curricula largely untouched.

4. Efforts to reestablish these programs coincided with the global crisis in higher education (Coombs, 1985); international programs appeared as "new kids on the block," and their funding was perceived to come at the expense of both established and newly emerging programs, such as diversity.

5. The most damaging consequence is that international education continues to be an add-on to established academic programs, expendable when funds run out.

The third phase, which can be called "defense through associations," began in the early 1980s, when the Reagan administration proposed enormous funding cuts to federal international programs, particularly the Fulbright program. By that time, private foundations had, for practical purposes, ceased funding international education, so that the Fulbright program, Title VI, and AID became the only defining funding agencies. Even then, with diminishing funds, each of these government agencies developed associated client groups that helped write grant guidelines to which educational institutions had to be fitted. The clientism further fragmented international educators, creating confusion in Washington that quickly spilled over to university campuses. On the other hand, government agencies that depended on universities to provide specialized programs felt academia did not deliver as expected. The conservative, economics-driven era turned international exchange programs into an export article, pitted universities against slick private consulting companies in Washington, and substituted national competitive interest for educational interests.

The third phase included the breakup of the Soviet Union, which precipitated an unprecedented and unexpected era driven by the paradigm of competitiveness, dominated by disciplinary reductionism and economic instrumentalism, and presided over by a consortium of dominant disciplines: political science, economics, management, science, informatics, and technology. International educators have still not adjusted themselves to a world dominated by economics, technology, and information. On the other hand, these disciplines have not usually seen higher education as partners, and where they have, international education has been made into an instrument of international trade and competition. These forces, both nationalist and global, tend to deal with the world pragmatically and simply, principally as a context in which they function, and to neglect long-term considerations. University education is rapidly finding itself replaced by "quick-fix" training and consulting agencies that have sprung up everywhere. Educational dollars that might have come to universities, had they been more flexible in addressing changing global needs, are being spent elsewhere.

THE CURRICULUM OF INTERNATIONAL EDUCATION AND THE INTERNATIONAL CURRICULUM

Global interest in international education has increased dramatically, causing the possible emergence of a fourth phase—one we might call "business not as usual" (borrowing from Mittroff's 1987 work by the same title). Universities must reexamine their curricula, scrutinize "more of the same" thinking, and tune in to the new "international order" of things by reconceptualizing their roles and reassigning priorities. It remains to be seen whether or not this fourth phase of international education will emerge. Despite frequent and urgent wake-up calls within and without universities, the process of reconceptualization and reprioritization is barely beginning, and its slowness hinders the wider participation of faculty and students in international education. Only a major cognitive shift will persuade universities that international education does not come at the expense of existing programs; rather, it may save them from continuous erosion and stagnation. Others have discarded the Brownie camera with its black-and-white film and have opted for more sophisticated equipment.

The Organization for Economic Cooperation and Development (OECD) has developed guidelines for evaluating the international curriculum; there are substantial conceptual differences about what it means to be "internationalized" and about what "curriculum" is among Europe, Japan, and the U.S. Europeans appear to define curriculum primarily in terms of structured academic programs, usually requiring the approvals of appropriate ministries or, more recently, of Commission 12 of the European Union. The Dutch exchange organization NUFFIC has just published a survey of these curricula under OECD contract (Bremer and van der Wende, 1996). Several conclusions strike home. The programs surveyed have small enrollments and are primarily established by outside agencies. Some are open only to international students; some 46 percent are dominated by business, economics, and management. None touch the traditional curriculum for domestic students, and all are more expensive than traditional higher education.

Most of the U.S.-inspired effort to internationalize the curriculum was also instigated by outside forces, especially by federal legislation known as Title VI, which initially supported individual faculty members interested in internationalizing their courses. International centers of various kinds have recently been included in this support. The Fulbright legislation was based on selecting outstanding individuals who combined the best of academic tradition with an interest in cultural diplomacy and a commitment to integrating international experiences in domestic instruction. Consequently, in the recent history of higher education in the United States, curricular degree programs were few, while the dominant assumptions about mainstreaming were based on American values of individual entrepreneurship, innovation, and experimentation that constantly searched to uncover opportunities for academic "marketing."

INTERNATIONAL RELATIONS, AREA STUDIES, AND FOREIGN LANGUAGES

Historically, the most solid, persistent, and sustained academic program—one that became the centerpiece of the American approach to international education—was the popular International Relations degree program for undergraduates. Only a dozen or so universities offer such degrees at the Master's level, but students must major in one of the defining disciplines—usually political science—rather than in a distinct, interdisciplinary international relations major intended to produce international affairs specialists. Area studies programs are occasionally assumed to be a part of such training, but there are some tensions between the two due to serious differences regarding dominant theories, the need for language training, undergraduate or graduate focus, and the depth and methods of analysis. Since the beginning of academic concern with internationalization, programs in international relations, area studies, and foreign languages have been supported liberally by foundations and government agencies. The administrators of these foundations and government agencies were themselves products of such programs, which worked well, not only for them personally and professionally, but for the national interests of the United States. A critical analysis of any of these components of the international curriculum is beyond the scope of this chapter, though such criticism has been leveled by the profession itself, which is in the same turmoil that exists inside most social science disciplines (Light and Groom, 1985; Lambert, 1989; George, 1994; Lapid and Kratochwil, 1996). One of the primary criticisms is that international and area studies and foreign languages have received most of the available funding, but have produced few results. Consider, for example, the fact that none of the scholars of the Soviet Union and related issues of security and deterrence predicted the conditions that led to the split of the country despite enormous amounts of funds spent on such studies.

Defining Disciplines

The second category of international courses is found in several "defining" disciplines, such as anthropology, psychology, sociology, communication, education, and management. These disciplines have defined important directions that help to explain the various portraits of international education. For example, anthropology has introduced the concept of "culture" not only into the curriculum in its own discipline (Geertz, 1973; Pitman, Eisikovits, and Lundy Dobbert, 1989; Marcus and Fischer, 1986; Clifford, 1988; Gerlach, 1990; Friedman, 1994; Spindler and Spindler, 1994) but also into many others that draw on anthropological concepts (Fischer, 1988; Hofstede, 1984; Kluckhohn and Strodtbeck, 1961; Stewart and Bennett, 1991). The "communication theory" has given ground to a proliferation of courses in intercultural communication that are offered by virtually every college in the United States (Paige, 1993; Wiseman, 1995; Landis and Bhagat, 1995; Bennett, 1993; Samovar and Porter, 1993). The communication concepts have also influenced the area of cultural diversity—not necessarily in the universities, but in consulting firms that specialize in cross-cultural training. Psychology, especially its recent "stepchild," cross-cultural psychology, provides important insights into the areas of cognition, socialization, and learning (Segall et al., 1990; Brislin, 1990; Landis and Bhagat, 1995). Sociology has provided concepts related to the nature of knowledge, the nature of professions, and, recently, to the nature of globalization (Robertson, 1992). Education's most significant contributions are in the areas of development education (Berg and Gordon, 1989; Melkote, 1991; Thirlwall, 1995; Weiss and Gordenker, 1996; Seligson and Passe-Smith, 1993), comparative education (McAdams, 1993; Fraser and Brickman 1968; Schriewer and Holmes, 1990; Altbach and Kelly, 1986; Thomas, 1990; Faegerlind and Saha, 1989), and educational psychology/counseling (Petersen et al., 1996). These areas have helped define the development of educational institutions and educational reforms. Management-oriented international courses appear to be dominated by traditional concepts of management, foreign trade, marketing, and financing, but a few studies have focused entirely on the role of culture in doing business, promising a new paradigm in global business relations (Adler, 1991; Johnston and Edelstein, 1993; Hofstede, 1984).

A review of the literature suggests that the above-mentioned disciplines have created and sustained many new international courses, usually as disciplinary subspecialties, without altering the mainstream of their disciplines (Bond, 1988; Segall, 1990; Higinbotham, 1984; Kleinman, 1988). In other words, they are driven by dominant disciplinary theories and paradigms. The international "specialists" within these disciplines are, therefore, in a minority, and must conform to the canon. In history, sociology, and political science, tension is often caused by a conceptual gap between those who study the United States, e.g., American Government, and those whose focus is international. In most instances, the process of internationalization originated with a few internationally minded or visiting foreign faculty. The schools of management that needed federal subsidies and special accreditation leverage to begin internationalizing themselves were the most resistant to internationalization.

Liberal and General Education

About every 20 years or so, our universities review the so-called liberal and general study requirements. They are part of a sustained and integrated curricular system based on the credit system, distribution requirements, and the interaction between the "breadth" and "depth" of knowledge. Until recently, these requirements did not typically include international components. International educators who made the effort to include international education as part of the foundation of education were frustrated by universities' tendency to lump a variety of new educational mega-goals into the stationary category of liberal and general education, in competition with growing numbers of other goals. I collected the proceedings, meeting minutes, and draft documents from 10 universities during the late 1980s and early 1990s, and learned that all ran out of available credits within this category. International and sometimes multicultural education were lumped together as a subcategory of a category, without recognizing the possibility that both international and multicultural should be mainstreamed into all other subcategories. In all cases, these universities did not compromise the quantity of credits required for academic majors (the depth of study).

The traditional philosophy of liberal education has informed American higher education since 1828, and it is so deeply entrenched that it is difficult to challenge. Nevertheless, it has been under the scrutiny not only of curricular theorists from divergent schools of thought, but also from the ranks of prominent liberal studies educators. For example, Lanham (1992), recounting briefly the history of liberal education, suggested that "we are debating the same issues 160 years later" (p. 34). The issues he includes are Western-oriented contextual readings; a traditional, content-centered canon; a core curriculum; tight admission standards; democratization of access; and, for an outcome, liberation of people's minds. Additional challenges come from abroad: from Japan, where these concepts were exported after World War II, and then quietly dismantled as irrelevant to Japanese culture; and from many European post-socialist countries, where the concepts have created serious confusion, primarily because they are difficult to explain in the light of dramatically changing times.

Many faculty in traditional disciplines support liberal education as the home of international education. Such a solution delegates international education to the breadth of field component and relieves the depth of field component from pressure to internationalize the disciplines. Relegating international education to liberal and general education requirements is particularly troubling because it introduces a complex and interdisciplinary field to conceptually underdeveloped students through a scattering of courses taken only once. The education for depth that follows moves from elementary to intermediate and advanced levels of knowledge that can be pursued further at the graduate level. This arrangement implies that international education does not have intermediate and higher levels of knowledge and that the disciplinary depth is universal.

Principal Method: Infusion

The principal method of internationalization, "infusion," can be found in most American institutions of higher education, including two-year colleges. If a sufficient number of courses are enriched with international content of some kind, the assumption goes, the cumulative effect will be an impressive international education, all the while preserving the self-regulating system of student choice. No known study has tested these assumptions. However, the American Forum for Global Education (1987) has published a collection of 360 syllabi from courses that claim to have been internationalized by grants from the Title VI program.

The results of this examination reveal some serious flaws in the assumptions of the infusion model. Some faculty did not change existing courses, but introduced entirely new ones. Others "sandwiched" some international content into existing courses, but accorded the infused part few contact hours. The infusion did not alter the traditional disciplinary content, which continued to dominate. Furthermore, the international content was obtained from the same disciplinary domain and was included without curricular explanation regarding depth, reasons for selection of the materials, sequencing, relationship to the rest of the course, cognitive competencies taught, or sufficiency to function in an international context. Evaluating those programs for theoretical strength, pedagogical fluency, learned competencies, interdisciplinarity, and attendance rate would make an excellent Ph.D. dissertation. The Title VI courses I evaluated used only American reading sources, and the texts were based on Western cultural paradigms assuming the universality of knowledge. These assumptions are the major source of resistance to internationalization of the curriculum and need to be addressed next. This chapter is based on the assumption that knowledge is not universal, but culture-specific, and that the infusion model merely adds to the existing traditional structure of knowledge without confronting its origin.

Assumptions of the Universality of Knowledge

Kenneth Gergen (1994) convincingly critiques the assumption of universality, which is nurtured by an entire tradition of knowledge systems, division of labor, pedagogical practices, examination systems, university rankings, and cultural knowledge based on enlightenment, objectivity, rationality, truth, freedom, and progress. Gergen was surprised by how deeply ingrained the entire intellectual tradition is, making nontraditional theoretical positions extremely difficult. Thus, divergent views do not have the opportunity to confront the convergent ones. Furthermore, the tradition is reinforced by professional identities and a sense of like-mindedness that make it difficult for faculty members to take opposing positions on issues. Yet, our academic tradition of critical thinking presumably supports discourse, openness, divergence, and respect for opposing views. In line with this thinking, international education has not confronted non-mainstream curricular issues that lie beyond disciplinary boundaries. The assumption that knowledge is universal has several major implications for international education.

The first implication concerns the disciplines that have declared themselves fully internationalized (Groennings and Wiley, 1990) and capable of functioning everywhere. Economics was one such discipline, yet a study conducted for the World Bank (Cernea, 1991) concluded that slightly more than half of the Bank's development projects that were studied failed to be either sustained or cost-effective because they did not take the cultural environment into account.

The second implication is the reverse of the first and relates to the way our own culture biases those who are called upon to work abroad or to interpret people from other cultures. The Asia Society (1976) study of textbooks about Asia is the classic example of such cultural biases and perceptions; the study found that a significant number of textbooks about Asia was grossly culture-bound. Jervis's (1976) seminal study of the role of perceptions in foreign policy is another example of the way perceptions based on cultural socialization have affected policymakers. The same types of perceptions that are based on American cultural experiences color our views about development (Joy, 1990). Similarly, those working with international students are familiar with the views those students have of the relevance of American education (1ee et al., 1981). Natural scientists and engineers consider themselves immune from cultural influence. However, they, too, are affected by cultural biases—their confidence in scientific solutions to problems and their belief that human errors cannot significantly influence technological systems, for example.

Third, the assumption of universality of knowledge implies comparing all cultures with ours. The most common symptoms of such comparative judgment are assertions heard frequently in connection with explanations of values or behavior across cultures—"everybody does it" or "we are all alike in this regard." This comparison suggests a common "human nature" that explains common human experiences. But such apparent similarities may be coincidental, because, according to Gergen (1994), the sociocultural system has a virtually infinite number of variables; some may indeed be similar in several cultures, but for various reasons. No known method can empirically establish the principle of universality of knowledge and no evidence supports the existence of a universal human nature.

The fourth implication is that the assumption of universality ignores genuine cultural differences (Hofstede, 1984; Bennett, 1993). Ignoring differences is often costly and creates future problems. Related to the differences is the opposite of universality, namely, "uniqueness." Both differences and uniqueness are difficult to deal with because they either require discontinuous thinking or suggest some form of relativism to resolve differences. Yet differences and uniqueness are evident in both domestic and international contexts and need some new conceptual infusion.

Books on international education do not sell well and have to be produced on a shoestring by high-risk, low-volume publishers. There is another paradox: while virtually all self-studies or surveys of international activities in our universities produce long lists of accomplishments and document large numbers of programs to verify the existence of a significant international component, the merits of these programs, enrollments in them, and their depth of internationalization remain to be examined. When one visits the campuses that pride themselves on having an international character, one finds many people who claim they are "doing" international education, but also finds many reasons to believe that the programs are shallow, that few people are involved in them, and that they often fail to accomplish the outcomes for which they were established. The same can be said of the courses that have been internationalized by outside grants. Clever grant writers often produce grant proposals that have little resemblance to what actually happens after the grant is received. Here again, a critical evaluation is urgently needed.

SEVEN PERSPECTIVES ABOUT INTERNATIONAL EDUCATION AND CURRICULUM

In the past, it has usually been sufficient to produce lists of international programs by the relatively self-contained categories in which they are located, without qualitative evaluations and critical assessment. Times have changed, and the need to probe into several issues that cut across the entire field is becoming urgent. One issue is to study the people who represent the international dimension; as Clifford Geertz (1973) often suggested, if you want to study a phenomenon, study the people who make it work. Much of my research was actually devoted to the profession of international educators. Another issue is to study resistance to the field. Many international educators assume that the antecedent of international education is ethnocentrism among the general public. However, international educators are themselves ethnocentric when it comes to their disciplines. The resistance to international education comes not only from the nationalist/ethnocentric public, but also from the fragmented parts of the international community itself.

Yet another issue is to understand the sources of resistance. To do that, one must place oneself inside the minds of international educators and their clients and examine their frames of reference. In cross-cultural education, that is equivalent to the emic approach that is essential to comparative thinking and understanding of a phenomenon. Unfortunately, the scope and nature of emic (from the inside looking out) and etic (from the outside looking in) thinking (Headland, Pike, and Harris, 1990) are neither popular nor relevant to the dominant objective research tradition in the social sciences. These approaches raise many questions about relativism and advocacy of foreign perspectives, and become entangled in the explanations of what international education is.

By studying these issues wherever they are found, rather than relying exclusively on the study of international units, we learn that there are several perceptions that underlie how different components of international education see themselves and others. For example, those working with international students know that this area is very much outside the mainstream of educational institutions. This is truly amazing, because there is a yawning gap between what we say about the importance of international students to the international dimension of higher education and what we actually do about them. We fail to translate their presence into the exceptionally valuable and hitherto unappreciated curricular educational resource it could be.

What are these "perceptions?" I chose seven such perspectives for this chapter because I consider them especially important to understanding this field. They add new dimensions to the curriculum and supplement the traditional unidimensional explanations that emphasize only the component units.

The Majority and Minority Status of International Education

Little attention has been paid to this perspective, partially because the center-pieces of international education are widely perceived to represent the national interests of the majority. Thus, international relations and international management, for example, are a part of the majority and mainstream interests, especially when the instrumental paradigm is international competitiveness. This is paradoxical, because international education is generally in the minority of educational concerns, while several components of it ally themselves with the majority.

Moscovici (1976) suggested that the relationships of majorities and minorities are always relationships of influence, and that the relationship is always mutual and reciprocal. While the majority exerts great influence over the minority, the minority also influences the majority. However, the degree and direction of the influence is not symmetrical. The majority traditionally wants the minority to conform to its view publicly, but allows the minority substantial freedom to practice nonconformity more or less privately. On the other hand, the minority does not trust the majority's public pronouncements of respect and support for the minority and wants the majority to "put its foot where its mouth is" by changing itself and proving it.

Such asymmetry exists in international education. On the one side are international student programs that must be justified publicly on the grounds that they represent our profitable "knowledge export," while privately the programs are sustained and supported, even if they have to be occasionally "hidden" from sight. On the other side is the traditional content-driven curriculum that dominates our universities and sets priorities for funding.

Because of this asymmetrical relationship, faculty traditionally do not accept responsibility for study abroad or international student programs, which they see as outside the majority mainstream. Important federal legislation is justified by appeal to the mainstream and the majority; the best example of this is the National Security Education Program (NSEP), which provides scholarships for undergraduate and graduate students in area studies and funds to universities to internationalize their curriculum. As the title indicates, this otherwise worthy program has to be justified on the grounds of national security, with the purpose of training area specialists for employment with security agencies. Testimonies that support Title VI and Fulbright appropriations also traditionally reflect the national interest perspective that has dominated the foreign policy establishment. To deal with this perspective, we need a new way of thinking about interdependence and cooperation, and new approaches to influencing the mainstream.

International Education as a Program of Change and Reform

Related to the first perspective is the idea that internationalizing the curriculum is actually an educational reform. This perspective is relatively silent in the discussions about international education and curriculum. As I indicated earlier, most international curricular programs do not challenge the nature of the curriculum or the paradigms on which it is based. Rather, the only problem with the curriculum is that it does not have a sufficient amount of international content. That is why the infusion model is popular; nobody can deny that our students lack knowledge about other countries. However, the model is silent with respect to the knowledge that is to be infused. Most commonly, this knowledge is content-based, randomly selected, and drawn from the mainstream-defining disciplines. Cultural considerations challenge the presumption of the universality of knowledge and are, therefore, unlikely to be taken into account by the mainstream.

Scholars who have been studying educational reform suggest that failures are common, and that they are primarily caused by an inability to take the complexity of change into account (Fullan, 1991; Sarason, 1993). International education is perhaps one of the most complex fields trying to change another complex system—higher education. Unfortunately, the university administrators who make decisions about international educational reforms do not have the broad interdisciplinary, intercultural, and pedagogical perspectives needed to make these decisions. They often make decisions based on the first solution that fits, rather than on the best solution chosen from a large number of possible alternatives.

The perspectives about educational reform that appear to be most lacking are knowledge about change, knowledge about identification of problems that need to be addressed, knowledge about strategies to affect the desired change without too much cost and bureaucracy, and knowledge about the future consequences of decisions. One piece of such knowledge that is relevant to international curriculum comes from the neglected cross-cultural perspective and is related to an orientation to the future. Paradoxically, some of the new paradigms about leadership and restoration of trust in organizations are based on future orientation. Leadership studies call it "vision-oriented leadership for change," and cognitive and social psychologists call it "need to restore trust and consensus in organizations" (Moscovici, 1976; Kramer and Tyler, 1996).

We should be particularly concerned with the problem of trust. Our competitiveness paradigm has created widespread distrust abroad about our motives and practices, yet international educators have not addressed these issues. For example, our message to international students that they help balance our trade deficits undermines their trust in us at a time when we need to insure that they trust the nature, quality, and relevance of our education for them. Trust is not only important among individuals, but within and among organizations, including universities and governments. In addition, the market economy and democracy depend on trust and confidence much more than economists, trade representatives, and political scientists realize. Trust, as the Japanese know well, is actually more important than the quality of products we market, the content we infuse in the curriculum, or the American democracy we export.

Kramer and Tyler (1996) make four important suggestions about trust that all appear to be relevant to international education. The first is that trust is asymmetrical; our desire for others to trust us is not the same thing as our trusting them. While we want others to trust us, trusting *them* requires us to surrender some power. The asymmetry of trust is applicable to the conceptualization of interdependence, which has been neglected because of the dominance of the theory of national interests. Such study of interdependence would also require interdisciplinary inquiries, which are neither common nor respected. The second suggestion about trust is related to future orientation. An initiation of trust depends on whether interacting parties visualize the need for and likelihood of continuing relationships. Third, breaches of trust are not easy to heal. To restore trust after it has been violated requires different dynamics and different cognitive skills. Moreover, the forces that determine whether trust has been violated are based on perceptions rather than on objective realities. We only need to look at the Middle East and the Balkans to appreciate this point. Finally, trust has three phases: deterrence, mutual knowledge among partners, and mutual identification. International education and relations are, unfortunately, in the first phase and lowest level of trust based on deterrence; we must trust each other because distrust carries negative consequences.

Yet, trust based on mutual knowledge and on identification is within reach of educational exchange programs if they reorient goals based exclusively on academic content knowledge. We need to infuse—if that is the favored term—not only content knowledge about other countries, but knowledge from the defining disciplines described here, provided these disciplines have already been internationalized. This merged knowledge will produce new skills, such as a high degree of self-reflection, individually and nationally. The trust based on deterrence that appears to be the rule in international political and economic relations may be working, but it also creates the perception that we are intimidating others into compliance. The next phase in trustful relationships, based on mutual knowledge, is only one step away from deterrence and is particularly suitable for international education.

The Nature and Application of International Knowledge

Gibbons et al. (1994) recently published a provocative book about the "new" production of knowledge that all international educators should take note of. This group of authors represents several cultures, but write as a collective. They suggest that the production of knowledge cherished by traditional academia is no longer useful. They call it "mode one," reducing variables to the smallest units of analysis that will permit a scientifically valid inquiry. Critics of this tradition call it "digging the well deeper and deeper"; new knowledge is produced gradually and cumulatively.

The emerging "mode two" is based on pieces of knowledge already known; knowledge is produced by combining and recombining, configuring and reconfiguring, while applying it to solve problems. Their suggestion that the pieces of knowledge already known should be drawn from many relevant disciplines is of special interest. However, interdisciplinary and integrative thinking have not been part of our mainstream, especially in research institutions, so that most people, including faculty, do not have knowledge of other disciplines or cultures. Somebody quipped that it takes 21 disciplines to understand a single culture other than our own. Although international education is not—and should not—become a discipline, it is a field that should be added to the list. This assumes that "mode two" knowledge cannot be taught to our students either in the two courses required by liberal studies or in the undergraduate programs in international relations. It also assumes that we teach our students about interdisciplinary thinking, which requires translating and recoding concepts from one knowledge domain to another.

We now have several knowledges: disciplinary subject-matter knowledge, knowledge about countries, self-reflective knowledge about our own culture, and meta-knowledge about international education that includes perceptual knowledge of these seven, and possibly more, perspectives. All of them contribute to the collage of portraits about international education. There are two complications. The disciplines that define parts of international education also define the use of that education, and the disciplines may be culture-bound to the intellectual tradition from which they came.

For example, when economic and management theories are the defining paradigms, international knowledge is composed only of those parts that will support the purposes for which these disciplines are taught, as, for example, the knowledge needed by missionaries to gain converts in other countries. When the defining concepts come from anthropology, the application is to areas of international education that need in-depth understanding and insight. Explaining ourselves to others and others to ourselves are examples of this use of knowledge. Psychology and its various branches apply to the needs of people who are involved in international educational dynamics. When communication theories define international education, the application is to reduction of uncertainty, which has given rise to two cross-cultural competencies on both individual and organizational levels: cross-cultural effectiveness/competencies and cross-cultural adjustment. When political science theories define international education, these theories apply to relations among states and their political interactions based on interests, balance of power, and influence.

Traditionally, students majoring in international relations expect to join the foreign service or international departments of corporations. Education theories are applicable to programs that depend on knowledge dissemination to varied target groups and on the role education plays in the development of people and nations. In this sense, it is the most interdisciplinary domain, applying learning theories to pedagogy and defining cognitive skills, that can be taught under varied circumstances. In sum, internationally educated persons need several kinds of knowledge to function. Only one, the traditional content- and discipline-oriented knowledge, dominates curricular discussions.

The Learning Perspective

Controversy over "the social construction of knowledge" has created turmoil in most social sciences. For international educators, the debate about "the cultural construction of knowledge" is just beginning. An increasing amount of evidence indicates that culture influences cognition, reasoning, and thinking, and that basic cultural differences exist in spite of the rapid convergence of cultures (much of the convergence is procedural and behavioral, influencing the culture only skin-deep). This means that culture is a major variable that influences not only how people from other countries organize their knowledge, but also how we organize knowledge in various disciplines.

The notion that our knowledge is universal and superior because it is based on objectivity, truth, and rationality still anchors many academics and policymakers. They seldom reflect on the relevance and consequence of their activities. Self-reflection is one of the cognitive skills in international education that is extremely difficult to teach and practice. It requires us to take into account a great deal of criticism of our individual and national thinking and behavior, much of which is subconscious. People who work with international students encounter these reactions every day of their lives; students are constantly searching for answers to puzzling cultural differences, meanings of concepts in our culture, and the possible application of these concepts to their own countries. International student advisers also know that what international students say and do influences the way they are perceived by the majority culture. Cross-cultural misunderstandings are often blamed on the "messengers," because most people assume that they have made themselves perfectly clear, so it must be the others' fault when they do not understand us.

If we hear only the criticism, we tend to discount it. And if the criticism is particularly negative, we return it in kind. If, however, we can sustain relationships in the face of criticism and misunderstandings, we find out that the attitudes perceived to be critical are actually motivated by a desire to help Americans correct what appear to be culturally arrogant or insensitive practices and behaviors. Cross-cultural learning is then not only based on culturally acquired values, behaviors, and cognition, but also on emotional reactions to self-reflection, outside criticism, and conditions of uncertainty, most of which are not part of traditional academic content knowledge. Most of these perceptions also come from conditions of interdependence that are or should be part of the study of international education.

Implicit—and occasionally explicit—in every academic discipline is the method of thinking about the discipline itself. These methods are called intellectual skills or competencies, and usually include critical and creative thinking. These, too, are culturally constructed. One only needs to attempt to teach them in Central and Eastern Europe to understand this. In international education, several other competencies are seldom taught explicitly. Comparative thinking has already been mentioned, but needs one additional clarification. The point of entry into another culture is always with the etic perspective (Headland, Pike, and Harris, 1990). This method allows cross-cultural comparisons, but such comparisons produce a different kind of knowledge than the emic perspective. When our data from cross-cultural research are based almost exclusively on the etic approach, as they are in practice and by tradition, we learn about others differently from how they see themselves, and vice versa.

Gardner (1993) adds another point based on his study of analogical thinking. Citing research studies on the subject, he suggests that we are socialized to learn analogical thinking early in life, based on similarities within a single domain, and then move to analogical thinking based on similarities across domains. Analogical thinking based on differences requires different intellectual skills than thinking based on similarities. This point is well made by the Bennett model of ethnorelativism that is based on cognitive assumptions of differences (Bennett, 1993). Many international curricular programs, including study abroad, are based on, or have implicit in them, comparisons (analogical thinking) within a single domain of their own discipline. While many faculty believe they are teaching comparative thinking, they are in fact teaching the lower form of it within a single domain. Similarly, critical thinking that is part of traditional academic and disciplinary knowledge may not be transferable to other domains.

If we consider seriously the "mode two" model of knowledge production of Gibbons et al. (1994), several new intellectual skills emerge from cross-cultural literature and from the study of international interactions. Many have already been described as cross-cultural competencies, such as cognitive flexibility (Paige, 1993; Wiseman and Koester, 1993), and others are known but seldom associated with international education, such as differentiation and cognitive complexity. A few new cognitive skills need to be added, all with the understanding that the need for them changes rapidly and that new cognitive skills may emerge as conditions of global interdependence change. Gergen (1994) suggests the following cognitive skills: a capacity for rapid conceptual alteration, a corresponding capacity for rapid changes in self-perception, a conceptual ability for self-perception, a capacity to operate contrary to the established system, and a capacity to envision alternatives autonomously. These intellectual competencies are needed in other human relations areas as well. Consider, for example, the difficulties people have in race or ethnic relations in coming to terms with the past.

The popular "add-on" concept of infusion might have challenged the nature of disciplinary knowledge if it had been done thoughtfully. For many, however, it provided an easy solution to a complex problem and thus obscured the need to develop a more suitable learning model that would integrate several of the knowledges mentioned earlier. The integrated portraits of international curriculum will feature the intersection of these three types of knowledge in which the results may be different each time, depending on the lenses used. Several of the defining disciplines do not represent only their subject matter, but also contain their own theories of learning, such as early socialization, development theories, or information processing theories. The infusion model is inadequate to take into account these additional perspectives. It only adds a little spice to the pot of familiar brew. Banks (1993) has been equally critical of the infusion model for multicultural education and has even suggested that it marginalized the entire scheme of human relations.

Curricular Perspectives about International Education

International educators have neither developed nor debated a unifying curricular perspective on international education. The traditional academic, discipline-oriented perspective has dominated the structured curriculum. That system is comprehensive, logically consistent, and well-institutionalized. It has served the American higher education system exceptionally well in the past, but does not appear able to adjust itself to the demands of changing times—the rapid explosion of knowledge, the integration of contrary perspectives, and the expansion of pedagogical practices. As Gergen (1994) suggests, it is particularly resistant to change in the face of possible implications from the Kuhnian theory of paradigmatic revolution. At the same time, Gergen maintains that the traditional perspective has not really produced any substantial conceptual and theoretical revolution in social and behavioral sciences comparable to those that occur regularly in the sciences and technology.

Several of the cognitive skills discussed in this chapter cannot be taught by a traditional approach to the curriculum. As Einstein is reputed to have said, major problems cannot be solved by the same paradigms that created them. Similarly, cognitive psychologists have produced experimental evidence that suggests knowledge gained through a medium of one mode cannot be decoded by another. Our problem is how to develop new pedagogical and curricular practices that introduce multivaried modes of thinking and learning without openly challenging the system, and how to educate the system itself to embrace change in the direction of the maximalist approach proposed here. I believe that, consistent with the suggestion by Gibbons et al. (1994) about the production of new knowledge, we can develop new pedagogical knowledge by combining and recombining various curricular perspectives, including experiential learning and development theories—all to the benefit and survival of the traditional model. As in culture learning, one does not have to accept everything from other cultures or from other curricular theories described in McNeill (1990) and Short (1991). Such expansion would revolutionize both study abroad practices and international student programs. We might learn a great deal from the Europeans, where enormous energy is being directed toward curricular reform as they search for new paradigms related to the forthcoming European integration and to its pedagogy. For example, British universities have developed a format for "studio learning" in which students in the same program accept responsibility, for credit, for their own learning and studying.

The traditional academic model is enamored with the idea of internships and supports them fully. On the other hand, it does not support the idea of an informal internship in the global laboratory that exists on our campuses every day. It assumes it by osmosis. This paradox is related to the basic perspectives about what constitutes learning and how it is sequenced. Most faculty assume it is essential for colleges to produce graduates who have a large amount of foundational and disciplinary knowledge that they can apply to practical situations on the job. When the job market was relatively secure, this assumption worked well in practice, and most employers cooperated with it by providing special on-the-job training following graduation. International education challenges this assumption in four ways.

First, it wants international components to be included in both foundational and disciplinary knowledge. Second, it seeks practical experiences not only as an extension of education for jobs, but as a method of integrating knowledge from several disciplines and cultures. The third challenge is controversial; some international educators wish to provide job-specific training, such as in management. This perspective is more in line with contemporary attitudes about returns from education. On the other hand, others want international education to stress the generic and self-regulating competencies needed in a changing world. Meta-learning skills are part of that expectation. Fourth, international curriculum challenges both the dualistic "either this or that" and the mechanistic "one plus one is two" mode. Expressed graphically, one and one is more than two, if we recognize the (+) as the process of addition that adds a new quality to the traditional equation.

With few exceptions (Harari, 1972, 1977, 1983, 1989a, 1989b, 1992; Groennings and Wiley, 1990; Tonkin and Edwards, 1981), the literature about international education is generally silent about the nature of the international curriculum, and yet every field and discipline in international education makes assumptions about what to teach, how to teach it, when and to whom, in what sequence, and of what quality and quantity. None cite any research findings on which this form of the "curriculum" is based. The time has come to make these assumptions explicit, so that the Cinderella programs of study abroad and international student exchanges can become legitimate curricular concerns.

Cost and Benefits of International Education

The recent Dutch self-study of the international curriculum (Bremer and von der Wende, 1996) concluded that it is more expensive than traditional education for domestic students. That was a curious conclusion, because the data showed that the reason for higher costs was the necessity of establishing separate institutes for international learners. No mention was made about the outcomes of learning at institutions in which domestic and international students studied together. Six basic issues related to the cost of international education should become part of the debate about internationalization.

First, the indicators of cost-effectiveness are always economic and are based on formal university structures with short-term benefits in mind. Yet international education is regarded to be perhaps the only long-term aspect of our national policy. Several noneconomic benefits would also require research about learning and instruction; unfortunately, funds for research are not available. Still, impressive pieces of research indicate that international students regard nonformal (incidental) learning as more important than learning from the fields of study (Lee et al., 1981). On the other hand, Lambert (1989) studied the outcomes of formal education in foreign language learning based on Title VI-funded programs and concluded that only a small percentage of fellowship holders actually could handle the language they studied.

Second, international education, or some of its parts, is widely perceived as designed to benefit foreigners, whether they are international students studying here or faculty working in development projects abroad. In reality, international student programs are fast becoming market-oriented as institutions around the world see the presence of international students as income producing. Unfortunately, the income is hidden in institutional financial structures that do not connect it with the programs.

Third, we tend to compartmentalize the university by vertical structures so that new programs require new structures. "Mainstreaming" through existing and available resources is not often an option. This practice hinders the horizontal mainstreaming of international programs that are funded initially from soft money. The programs die when income stops. That is the cost of not managing international education as a system.

Fourth, the curriculum itself is fragmented into distinct and discrete chunks of knowledge that are each so tightly organized as to exclude related functions, concepts, and skills. Students often complain about redundancy among courses offered by different disciplines that draw on the same conceptual content and readings. Often these "redundant" courses are organized separately because we do not know how to cooperate across disciplines to provide different or competing perspectives from those offered in our own departments.

Fifth, many universities have not developed sophisticated administrative structures for international education, and treat it as just another bureaucracy. People tend to organize themselves the way they think. Yet, international education administrators perform a vast number of functions that correspond to the complexity of the field. When they do not perform them, or the structure ignores them, a hidden but significant administrative cost arises from constant jockeying for power, the need to access central administration, jurisdictional conflicts, competition, undermining, and a flurry of memos and position papers requiring clarifications, explanations, and solutions to disputes. Canon (1976) studied the fiscal consequences of such power struggles and "turfism" within just one organization of a university and reported how enormously costly such jurisdictional disputes are. Students usually catch on to these gaps and contribute to the costs by challenging the system and seeking individual attention.

Sixth, international educators have always been cost-conscious, if for no other reason than majority perceptions kept reminding them that support for international education depended on losses to traditional departments. These perceptions survive because we have not yet succeeded in persuading the educational establishment that international education is for everybody.

We need a serious debate about direct and indirect costs. Such a debate may reveal that we pay dearly not for international programs, but for our inability to manage multipurpose and complex learning tasks, and for our inability to integrate fragmented segments of international education into the mainstream system of academia. Several years ago, the Dag Hammarskjold Foundation in Stockholm produced an interesting publication about the new "human scale development" paradigm for development schemes (Development Dialogue, 1989) that are based on motivational theories of needs satisfaction. The paradigm was based on the idea that existing theories are inadequate for development because they ignore the different levels of needs to be satisfied and thus the different satisfiers. These needs range from (1) pseudo needs to (2) inhibiting needs, (3) single needs, and (4) synergistic needs. Consequently, the programs became either "pseudo satisfiers," "inhibiting" satisfiers, "singular" satisfiers, or "synergistic" satisfiers. This paradigm may also be applicable to learning needs not taken into account by this Swedish publication. For example, among the pseudo-learning satisfiers might be stereotyping of others, promotion of national interests, or disciplinary reductionism. An inhibiting satisfier is, for example, rigidity about enforcement of rules and authoritarian teaching style. Single satisfiers are educational loans, nationalism, and making restrictive rules. The synergistic-learning satisfiers produce learning that continues to produce learning, e.g., meaningful interpersonal relationships of an intellectual nature with people from other cultures; meta-learning; and multiple purpose programs, or structures that encourage self-regulation, self-motivation, self-reflection, and a capacity for conceptual alteration.

Cross-Cultural Perspectives on International Education

Cross-cultural perspectives add still more complexity to international education. Culture's portrait is not a single frame, but a collage of constantly changing pictures taken with different equipment under varying conditions.

Most faculty who have internationalized their courses add domain-specific content. This is how most of us are programmed; knowledge is content. Students enrolled in such courses learn, for example, about the government, history, economics, or geography of a selected country. Culture is commonly associated with anthropology, so we tell students if they want to learn about the cultural aspects of their field, they should take courses in anthropology. That does not happen often, however. It was reported that a cross-cultural sequence, part of Stanford's international relations program, was not taken by a single student after 10 years of operation. It appeared to be irrelevant to them.

Difficulty arises when we are not aware that our own culture is part of our discipline and then infuse part of another culture into our field of study. The "foreign" culture is commonly reduced to a variable of our discipline, where it becomes subordinated to the major disciplinary theories. For example, psychologists often treat culture as attitudes and proceed to study them accordingly. Similarly, in communication departments culture is assumed to be synonymous with communication so that it is studied as the context in which communication takes place. Much research evidence suggests that culture is a higher-level concept than disciplines, and that disciplinary theories are derived from their cultural context (Hofstede, 1984; Stewart and Bennett, 1991; Adler, 1991; Gergen, 1994). This kind of cross-cultural perspective has advantages. It helps identify the general principles that influence disciplines, and that should be helpful in internationalizing the curriculum. Furthermore, it does not confront us with the troublesome question about how many cultures it takes before we know when knowledge from one can be transferred to another.

Virtually every task and function of international education eventually confronts the concept of culture. We can study culture as its own subject, as a dependent or independent variable, or as the context in which people work, study, teach, or conduct research. Culture is a variable when we study what happens to people involved in such activities, and on a higher level of abstraction, how culture influences the production of knowledge in general and in the disciplines in particular. This perspective provides tools for comparison and evaluation of not only cultural variables, but other disciplines as well, including science, technology, and business. It addresses issues such as the transfer of knowledge, the dynamics of culture contact, social change, conformity, identity, and roles. It relates individuals to institutions and speaks to the division of labor, ways of organizing, and, most importantly for international education, ways of thinking and reasoning.

Culture is not just one *thing*; it includes many variations. And culture does not *do* anything, it just is. I heard an economist blame culture for making it impossible for economics to work; that notion is a reflection of the same perspectives people have about culture that are discussed in this chapter. This chapter subscribes to the opposite perspective, that the disciplinary knowledge being applied to other countries is culture-bound and thus may be inappropriate in the host culture. One does not have to become a cultural anthropologist to use cultural concepts. Some anthropologists may not like it when parts of their domain are taken away from its whole, but that is the reality of the world in which we live. The world is not organized the way the disciplines are, and knowledge is in a glass bowl for everybody to see. People are the principal carriers of culture, and when they travel or appear on global television networks, they contribute to the same glass bowl effect whether they are aware of it or not. That is why study abroad and international student programs fail to achieve their educational potential when they ignore the fact that exchange activities are defined by culture more than by the disciplines, and when they fail to take advantage of people as cultural carriers. Moreover, students and scholars provide a more refined, educated, and sophisticated picture of culture than television images.

Cultures also have their borders and have invisible mirrors attached to them. The borders define who the insiders and outsiders are. Borders restrict vision beyond themselves, and the mirrors confront those looking with their own identities. The "mirror" learning analogy (Morris, 1960) has three meanings: (1) seeing another culture as we see ourselves, (2) seeing another culture as a mirror image of our own, and (3) not seeing another culture because the mirror is in the way and makes us see only ourselves. All these metaphors have learning, and also teaching, implications. Education is a sector of public life that reflects its cultural context more than any other sector, primarily because it is designed in part to perpetuate that culture. In a more dynamic sense, the same mirror-effect encounter occurs when we merge, fuse, or otherwise connect the major learning systems; namely, the discipline, the culture, and perspectives about both.

Cross-cultural analysis helps explain a number of things that are important to international relations, international understanding, and international interactions. For example, whom we can trust and why; how institutions are organized; what authority exists in these institutions; what kind of social structure and hierarchies exist in them; how people relate to the past, present, and future; what control they have over their affairs; how they relate to each other and to outsiders; who these insiders and outsiders are to begin with; how they think and solve problems; what evidence they seek for decisions; what activities they are involved in, and how these activities relate to jobs and careers; whom they punish for what and why; and so forth. Time and space do not permit a more detailed analysis of these variables, but it may be useful to elaborate on at least one of them, the "time" variable that I described earlier in connection with educational reform, social change, development programs, and the building of trust and confidence.

The time variable also provides a cognitive map for the members of a culture to remember the past, to assess guilt and punishment for wrongdoing, and to focus attention on development projects for the future. From this variable also flow perspectives about how individuals change. Take, for example, the life-span theory, which suggests that peoples' earliest socialization experiences influence them for life. Translated to cultural conditions that require people to make major personal and conceptual changes, it means that people cannot change. For example, once a communist, always a communist; once a racist, always a racist; once a colonizer, always a colonizer. When regimes change as rapidly as they do, those associated with the ousted regimes often protest that they have changed, but their claims are usually disbelieved, on the ground that they say so to hold on to their positions and power.

International education stands clearly for change and should be future oriented. Students learn today so that they will have the knowledge and skills tomorrow. This should be the basic question for universities: Are we educating our students for the future? The competitiveness paradigm tends to reinforce a survivor mentality—it is present time oriented.

CONCLUSION

Most Americans, including college and university faculty, do not realize how profound are the changes around us. This chapter is motivated by a desire to urge equally profound changes in our curriculum that will meet the needs of the future. People often want others to change, but don't realize that in that process, they have to change themselves. The idea that a little internationalization is better than nothing—at least it is a "good start"—is dangerous and misleading to students, who may believe two courses are all they needed to be globally competent. Besides, we have been hearing this about international education for over 50 years, with little progress. To effect change, one needs to begin with the recognition that the present system is inadequate to meet future needs. Those who do not think so will only apply Band-Aids. Since massive educational reforms usually do not succeed, we need to design an incremental, but systemwide program of change that will allow faculty participation. Other universities are taking internationalization seriously; for example, Nannerl Keohane, the President of Duke University, has declared international education Duke's top priority, and intends to implement dramatic changes (Tiryakian, 1990).

Before any curricular changes can be implemented, two things must happen: ways must be found (1) to merge various cognitive systems, and (2) to render intelligible the diverse perspectives of the "minority" of international educators. Creative ideas about specific curricular changes are known and available, provided we can accomplish a cognitive shift about the nature of international knowledge.

Although most of the defining disciplines come from social sciences and humanities, it would be a mistake to limit the discussion to these disciplines. At a time when international relations are dominated by science, technology, business, information, and industry, both these areas and the rest of society need the perspectives that internationalized social sciences and humanities can offer.

There is another, hitherto silent, dimension. The original euphoric phase was based on the idea that international education would produce improved international relations and understanding. That assumption was not limited to official diplomacy, but extended to public and cultural diplomacy as well. The need to reevaluate the basic objectives of international education in these terms remains. I may not be meeting the same people many university students, faculty, and administrators do, but what I hear gives me cause for concern about the poor image we have as individual Americans, as a country, and even as academics.

There is a great deal of anti-Americanism out there, based on valid or invalid causes, expressed and latent. Many Americans deal with it naively and ignorantly, showing little concern. When they do, they attribute this anti-Americanism to envy of our international power, or to others' projections of dissatisfaction with their own societies. What is even more disturbing is that these criticisms come not only from the sources from which we have traditionally expected anti-Americanism to come, but increasingly from our European friends, especially those connected with higher education. International students often feel themselves the least welcome group in our society and thus share the negative perceptions which, in turn, distance Americans from them. The idea of student mobility has become a global enterprise; we can no longer take the presence of international students for granted. Instead of being blinded by euphoria, thinking that we have won the Cold War and that things are going our way, we should realize that instead our democracy and economic system are on probation and that we should quickly reeducate ourselves to meet these and other still unknown challenges.

Professor Tiryakian's inspiring chapter in Groennings and Wiley (1990) is entitled "Sociology's Great Leap Forward." In it, he expressed delight with the opportunities that internationalization presents to what he termed the stale and dull discipline of sociology, that urgently needed the infusion of new knowledge and perspectives for its own growth and survival. Given the great turmoil in our disciplines, Tiryakian's challenge may well extend to others. Many faculty are now overwhelmed with work and demoralized by the pressures placed on them and their cherished institutions. If they can take a step back, take a retrospective look, and reach out to these new ideas, they may gain more than they realize. As history shows us, international initiatives have not come from within universities; if we will not cultivate international education more seriously, other already-existing or to-be-established institutions will, thus contributing to the further decline of universities.

To internationalize or not to internationalize the curriculum? This question is often decided by attempting to weigh the consequences of either decision. Yet the consequences are not symmetrical. To make a serious effort to internationalize the curriculum, at some cost, and then find it was not necessary to do so would waste some human resources—if learning something can be regarded as waste. On the other hand, failing to internationalize the curriculum now and later finding that it *was* necessary may waste an entire generation of students, who will be denied the choices that would give them some control over their lives and careers.

The final portrait of international curriculum is now emerging. It is a composite collage of an X-ray picture (for the inside and unseen perspective), with the holograph (containing both the whole and the parts), and a video, showing a few runners reaching the finish line, while another, larger group, stands still, looking backward to see what happened.

REFERENCES

Adler, N. J.(1991). *International dimensions of organizational behavior*. 2nd ed. Belmont, CA: Wadsworth.

Altbach, P.G. and Kelly, G.P. (Eds.). (1986). *New approaches to comparative education*. Chicago: University of Chicago Press.

American Forum for Global Education. (1987). *Research for education in global issues*. New York: Global Perspectives in Education.

Amir, Y. (1969). Contact hypothesis in ethnic relations. *Psychological Bulletin* 71, 319–42.

Asia Society. (1976). *Asia in American textbooks*. New York: Asia Society, Inc.

Banks, J.A. (1993). *Multiethnic education: Theory and practice*. 3rd ed. Boston: Allyn and Bacon.

Baron, M. (1979). *The relevance of U.S. graduate programs to foreign students from developing countries*. Washington, DC: NAFSA.

Beals, R.L. and Humphrey, N.D. (1957). *No frontier to learning: The Mexican student in the United States*. Minneapolis: University of Minnesota Press.

Bennett, John W., Passin, Herbert, and McKnight, Robert K. (1954). *In Search of Indentity*. Minneapolis, MN: University of Minnesota Press.

Bennett, M.J. (1993). Towards ethnorelativism: A developmental model of intercultural sensitivity. In R.M. Paige (Ed.), *Education for the intercultural experience*. Yarmouth, ME: Intercultural Press.

Berg, R. and Gordon, D.F. (Eds.). (1989). *Cooperation for international development*. Boulder, CO: Lynne Rienner Publishers.

Bogner, M. (1994). *Human errors in medicine*. Hillsdale, NJ: Lawrence Erlbaum Associates.

Bond, M.H. (Ed.). (1988). *Cross-cultural challenges to social psychology*. Newbury Park, CA: Sage.

Bornstren, R.F. and Pittman, T.S. (Eds.). (1992). *Perceptions without awareness*. New York: Guilford Press.

Bremer, L. and van der Wende, M. (1996). *Internationalizing the curriculum in higher education*. The Hague, Netherlands: NUFFIC (Netherlands Organization for International Cooperation in Higher Education).

Brislin, R. W. (1990) *Applied cross-cultural psychology*. Newbury Park, CA: Sage.

Butts, R. F. (1963). *American education in international development*. New York: Harper & Row.

Canon, H.J. (1976). A development model for divisions in student affairs. *Journal of College Student Personnel*. 17:3, 178–180.

Cernea, M.M. (1991). *Using knowledge from social science in development projects*. World Bank Discussion Paper #114. Washington, DC: The World Bank.

Cleveland, H., Mangone, G.J., and Adams, J.C. (1960) *The overseas Americans*. New York: McGraw Hill.

Clifford, J. (1988). *The predicament of culture*. Cambridge, MA: Harvard University Press.

Coelho, G.V. (1958). *Changing image of America: A study of Indian students' perceptions*. Glencoe: Illinois Free Press.

Cole, F. (1958). *International relations in institutions of higher education in the south*. Washington, DC: American Council on Education.

Coombs, P.H. (1985). *The world crisis in education: The view from the eighties*. New York: Oxford University Press.

————. (1964). *The fourth dimension of foreign policy: Educational and cultural affairs*. New York: Harper and Row.

Development Dialogue. (1989). *Human scale development*. Uppsala, Sweden: Dag Hammarskjold Foundation.

DuBois, C. (1956). *Foreign students and higher education in the U.S.A.* Washington, DC: American Council on Education.

Education and World Affairs. (1967). *The professional schools and world affairs*. Albuquerque: University of New Mexico Press.

————. (1965). *The university looks abroad: Approaches to world affairs at six American Universities*. Albuquerque: University of New Mexico Press.

————. (1964). *The college and world affairs: Report of the committee on college and world affairs*. Albuquerque: University of New Mexico Press.

Ennis, R.H. (1996). *Critical thinking*. Upper Saddle River, NJ: Prentice Hall.

Faegerlind, I. and Saha, L. J. (1989). *Education and national development*. Oxford: Pergamon.

Fischer, G. (1988). *Mindsets: The role of culture and perception in international relations*. Yarmouth, ME: Intercultural Press, Inc.

Ford Foundation. (1960). *The university and world affairs: Report of the committee on the university and world affairs*. New York: The Ford Foundation.

Frankel, C.E. (1965). *The neglected aspect of foreign affairs: American educational and cultural policy abroad*. Washington, DC: Brookings Institute.

Fraser, S.E. and Brickman, W.W. (1968). *A history of international and comparative education*. Glenview, IL: Scott, Foresman and Company.

Friedman, J. (1994). *Cultural identity and global process*. Thousand Oaks, CA: Sage.

Fullan, M.G. (1991). *The new meaning of educational change*. New York: Teachers College Press, Columbia University.

Fuller, C.D. (1957). *Training of specialists in international relations.* Washington, DC: American Council on Education.

Gange, J. (1958). *University research on international affairs.* Washington, DC: American Council on Education.

Gardner, H. (1993). *Frames of mind: The theory of multiple intelligences.* New York: Basic Books.

Garrity, J.A. and Adams, W. (1959). *From Main Street to the Left Bank.* East Lansing, MI: Michigan State University Press.

Geertz, C. (1996). *After the fact.* Cambridge, MA: Harvard University Press.

————. (1973). *The interpretation of cultures.* New York: Basic Books.

George, J. (1994). *Discourses of global politics.* Boulder, CO: Lynne Rienner Publishers.

Gergen, K. (1994). *Toward transformation in social knowledge.* Thousand Oaks, CA: Sage.

Gerlach L. (1990). Cultural constructs of the global commons. In R.H. Winthrop (Ed.). *Culture and the anthropological tradition.* Lanham, MA: United Press of America.

Gibbons, M. et al., (1994). *The new production of knowledge.* London: Sage.

Groennings, S. and Wiley, D.S. (1990). *Group portrait: Internationalizing the disciplines.* New York: The American Forum.

Hanson, K.H. and Meyerson, J. (1995). *International challenges to American colleges and universities: Looking ahead.* Phoenix, AZ: American Council on Education and Oryx Press.

Harari, M. (1992). Internationalization of the curriculum. In Klasek, C. B. (Ed.) *Bridges to the future: Strategies for internationalizing higher education.* Carbondale, Ill: Association of International Education Administrators.

————. (1989a). *Internationalization of higher education: Effecting institutional change in the curriculum and campus ethos.* Long Beach: Center for International Education, California State University

————. (1989b). *Internationalization of higher education report no. 1: Occasional report series on the internationalization of higher education.* Long Beach: Center for International Education, California State University

————. (1983). *Internationalizing the curriculum and campus: Guidelines for AASCU institutions.* Washington, DC: American Association of State Colleges and Universities

————. (1977). *Trends and Issues in Globalizing Higher Education.* Washington, DC: AASCU

————. (1972). *Global Dimension in US Education: The University.* New York: Education Commission of the International Studies Association.

Headland, T.N., Pike, K.L., and Harris, M. (1990). *Emics and etics: The insider/outsider debate.* Frontiers of Anthropology. Volume 7. Newbury Park, CA: Sage.

Higinbotham, H.N. (1984). *The third world challenge to psychiatry.* Honolulu, Hawaii: University of Hawaii Press.

Hofstede, G. (1984). *Culture's consequences: International differences in work and related values.* Beverly Hills, CA: Sage.

Houle, C.O. and Nelson, C.A. (1956) *The university, the citizen, and world affairs.* Washington, DC: American Council on Education.

Jervis, R. (1976). *Perceptions and misperception in international politics.* Princeton, NJ: Princeton University Press.

Johnston, J.S. and Edelstein, R. (1993). *Beyond borders: Profiles in international education.* Washington, DC: Association of American Colleges and American Assembly of Collegiate Schools of Business.

Joy, C. (1990). *Believing is seeing: Attitudes and assumptions that affect learning about development.* New York: National Clearinghouse on Development Education.

Kleinman, A. (1988). *Rethinking psychiatry.* New York: The Free Press.

Kluckhohn, F. R. and Strodtbeck, F.L. (1961). *Variations in value orientations.* Westport, CT: Greenwood.

Koester, J. (1987). *A profile of U.S. students abroad.* New York: Council on International Educational Exchange.

Kramer, R.M. and Tyler, T. R. (1996). *Trust in organizations.* Thousand Oaks, CA: Sage.

Lambert, R.D. (1989). *International studies and the undergraduate.* Washington, DC: American Council on Education.

————. (1954, September). America through foreign eyes. *The Annals of the American Academy of Political and Social Science.*

Lambert, R.D. and Bressler, M. (1956). *Indian students on an American campus.* Minneapolis: University of Minnesota Press.

Landis, D. and Bhagat, R.S. (Eds.). (1995). *Handbook of intercultural training.* Thousand Oaks, CA: Sage.

Lanham, R.A. (1992). The extraordinary convergence: democracy, technology, theory and university curriculum. In D.J. Gless and B.H. Smith (Eds.), *The politics of liberal education.* Durham, NC: Duke University Press.

Lapid, Y. and Kratochwil, F. (1996). *The return of culture and identity in international relations theory.* Boulder, CO: Rienner Publishing.

Lee, M.Y. et al. (1981). *Needs of foreign students from developing nations at U.S. colleges and universities.* Washington, DC: NAFSA: Association of International Educators.

Light, M. and Groom, A.J.R. (1985) *International relations: A handbook of current theory.* Boulder, CO: Lynne Rienner Publishers, Inc.

Marcus, G.E. and Fischer, M.M. (1986) *Anthropology as cultural critique.* Chicago: University of Chicago Press.

McAdams, R.P. (1993). *Lessons from abroad.* Lancaster, PA: Technomic Publishers.

McNeill, J.D. (1990). *Curriculum: A comprehensive introduction.* Glenview, IL: Scott, Foresman, & Company.

Melkote, S.R. (1991). *Communication for development in the third world.* Newbury Park, CA: Sage.

Mitroff, I.I. (1987). *Business not as usual.* San Francisco: Jossey-Bass.

Morgan, G. (1986). *Images of organization.* Newbury Park, CA: Sage.

Morris, R. (1960). *The two-way mirror: National status of foreign students' adjustment.* Minneapolis: University of Minnesota Press.

Moscovici, S. (1976). *Social influence and social change.* London: Academic Press.

Oyen, E. (Ed.). (1990). *Comparative methodology: Theories and practice of international social science research.* Newbury Park, CA: Sage.

Paige, R.M. (1993). *Education for the intercultural experience.* Yarmouth, ME: Intercultural Press.

Petersen, P.B., Draguns, J.G., Lonner, W.J., and Trimble, J. (1996). *Counseling across cultures.* Thousand Oaks, CA: Sage.

Pitman, M. A., Eisikovits, R., and Lundy Dobbert, M. (1989). *Culture acquisition: A holistic approach to human learning.* New York: Praeger.

Robertson, R. (1992). *Globalization: Social theory and global culture.* Newbury Park, CA: Sage.

Samovar, L. and Porter, R. (1993). *Intercultural communication: A reader.* Belmont, CA: Wadsworth.

Sanders, I.T. and Ward, J.C. (1963). *Bridges to understanding*. Carnegie Commission on Higher Education. New York: McGraw Hill.

Sarason, S.B. (1993). *The case for change: Rethinking the preparation of educators*. San Francisco: Jossey-Bass.

Sarles, H. (n.d.) Comparative thought. Unpublished Paper. Minneapolis: University of Minnesota.

Schriewer, J. and Holmes, B. (1990). *Theories and methods in comparative education*. Paris: Peter Lang.

Scott, F.D. (1956). *The American experience of Swedish students*. Minneapolis: University of Minnesota Press.

Segall, M.H. et al. (1990). *Human behavior in global perspective*. Boston: Allyn & Bacon.

Seligson, M.A. and Passe-Smith, J.T. (1993). *Development under development: The political economy of inequality*. Boulder, CO: Lynne Rienner.

Selltiz, C., Cook, S.W., and Christ, J.R. (1963). *Attitudes and social relations of foreign students in the U.S.* Minneapolis: University of Minnesota Press.

Sewell, W.H. and Davidson, O. (1961). *Scandinavian students on an American campus*. Minneapolis: University of Minnesota Press.

Short, E.C. (1991). *Forms of curricular inquiry*. Albany, NY: SUNY Press.

Spindler, G. and Spindler, L. (1994). *Pathways to cultural awareness*. Thousand Oaks, CA: Corwin Press.

Stewart, E.C. and Bennett, M.J. (1991). *American cultural patterns*. Yarmouth, ME: Intercultural Press.

Swift, R.N. (1959). *World affairs and the college curriculum*. Washington, DC: American Council on Education.

Taba, H. (1953). *Cultural attitudes and international understanding: An evaluation of an international study tour*. Occasional Paper No. 5. New York: Institute of International Education.

Thirlwall, A.P. (1995). *Growth and development: With special reference to developing economies*. Boulder, CO: Lynne Rienner.

Thomas, R.M. (Ed.). (1990). *International comparative education*. Oxford: Pergammon.

Tiryakian, E.A. (1990). Sociology's great leap forward. In S. Groennings, and G. Wiley, (Eds.), *Group portrait: Internationalizing the disciplines*. New York: The American Forum for Global Education.

Tonkin, H. and Edwards, J. (1981) *The World in the Curriculum*. New Rochelle, NY: Change Magazine Press.

Useem, J. and Useem, R.H. (1955). *The Western educated man in India*. New York: Dryden Press.

Weidner, E.W. (1962). *The role of universities*. New York: McGraw Hill.

Weiss, T.G. and Gordenker, L. (1996). *NGOs, the U.N., and global governance*. Boulder, CO: Lynne Rienner.

Wilson, H.E. (1956). *American college life as education in world outlook*. Washington, DC: American Council on Education.

———. (1951). *Universities and world affairs*. Washington, DC: American Council on Education.

Wiseman, R. (Ed.). (1995). *Intercultural communication theory*. Thousand Oaks, CA: Sage.

Wiseman, R. and Koester, J. (1993). *Intercultural communication competence*. Thousand Oaks, CA: Sage.

CHAPTER 2

Culture in Curriculum

Internationalizing Learning by Design

by Kerry Freedman

C urriculum design is based on particular attitudes, values, and beliefs. As a result, curriculum reflects underlying assumptions about the appropriate purposes and practices of education. This chapter is based on such an underlying assumption: increased internationalism in the higher education curriculum will benefit students. The chapter focuses on conditions of curriculum that would enable such a change.

The chapter has three main parts. The first part is a brief summary of several historical, theoretical approaches to curriculum and curriculum issues. It concludes with a recommendation as to which approach to internationalizing higher education curriculum would be most appropriate. The second part is a discussion of a common model of learning in higher education and its limitations in the context of internationalization. The third part focuses on two types of content that could be used in conjunction with the recommended approach to design and conceptualization of learning to promote internationalization in higher education.

CURRICULUM DESIGN: APPROACHES AND ISSUES

Curriculum design is a plan for teaching and learning in which information is organized into parts (such as lessons, units, or courses) that support the educational purpose of the whole. Good curriculum design should result in something like a Gestalt: the value of the curriculum as a whole is more than the sum of its parts. The term "design" is appropriate because it suggests that careful planning must occur, that the endeavor is creative, and that curriculum has aesthetic qualities. Good curriculum is also a process of continual redesign and may be based on a particular style or approach.

Four Approaches to Curriculum

Historically, experts in the field of curriculum studies have delineated several historical, theoretical approaches to curriculum, each based on different assumptions about the purpose of education (e.g., Eisner and Vallance, 1974; McNeil, 1975, 1990, 1996). These underlying assumptions are reflected in the planning, implementation, and evaluation of curriculum. For example, McNeil describes four approaches that have been particularly influential in the past: (1) the academic approach, (2) the humanist approach, (3) the technological approach, and (4) the social reconstructionist approach.

The Academic Approach. The purpose of the academic approach to curriculum is the dissemination of information from the professional disciplines and the conservation and maintenance of traditional knowledge. A strong emphasis on truth, and the search for it, is inherent. Roots of the approach go back to the eighteenth and nineteenth centuries, and long before. However, a resurgence of the academic approach followed the Second World War when international competition became an increasingly important political and economic issue.

Support for the academic approach to curriculum has come from a variety of sources, including contemporary scholars who subscribe to the idea that discretely different forms of knowledge exist. For example, Howard Gardner (1991) supports this approach through his argument that students should be guided away from their intuitive understanding of the world toward knowledge developed by professional communities (McNeil, 1996). The perspective of cultural literacy espoused by such scholars as E. D. Hirsch and Allan Bloom supports this approach through its focus on schooling as a means of passing on traditions of excellence.

The Technological Approach. The primary purpose of the technological approach to curriculum is the efficient and systematic delivery of information to students. In the early decades of this century, such educators as Franklin Bobbitt and David Snedden sought to make schooling more efficient through recommendations derived from task analyses and time management studies. The work of behavioral psychologists added support to the approach, which has focused heavily on maximizing student achievement on standardized tests and in vocational training for business and industry.

Based on this approach, complex concepts and skills are reduced to simple, concrete, step-wise learning activities that are assessed through testing. Systems frameworks for curriculum, such as "teacher-proof" curriculum packages, mastery learning, and outcome-based education, are generally considered to be based on this approach because they tie learning to a hierarchy of tasks that are assumed to result in an acquired concept or skill that is conceptualized as an end product.

The Humanist Approach. The purpose of the humanist approach to curriculum is the personal fulfillment of each individual. McNeil (1996) argues that this conception of curriculum draws on the notion of self-actualization and Maslow's framework for a healthy psychology that is dependent on self-expression and peak experiences. However, the roots of this approach are older than Maslow's work. They go back to the early student-centered experimental schools of the 1910s and 1920s, and are based, in part, on the work of John Dewey. In contrast to Dewey's work, the humanist approach has focused on a conception of individuals as somewhat independent of social context. Recently, however, humanist curriculum theorists have begun to respond to critics' complaints that their approach does not take into account the social aspects of individualism by drawing upon, for example, social psychology.

A humanist curriculum centers on the development of self-reflection, self-directedness, creativity, and broad-mindedness in students. Personal development, such as in the areas of morality and self-esteem, are as important as intellectual development. Within this approach, helping students to generate personal responses to academic knowledge is a vital aspect of teaching, and problem-solving is often the basis of educational experience. Affective teaching techniques are commonly used, including techniques involving fantasy and imagination.

The Social Reconstructionist Approach. Historically, the social reconstructionists have also borrowed from Dewey. However, the most influential early social reconstructionists were George Counts and Harold Rugg, who argued that a new social order could be created through education. The modern perspective of this approach is grounded, for example, in the work of critical theorists, feminists, cultural critics, and such revolutionary educators as Paulo Freire. These theorists argue that education should help prepare students to transform their world in ways that will improve life for all. One purpose of a social reconstructionist curriculum is to make sociocultural conditions and human interactions more equitable through schooling. As a result, the current debate between, for example, Dinesh d'Souza and others about diversity and conceptions of excellence exemplifies conflicts related to this approach.

Knowledge is represented as socially constructed in curriculum based on this approach. Students are taught to think critically and analyze information in relation to social ideals. Learning involves group activities that include negotiation of various types, and that avoid competition. Curriculum extends beyond the institution and students are expected to enact their learning through, for example, their interactions with peers and community. Complex concepts are addressed in their complexity, rather than through atomistic reduction.

The theoretical approaches briefly summarized above are only models. In practice, curriculum is not so neat and usually reflects more than one approach. Higher education curriculum in the United States is large in scale and certainly includes all these approaches, depending on disciplinary boundaries, alliances within disciplines, and the work of individual faculty. However, the models can help us to think about some of the characteristics of a desired curriculum and the ways in which to achieve that curriculum.

Critical Issues of Curriculum

Regardless of which of the four approaches is given emphasis, the design of good curriculum includes a consideration of at least five sets of issues: epistemological, informational, developmental, outcome, and structural.

Epistemological issues concern the ways in which knowledge is conceptualized in relation to formal education. The four approaches to curriculum discussed above each reflect a different conceptualization of knowledge. Depending on the approach, knowledge is assumed to involve varying degrees of logic, affectivity, and verisimilitude. A consideration of knowledge from an international standpoint might support the idea that knowledge is socially constructed, based on forms of consensus and conflict, reproduced through efforts to maintain tradition, and transformed in relation to time and place.

Informational issues concern the representation of knowledge in curriculum. Curriculum is inherently selective. It emerges through written texts, human interactions, visual media, and other educational experiences. The production of each of these forms of representation changes knowledge into information in various ways. An internationalized curriculum must include the information students need to understand and make judgments about global affairs.

Developmental issues concern the developmental level of the students for which a curriculum is designed. That level determines important aspects of learning. In higher education, developmental level usually refers to educational level, such as undergraduate, masters, or doctoral, rather than to the psychobiological growth of a student. Consideration of developmental issues in the context of an internationalized curriculum should also include a focus on the level of knowledge students have about global affairs. Curriculum should help students develop to a higher level of social consciousness and a greater awareness of the experience of others.

Outcome issues concern the aims, goals, and objectives of a curriculum. The aims of a curriculum are the large ideals on which the curriculum is based. For example, one common aim of curriculum in the United States is the creation of a democratic consciousness in students. The goals of a curriculum must be accomplished to meet these aims. In a context of internationalization, curriculum goals should reflect global perspectives. For example, such goals could focus on students attaining multicultural sensitivity or ecological awareness. The learning objectives would then spell out the knowledge students should gain and the activities to be undertaken to attain those goals.

Structural issues pertain not only to how knowledge is represented through information and the ways in which knowledge is organized, but also the ways in which curriculum is implemented. The structure of a curriculum is crucial to its success. In higher education, curriculum should be organized to permit students to see concepts in their complexity. From the perspective of internationalization, the structure of curriculum should promote the learning of both deep and broad knowledge and focus less on sequential, hierarchical knowledge and more on flexibility, interpretive analysis, and interactive instruction.

The consideration of these issues in relation to internationalization leads me to recommend that we build on a foundation of social reconstructionism, but that a new approach is needed for higher education in the future. The interests of global awareness and involvement are consistent with the assumptions on which social reconstructionism is based. To build on this foundation, the next section of this chapter includes a discussion of the nature and limitations of a common model of student learning that is often reflected in the higher education curriculum. In the final section, I illustrate why and how we might develop a new approach to higher education curriculum.

RELATIONSHIPS BETWEEN CURRICULUM AND STUDENT LEARNING

Unfortunately, curriculum design has not always been given the attention it deserves in higher education. In the past, courses and programs have often been designed based on the academic approach to curriculum and have been more influenced by the expertise of faculty than the knowledge base for which students should be responsible. This practice can leave gaps in students' educational experience and lead students to wrongly believe that faculty are responsible for student learning. Fortunately, this condition is changing in higher education. Educators are now focusing more on what students need to know and on ways of helping them develop knowledge that goes beyond the simple delivery of information in a lecture format.

Educators now generally agree about the importance of student development in the construction of curriculum. However, debate continues about the character of that development, particularly in adults. What conception of development has shaped higher education curriculum? How should curriculum be structured to best promote student development? To answer these questions, we must consider the ways in which learning is generally thought of in higher education.

The Expert-Novice Conception of Learning

The psychological conception of adult learning that has particularly influenced higher education curriculum is reflected in *expert-novice* models of learning that are based on the steps required to advance from novice knowledge to higher-order expertise. Expert-novice models represent learning in terms of increasingly complex levels of a particular domain of knowledge. They are stage-based in the sense that students are expected to move naturally in a fairly linear manner through these levels. Although authors of such models refer to development as dependent to a greater or lesser extent on interaction with the world, the models are fundamentally representations of internally motivated behaviors (and, to a lesser degree, thought processes) that demonstrate learning has taken place.

Psychologists and other educational researchers began seriously studying expert-novice conceptions of learning in the 1960s, when they shifted from a focus on traditional behavioristic research to research concerning complex performances and, by the late 1970s, learning processes (e.g., Baars, 1986; Langley and Simon, 1981). In a sense, cognitive psychology reopened the possibility of theorizing about internal psychological processes, which had been closed for a time by the focus on behaviorism. The mid-twentieth century cognitive revolution was, in part, responsible for changes in curriculum. However, other influences also resulted in change related to expert knowledge. For example, psychologist Jerome Bruner and others argued that education should more closely resemble its parent disciplines for social, political, and economic reasons. A greater understanding of the ways in which proficiency was gained in disciplinary domains was required if such a curriculum was to be developed. Scientific expert-novice models gained credibility as educators were pressed to create discipline-based curriculum.

Cognitive theory researchers generally agree on the importance of incorporating or modifying prior knowledge in learning (e.g., Joyce and Weil, 1986; Marzano, 1992; Vosniadou and Brewer, 1987). Although subtle changes in knowledge occur on a continual basis, radical restructuring of knowledge seems to emerge with age or expertise. This periodic restructuring of knowledge, considered by Piaget and others to be a global developmental change, involves interaction with the world. Researchers are in debate about whether a global approach to learning, such as Piaget's, should be replaced by one that is more domain-specific, in part, to explain developmental differences between novices and experts.

Expert-novice research has suggested that age may not be the most important determining factor in development. Formal knowledge is also dependent on the structure of domain-specific information. Experts in a field, for example, physics (Larkin, 1981), follow different strategies for learning and organizing formal knowledge than do novices. Unlike novices, experts can draw on multiple levels of knowledge when solving problems. Even adults who know about the materials and processes of a particular domain, and are highly proficient in their use, use processes that reflect novice thinking when learning to use a new medium, such as a computer (e.g., Freedman and Relan, 1992).

Recent analyses of expert-novice development has focused on several areas of expertise, such as artistic production and response (e.g., Koroscik, 1990; Parsons, 1987). However, particular attention has been given to expert-novice development in science and math education. This research suggests that theorists should shift from the idea of a global restructuring of knowledge, suggested by a stage-dependent conception of development, to a cognitive perspective of learning dependent on the integration of specific concepts (Novak, 1977).

Expert-novice models have helped researchers and educators more fully understand the character of learning and applying formal knowledge. However, attempts to devise expert-novice stage models have had inherent sociological problems on at least three levels. First, the learning of informal knowledge, which is also an important aspect of schooling, is not taken into account. Second, the social attributes of knowledge construction have not been given serious attention. Third, the social construction of professional disciplines has not been analyzed in relation to expert-novice development. Each of these issues is extremely important in the context of an internationalized curriculum.

Sociological Shifts in Conceptions of Learning and Curriculum

Recent research suggests that development is more dependent on learning than previously thought. Because formal learning is an inherently social enterprise, a sociological understanding of development and curriculum is required. As a result, sociocultural aspects of each of the curriculum issues discussed above must be viewed as important dimensions of education.

As American psychologists became interested in cognition after the Second World War, the influences of society and culture on development and learning became increasingly apparent. At the same time, the work of sociologists and anthropologists became more closely associated with the ways people's minds worked and the boundaries between these and other social sciences began to blur. By the 1970s, through influences ranging from changing educational populations to Frankfurt School sociology and Soviet psychology, new sociological conceptions of development and curriculum emerged that took into account previously ignored sociocultural influences.

The sociological direction taken in education is reflected in new visions of social reconstructionism and constructivist learning theory, which have roots in the work of Dewey, Piaget, and others. This learning theory research suggests that learning is *situated*, or closely related to the circumstance in which it takes place (see e.g., Prawat, 1989; Vosniadou and Brewer, 1987; Walkerdine, 1988). Development, then, is bounded by students' construction of knowledge as they learn. Students learn by appropriating information and restructuring it in relation to what they already know. Such restructuring actually influences the processes used to learn further information. If this information is consistent with previous knowledge, it will be assimilated. If it is inconsistent, it may be rejected or changed to fit what is already known.

Curriculum influences not only what students know, but how they come to know. Constructivists argue that students learn best through deep engagement in activities of medium complexity that reflect life experiences and provoke several levels of thought. From a constructivist perspective, curriculum should be designed to enable students to make connections between various arenas of knowledge and experience. Curriculum that includes multi-layered cultural and interdisciplinary experiences, such as cooperative learning, educational immersion, and faculty mentorship, advance knowledge precisely because they help students connect and construct meaning of the synthetic sequence of information that makes up much of higher education curriculum.

Expert-novice models help us understand something about the psychological processes of building domain-specific knowledge. However, they do not help us to effectively design curriculum that gives attention to the sociocultural aspects of knowledge and knowing. To reflect such attention, curriculum must be seen as an interactive process between students and a range of people through various types of texts and images involving many communication practices, cultural norms, ideals, and other social conditions that should help the students live successfully in the new global environment.

GLOBAL VISUAL CULTURE AND INTERDISCIPLINARITY AS EXAMPLES OF CURRICULUM CONTENT

The new global technology and unstable borders of culture have made popular culture pedagogical, as well as political (Giroux and Simon, 1989). The technological developments that enable mass communication have increased the availability of visual representations of all sorts to anyone who has access to television, computers, film, and other mass media. Visual forms of culture have become more accessible than literary forms. Although Americans have more televisions and video recorders and spend more on advertising per capita than any other nation, the case is similar in other industrialized countries. Representations of information, from entertainment to curriculum, have blurred the boundaries of truth, culture, and country.

All this has two important meanings for curriculum. First, the character and content of various forms of international visual culture are now part of global, social knowledge. Visual culture has become an essential way to learn about the world. As a result, the power of visual culture of all forms (mass media, visual arts, scientific computer visualization, popular culture, marketing and advertising, etc.), including those dependent on new technologies, should be critically addressed in all educational situations

Second, references to knowledge now come from a variety of sources outside school, and not only from the professional community of a parent discipline. These fragmented, often conflicting, and multidisciplinary references may have more to do with student understanding of a subject than does a course based on the structure of a discipline. As a result, the conflicts and interdisciplinary connections between bodies of knowledge should be included in any internationalized curriculum.

Communication and Global Visual Culture

Communication theory can shed light on the process of curriculum design in relation to global visual culture (Freedman, 1997). For example, perspectives on the relationship between objects and audiences have recently changed (e.g., Best and Kellner, 1991; Morley, 1992; Thompson, 1994). Early communication theorists such as Theodor Adorno and Max Horkheimer, as well as structuralists and semioticians, focused to a great extent on the sending and receiving of intended messages in their analyses of technological communications, but little on the appropriation of information by audiences. Theory now focuses more on the suggestiveness of signs and the ways in which meaning is constructed by audiences. In contrast to the earlier view, that an author or artist controls the message that will be taken from his or her work, response theory begins with the assumption that each member of an audience constructs his or her own meaning. Based on hermeneutics, this perspective of audience involvement gives attention to the interpretation of literary and visual texts as dependent on individual, lived experience.

However, as British sociologist and communication theorist David Morley (1992) argues in relation to encounters with the mass media, neither of these dichotomous approaches to the way in which messages are received and understood are plausible because they do not take into account the important sociocultural conditions of the process. For example, the process of learning in the context of curriculum involves a highly interactive relationship between sources of information and students; this relationship is both similar and different for individuals and groups. Cultural readings may generally glean intended meanings, while personal readings may result in the unintentional. Differences are due, in part, to different cultural experiences among social, ethnic, and gender groups and the ways members of these groups interpret experience. And yet, the contribution of the audience is not entirely unique and individual because similar people have similar experiences from which to draw, interpret, and integrate new experience.

Case studies of student interaction with visual and textual sources of information can help us understand how people appropriate information. Such studies have suggested that adolescents and adults place themselves in fictional realities (e.g., Beach and Freedman, 1992; Freedman and Wood, 1996; Radway, 1984). For example, Radway drew this conclusion from her study of women reading fiction, and Beach and Freedman's study of the appropriation of representations of gender demonstrated that students act this way when reading short stories and looking at advertising images. Beach and Freedman's research indicated that students do not view such sources critically unless they are specifically taught how to do so, and knowing how to analyze written texts does not necessarily transfer to visual images. As a result, student appropriation of information from images results in knowledge that may be, for example, inconsistent with the social equity goals of American education.

Such research suggests that student encounters with multiple, even fictional, realities are appropriated and transformed into knowledge and that many of these encounters involve an array of visual sources. In other words, the vast number of globally distributed, visual representations that students encounter daily become part of their previous knowledge when they come to school, and should be taken into account as are other aspects of foundational knowledge. Helping students analyze visual culture would aid them in increasing their understanding of the world.

Interdisciplinary Knowledge: Connections and Conflicts

Curriculum aids in the development of student knowledge, in part, through the dissemination of information about the professional disciplines. Recent research has indicated that students only learn when they can attach new information to what they already know (see e.g., Prawat, 1989; Vosniadou and Brewer, 1987). However, as suggested above, prior knowledge may not be tied to a particular discipline and much educational discourse reflects the belief that students' lives outside school can, and should, be left at the classroom door. In a sense, faculty are expected to actually overcome student experience outside the classroom.

In part, this perspective is common because the determination of what is appropriate curriculum content is often based on the idea of promoting consensus. Educators tend to be concerned that conflict in curriculum will only confuse students, and teachers tend to be careful not to teach about professional conflicts in school (Graff, 1987). However, if we want education to be intellectually challenging, we must teach about meaning, including conflicts of meaning, and how things come to mean. If schools in a democracy are to educate enlightened citizens who take part in political decision-making and work together to improve cultural conditions, then conflicts of meaning must be included in the discussion.

An important reason for the focus on consensus and isolated content is a dependence on traditional conceptions of disciplinary knowledge. In different cultures, the divisions between the professional disciplines on which Western (Euro-American) curriculum is built do not always exist. For example, some cultures do not have a word for art because the artifacts that we conceptualize as art are so completely integrated into their daily life. Even in such European countries as Sweden, the boundaries between, for example, semiotics and education are drawn differently than in the U.S.

Cultural overlaps and contradictions are part of what make up our definitions of knowledge. For example, any of the dichotomies suggested by representations of knowledge may effectively be thought of as dualities because both parts are integral to knowledge. In a sense, these dualisms are part of the complexity of knowledge and drawing on these conflicts in curriculum could help students understand how people come to know. Because knowledge is built on conflicts and multiple meanings, interdisciplinary content should be seen as an important part of any curriculum, but particularly in the context of internationalization.

CONCLUSION

I have argued that a sound international curriculum needs to be designed with an eye toward *social transformation, constructivist principles of learning, interdisciplinary content,* and *diverse modes of representation.* Such an education must reflect the complexities of global existence and be based on visual as well as textual and numerical cultural carriers as reflected by the following recommendations for practice.

1. Begin curriculum design with a social reconstructionist perspective.
2. Broaden this perspective through the application of new approaches to learning.
3. Present knowledge in terms of sociocultural, as well as disciplinary, contexts.
4. Think of culture as being local and global, as well as national.
5. Include in curriculum the various forms of international visual culture that influence global knowledge.
6. Reference knowledge from international sources, including sources that may be fragmented, conflicting, and multidisciplinary.

7. Help students directly and constructively address professional and cultural differences.

Obviously, the process of internationalizing is large scale. Such a change in higher education curriculum will not take place easily. However, work currently being done within colleges of education could take us toward this transformation and help make us citizens of the world.

REFERENCES

Baars, B. J. (1986). *The cognitive revolution in psychology*. New York: Guilford.

Beach, R. and Freedman, K. (1992). Responding as a cultural act: Adolescents' responses to magazine ads and short stories. In J. Many and C. Cox (Eds.), *Reader stance and literacy understanding* (pp. 162-88). Norwood, NJ: Ablex.

Best, S. and Kellner, D. (1991). *Postmodern theory: Critical interrogations*. New York: Guilford.

Eisner, E.W. and Vallance, E. (1974). *Conflicting conceptions of curriculum*. Berkeley, CA: McCutchan.

Freedman, K. (1997). Representations of fine art in popular culture: Curriculum inside and outside of school. *Journal of Art and Design Education, 16*(2), 137-46.

Freedman, K. and Relan, A. (1992). Computer graphics, artistic production and social processes. *Studies in Art Education, 33*(2), 98-109.

Freedman, K. and Wood, J. (1996, April). Student knowledge about visual culture: Images inside and outside of social studies classrooms. Paper presented at the meeting of the American Educational Research Association, San Francisco, CA.

Gardner, H. (1991). *The unschooled mind: How children think and how schools should teach*. New York: Basic Books.

Giroux, H. A. and Simon, R. I. (1989). *Popular culture: Schooling and everyday life*. Bergin and Garvey.

Graff, G. (1987). *Professing literature: An institutional history*. Chicago: University of Chicago Press.

Joyce, B. and Weil, M. (1986). *Models of teaching*. Englewood, NJ: Prentice-Hall.

Koroscik, J. (1990). Novice-expert differences in understanding and misunderstanding art and their implications for student assessment in art education. *Art and Learning Research, 8*, 6-29.

Langley, P. and Simon, H. A. (1981). The central learning in cognition (pp. 361-80). In J. R. Anderson (Ed.), *Cognitive skills and their acquisition*. Hillsdale, NJ: Erlbaum.

Larkin, J. (1981). Enriching formal knowledge: A model for learning to solve textbook physics problems. In J. R. Anderson (Ed.), *Cognitive skills and their acquisition*. Hillsdale, NJ: Erlbaum.

Marzano, R. J. (1992). *A different kind of classroom: Teaching with dimensions of learning*. Alexandria, VA: Association for Curriculum and Supervision.

McNeil, J. (1996). *Curriculum: A comprehensive introduction* 5th ed. New York: HarperCollins.

————. (1990). *Curriculum: A comprehensive introduction*. 4th ed. New York: HarperCollins.

————. (1975). *Curriculum: A comprehensive introduction*. New York: HarperCollins.

Morley, D. (1992). *Television, audiences, and cultural studies*. London: Routledge.

Novak, J. D. (1977). An alternative to Piagetian psychology for science and mathematics education. *Science Education, 61*, 453-77.

Parsons, M. J. (1987). *How we understand art: A cognitive development account of aesthetic experience*. Cambridge: Cambridge University Press.

Prawat, R. S. (1989). Promoting access to knowledge, strategy, and disposition in students: A research synthesis. *Review of Educational Research, 59*(1), 1-41.

Radway, J. (1984). *Reading the romance: Women, patriarchy and popular literature*. Chapel Hill, NC: University of North Carolina Press.

Thompson, J. B. (1994). Social theory and the media. In D. Crowley and D. Mitchell (Eds.), *Communication theory today* (pp. 27-49). Stanford, CA: Stanford University Press.

Vosniadou, S. and Brewer, W. F. (1987). Theories of knowledge restructuring in development. *Review of Educational Research, 57*(1), 51-67.

Walkerdine, V. (1988). *The mastery of reason: Cognitive development and the production of rationality*. London: Routledge.

CHAPTER 3

The Impossibility of Internationalizing Students by Adding Materials to Courses

by Marion L. Lundy Dobbert

INTRODUCTION

One common proposal for internationalizing a university curriculum is to add international elements to a large number of classes. It is assumed that when a high level of curricular internationalization has been reached, the institution will have created a globalized university culture.

Using the analytic point of view of modern structural anthropology, I will demonstrate in this chapter the impossibility of this proposal. First, universities per se cannot "have" culture. To say that a university has a culture is to use a dangerous form of academic shorthand that reifies culture and permits us to employ a reductionistic fallacy. To use the idea of a university culture without examination is to fall into the trap of believing that we can fix or improve a university by direct action upon its parts, in this case, its curriculum and courses. Such sloppy thinking smoothes over the real difficulties of globalizing or internationalizing a university. Culture is not a thing; it is a process. Only people who form an interactive social group can have a culture. Culture may be seen only in patterns of continuous social interchange. Thus, internationalization can only occur by changing interaction patterns within the university.

Unfortunately, educational systems-based factors make course-by-course curriculum change for maximal internationalization difficult and probably impossible. Two inertial factors in college and university curriculums militate against course-by-course internationalization: (1) discipline-based curricular organization and (2) the need for more time to teach new content. The standard types of university teaching—lecturing on international subjects, assigning texts that include global viewpoints, or insisting on a term paper that contains global material—will not internationalize either students or the university. Regardless of the inclusion of new internationalized materials and requirements, lectures, texts, and assignments permit only passive, cognitive learning. Personal globalization, on the other hand, requires active participation in acquiring new social and behavioral patterns that make up an internationalized culture. In real life, internationalization occurs in a nonlinear fashion. The main forces for internationalization are events that initiate new processes in the lives of individuals, not formal curricular or class-based cognitive learning.

To create a genuinely globalized and internationalized university, faculty, administration, teaching assistants, and students must build new patterns of interaction. They must build a new university culture with new and very different patterns. And, as will be discussed later in this chapter, they must undertake an enormous transformation.

The teaching of foreign languages provides an excellent example of the problems involved in creating a real internationalism. One might think that foreign languages are by definition internationalized. However, a large volume of cross-cultural training research demonstrates that the opposite is more frequently true. When students leave foreign language classes at both the secondary and university levels, they usually speak a version of the language that is "culturized"[1] by U.S. interaction patterns. An extraordinary instructor of, say, Spanish, would avoid this failing by interweaving Spanish or Mexican behavior patterns into his or her course offering. For example, the instructor could teach how to politely excuse one's self to go to the toilet in Latin American cultures and how this is done by males and females to either or both males or females. Knowing how to go to the bathroom (a commonly used U.S. euphemism) is only one small behavioral trait. Even teaching several hundred behavior traits does not enculturate class members because culture is not made up of a set of traits. Thus, foreign language students become no more internationalized than calculus students.

Another approach to achieving globalization in universities relies on the globe-spanning technology of the Internet and the World Wide Web. This technological highway, as it now exists, can give only limited help with internationalization and globalization. E-mail and network webs create only partial contact that is essentially cognitive and issue oriented. Currently, full

---

[1] The use of the word culture as a verb is not common in anthropology, but Beatrice Diamond Miller (1979) has argued eloquently and convincingly for this verbalized usage.

contact with alternative social systems cannot be supplied due to this limit on interaction via any electronic medium of cross-national contact.

All the approaches listed above are based on weak cognitive definitions of culture. If culture is defined as knowing the values and beliefs of a selected group of people, such as the Vietnamese, or upon the concept that culture is a game that one joins by learning the rules, much of what social and materialist anthropologists consider culture is omitted: (1) patterns of social interaction between individuals engaged in group processes; (2) patterns of relationships between individuals, groups, and the society as a whole; and (3) the relationships between sociocultural patterns and the natural eco-environment. These are either ignored or transformed into rules. However, because the use of cognitive definitions fits well with North Euro-American cultural emphases on individualism, the resulting personality-based explanations of cultural life contain an inherent and unrecognized reductionistic fallacy. This type of cognitive fallacy is different from the one mentioned earlier. This one reduces being to a mental process.

As we can see, the rhetoric of globalizing the curriculum hides the real issues of creating internationalized institutions and persons. In this chapter, I will uncover those issues. I will begin by examining some plans for internationalization that are more comprehensive than the curricular change model. I will provide a thought experiment that uses a visual simulation of cultural complexity that is strong enough to serve as a pattern for thinking accurately about cultures and what is needed to create internationalized individuals. I will discuss the way in which whole cultures are learned. Finally, I will make some modest recommendations about what universities can do to support globalization.

FIVE MODELS OF INTERNATIONALIZATION

Anthropologist Margaret Gibson (1976) has studied proposals for creating multiculturalism in U.S. public schools. She discovered that multicultural proposals could be divided into five paradigms: (1) the model for educating the culturally different; (2) the cultural understanding model; (3) the education for cultural pluralism model; (4) the bicultural education model; and (5) the multiculturalism as the normal human experience model. Gibson's five classes, with some modification, are equally useful for the examination of proposals for globalizing/ internationalizing colleges and universities.

Educating the Culturally Different

The first model, educating the culturally different, which Gibson calls benevolent multiculturalism, might also be called the default setting. Educational institutions following this model assume that individuals who enter but do not match the culture of the institution need to be given remedial work. Many universities screen international students via the TESOL or provide remedial English as a second language classes. Because these classes meet four or five days a week for several hours, they lock many international students out of the mainstream culture of the university. American students who are ethnically or socioeconomically different are also assigned to remedial classes in English and other subject matter courses. Such classes also separate them from the mainstream culture of the university. Separate treatment stigmatizes these students and creates a barrier that blocks other faculty and students from learning multicultural skills through interaction with them. Such separation prevents everyone from increasing the breadth of his or her cultural repertoire and impoverishes the entire university culture.

Cultural Understanding

Gibson's second model is termed the "educating about cultural differences" or the "cultural understanding" model. Institutions using this model provide courses and activities from which all students can study different cultures and learn to accept their varied styles of being and doing. Educational institutions espousing this model believe that cultural pluralism is a vital and positive force that enriches everyone. Large universities are bastions of this model, with centers or departments of East Asian cultures, Scandinavian cultures, African cultures, Native American cultures, etc.

Nevertheless, Gibson finds fault with the education for cultural understanding model because it tends to emphasize differences, working outward from North Euro-American culture. In so doing, the "education about" model can actually increase stereotyping. This situation is a result of the unrecognized assumption that culture is an entity, that examiners, in some way outside and above the culture being studied, can turn over, prod, and poke until complete understanding is reached. This happens in universities not through purposeful malice or the ignorance of those who teach about other cultures, but as a byproduct of a university structure that is divided into small boxes by disciplines or areas.

Education for Cultural Pluralism

Education for cultural pluralism, Gibson's third classification, is conceptually distinct from the first two models because its strongest advocates are generally people of color and members of identifiable ethnic groups. This model's advocates seek to preserve heterogeneity and egalitarian pluralism and reject and resent the political dominance of North Euro-Americans. According to Gibson, they believe that controlling cultural pluralism will increase their political power. The results of the movement for cultural preservation were seen in universities and colleges with programs in Native American Studies, Black Studies, and Hispanic Studies.

At the same time institutions set up these programs, they realized that higher education environments were not comfortable for students from these so-called minority groups, and advising offices that included advisors who were members of the target ethnic group were established for students of color. Because this model is generally confrontational (Gibson, 1976), it could easily provoke increasing resistance from and conflict with the North Euro-American group that controls much of higher education. Gibson also observed that this movement lacked a plan for creating a stable, heterogeneous, egalitarian nation.

Nevertheless, the idea of education for heterogeneity and egalitarian pluralism on a world scale is intellectually attractive. Further, the model can fit comfortably into an environment that supports critical social analysis and movements for grassroots democracy. It has some clear advantages over the cultural understanding model, especially when self-critique is built into its curriculum. Nonetheless, the model has two problems. First, a program for achieving internationalization with this model would require a teaching faculty drawn from the nations or cultures under study. Second, it would have some of the same problems as the education for cultural understanding model if the target cultures are taught primarily through classes, although these problems would be in part alleviated by the presence of faculty acculturated outside North Euro-American social and ideological systems.

Bicultural Education

Gibson's fourth classification covers proposals for bicultural education. Proponents of this model, like those supporting education for pluralism, reject plans for creating uniformity and similarity and desire to promote heterogeneity. Advocates of this model believe that all school children should achieve competence in at least two cultures, the so-called U.S. mainstream culture, and at least one other, a so-called ethnic culture. Since abundant research has shown that bicultural individuals tend to be more creative and tolerant than monocultural individuals, supporters of this plan believe it will greatly benefit the nation. However, Gibson points out that this plan carries an assumption that U.S. culture will continue to be dominated by North Euro ethnic groups and is therefore supportive of the status quo. Now, nearly 20 years since Gibson commented on the status of multicultural education, we recognize the weakness of this assumption because we have on one hand the example of Quebec, and on the other hand population estimates that show that Spanish speakers will soon predominate in the U.S. Both these examples underscore the need for biculturalism. The problems with implementing this model, whether at the K-12 level or the university level, are nearly identical to those for the second and third models described above.

Multiculturalism as the Normal Human Experience

Gibson's fifth model, multiculturalism as the normal human experience, is adopted from the work of Ward Goodenough, an anthropologist well known for his analyses of applied social and technological change projects. Goodenough (1976) argues that we are all already multicultural. We can operate in commercial-economic environments, medical environments, workplace environments, formal political environments, and religious environments, to name a few. In commenting on this model, Gibson notes that people do not learn this type of multiculturalism in schools because they are too over-focused on formal education as a solution to our problems with pluralism. Gibson argues that we ignore the ways that people actually learn to be multicultural. Several generations of anthropologists who have studied the acquisition of cultural competence know that competency can only be attained through frequent (or continual) and intense interaction with members of the target culture. Thus, the strategy of those who support this model is to take the focus off schools and to arrange our social structure to provide multicultural or international experience in many different situations. Although this model avoids stereotyping, Gibson believes we lack the mechanisms to implement it. Nevertheless, the multiculturalism-as-the-normal-human-experience model is the only model that can actually produce bicultural or multicultural individuals at the national or international levels, we must adopt this model if we aim to produce internationalized or globalized students through programs at our colleges and universities.

THE NATURE OF CULTURE: AN ILLUSTRATED THOUGHT EXPERIMENT

If we are planning to globalize our students, then we must make an estimation of the size of the task. How much do we need to teach them to have them become multicultural?

Any sociocultural system has 12 bases: activities, social responses, use of space, relation to its ecology, a tool system, social groupings, social interaction patterns, social roles, fixed institutions, defined relational expressive/emotional systems, communication, and priorities and values. These can be imagined to form a 12-sided solid (see Figure 3–1). The origin of these patterns is biological and we share them with most mammals Part of the uniqueness of any mammal, including humans, is found in the hormonal patterns that create emotions and in the unique social response repertoires of each individual.

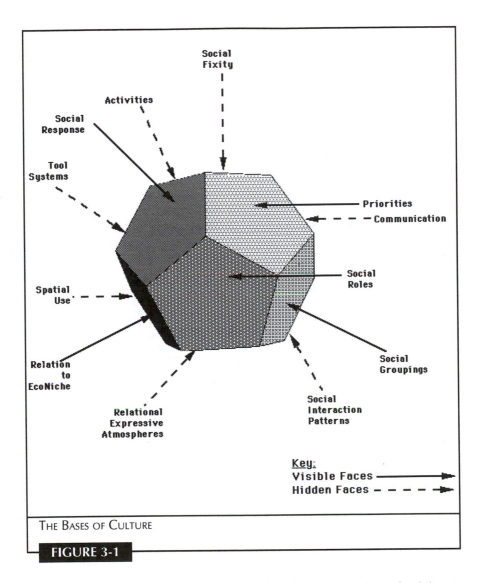

Social
Fixity

Activities

Social
Response

Tool
Systems

Priorities

Communication

Spatial
Use

Social
Roles

Relation
to
EcoNiche

Social
Groupings

Relational
Expressive
Atmospheres

Social
Interaction
Patterns

Key:
Visible Faces ——————▶
Hidden Faces – – – – –▶

THE BASES OF CULTURE

FIGURE 3-1

Thus all mammals have flexible sociocultural patterns. This flexibility is fundamental to survival and has been well documented.

Although human culture is founded on our mammalian inheritance, it is not limited to it. James G. Miller (1979) has developed a concept that suggests that greater and greater complexity is created when simple functions are developed, more complex functions arise, and novel structures evolve to support them. Figure 3-2 pictures the above 12 sociocultural bases pushed out to make a hollow star with 12 five-sided points that represent added complexity.

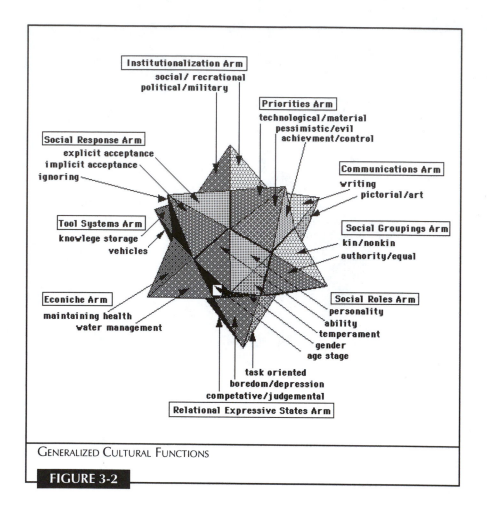

Institutionalization Arm
social / recreational
political / military

Priorities Arm
technological/material
pessimistic/evil
achievment/control

Social Response Arm
explicit acceptance
implicit acceptance
ignoring

Communications Arm
writing
pictorial/art

Tool Systems Arm
knowlege storage
vehicles

Social Groupings Arm
kin/nonkin
authority/equal

Econiche Arm
maintaining health
water management

Social Roles Arm
personality
ability
temperament
gender
age stage

task oriented
boredom/depression
competative/judgemental
Relational Expressive States Arm

GENERALIZED CULTURAL FUNCTIONS

FIGURE 3-2

In total there are 60 complex functions.

Social Fixity/ Institutionalization:	informal organization, social/recreational, economic, political/military, instructional/religious
Activities:	individual acts/states, curing/caring for, multipurpose socializing, obtaining, making, maintaining, entertaining
Social Response:	explicit acceptance, implicit acceptance, explicit denial, implicit denial, ignoring
Spatial Systems:	personal space, group living space, architecture, land use, geographical concepts
Social Interaction:	discussing/gossiping, watching, joking/teasing, feasting/gifting, conflict activities

Grouping Principles:	age/gender, kin/nonkin, familiar/strange, purposeful/authority/equality
Social Roles:	ability, personality, temperament, age stage, gender
Relational/Expressive Emotional Systems:	relaxation/affection, happiness/elation, task oriented boredom, depression, competitive/judgmental
Communication:	verbal, singing, writing, pictorial/art, nonverbal/dance
Priorities and Values:	technological/material, scarcity/gain, lawfulness/harmony, achievement/control, pessimistic/evil
Relation to Econiche:	gathering/hunting, horticultural/agricultural, extraction/manufacturing, water management, maintaining health
Tool Systems:	simple tools, machine tools, vehicles, communication tools, knowledge storage tools

Place yourself at the center of the star and imagine that the 60 sides belong to a culture that is not your own, but is that of a culture in which you wish to become fluent. It is clear that knowing the 60 facets of culture is an enormous task. It is equally clear that the 60 aspects listed here do not even begin to touch the richness of cultures. As we stare in dismay at the points, we realize with alarm that the surface labels are generic; they label types of things but there are no culture items from any culture to be seen anywhere.

Now imagine that each of the star points has on it eight smaller three-sided points. This means that each now bumpy star arm now has 24 new surfaces on it. On one arm, the three sides of the new little points represent activities in the culture's econiche like getting salt, processing food, preserving food, obtaining fuel, making fire, tending fire, cooking, tending food, herding animals, feeding animals, pasturing animals, driving herd, marking/branding, milking, butchering, breeding, hunting, foraging, digging, fishing, irrigating, hoeing, plowing, and planting. On another arm of the star, the 24 small surfaces include body-oriented activities—dressing, bathing, brushing teeth, decorating body, cutting hair, arranging hair, piercing the body, scarring the body, day dreaming, dreaming, imagining, having visions, drug-induced states, meditating, sleeping, resting, being ill, having a nocturnal emission, having menstruation, being in pain, having surgery, being pregnant, giving birth, and dying.

Counting all the sides of all the new points gives us 1,540 new surfaces representing subsystems of culture. These two lists have been obtained from ethnographic information my colleagues and I used to code data about learning culture (Pitman, Eisikovits, and Dobbert, 1989). As was the case with the cultural categories for the 60 main star points, these categories are generic. Each culture does these activities in its own way. If we were to try to specify the exact cultural content for a specific culture, it would be necessary to add points to our point and points onto those points, until we would have a very bristly star indeed. But for our purposes of answering the question of how much information we would need to know to learn another culture, we would have come far enough with respect to listing types of cultural phenomena. Nevertheless, this is an extremely conservative listing. I believe it is justified to use such a conservative estimation because we are not expecting our globalized students to become cultural natives.

All the actions, beliefs, technologies, etc. placed on the 1,440 sides of the star are related to each other by social and individual processes. The number of pairs of the 1,540 cultural items is 43,275 followed by 3,920 significant numbers, an unimaginably large number ($43,275 \times 10^{392}$). However, there are actually four primary ways of relating any two items—through socially approved means, socially approved ends, disapproved means, and disapproved ends (Spindler, 1976). This produces four combinations: approved means to approved ends, approved means to disapproved ends, disapproved means to approved ends, and disapproved means to disapproved ends.

Further, as the bearers of a culture go about their business using patterns by thinking, feeling, acting, and behaving individually and socially, they push, pull, and twist on the patterns as their individuality shapes culture just as culture shapes them. We stand with our mouths dropped open in disbelief that someone should expect us to be able to internationalize ourselves and learn many of these patterns for any culture, be it Spanish, Polish, or Tamil.

If we work hard on the language and find full members of the culture to live with and work with; and if we are observant and sensitive, we will probably be able to pass a surface inspection in a few years.

LEARNING CULTURES

How, then, can we learn culture(s) and become functionally multicultural and international persons? We are able to learn cultures because we, along with other higher primates, are genetically and operationally generalists and therefore designed to be learners. We are also polyphasic learners (Henry, 1960). Figure 3-3 depicts a schematized polyphasic learner. As polyphasic learners, we are always ingesting information in multiple simultaneous ways. For example, starting in some kindergartens and many first grades, we learn that education is acquired by sitting on our posteriors; formal education is done at the ever-present desk or table.[2] We absorb this generally unconscious lesson so well in our culture that we tend to forget that life, breathing, and learning

---

[2] In contrast, traditional leaning in the Jewish shtetls of eastern Europe occurred on foot as the students crowded about the rabbi (Zborowski, 1955) to fiercely debate critical issues of faith and life.

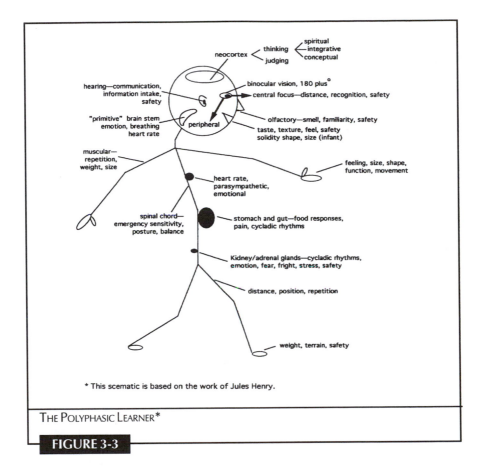

THE POLYPHASIC LEARNER*

FIGURE 3-3

are all simultaneous and all equally necessary through every moment of our time on earth. We cannot be what we most essentially are, social beings in interaction, without accommodation and change to the living and evolving others surrounding us every day. Nor can we stand still when the cultural and environmental processes in which we are embedded undergo continual transformation. The polyphasic learner, then, is the human response to complexity.

The model of the polyphasic learner in Figure 3-3 depicts 67 simultaneous learning modes, by no means an exhaustive list. The five major senses—sight, hearing, smell, taste, and touch—and our adrenal emotions, immediate spinal chordal response, and motor systems form part of each individual's primary safety structures. Other parts of our bodies—the heart, muscles, limbs, and primitive brain stem—are all involved in the way humans learn to deal with time and rhythm. None of these are turned off just because we are sitting at a desk or table reading, doing math, or writing; these systems and many others continue to operate, and we subsequently learn through them even if they are not part of our conscious focus. Just as information is learned via all parts of the body, it is stored in complex combinations of brain, hormonal, musculo-skeletal, and involuntary systems. If, for example, we have learned to play a Vivaldi concerto, we find that our fingers, hands, arms, and possibly our breath know more about how to play that same Vivaldi piece after 15 years of not playing then does the cognitive part of our brain. To learn the complexities of a new culture all these modes for learning and storing data are at our service for learning *if we are immersed in that culture.*

Studies of wild primate and human learning have identified five major holistic learning processes.

- Habitat Learning
- Modeling and Imitation
- Social Experience
- Social Conflict
- Play

Each process calls for the use of the multiple modes of the polyphasic learner. Each of them operates under the presumption that the learner is immersed in the process that is the learning target. Each calls for social interaction over a time period proportional to the complexity of the learning to be gained. An adult joining a new club that meets monthly within the framework of his or her primary culture could probably learn the club's ways and peculiarities in six months to a year using the first four learning processes. A human child learning its native culture has, as a polyphasic learner, a much more complex task. Because culture is so complex, play, which is free experi-mentation with the elements of that culture over many years in a safe and sheltered context, becomes the major mode for optimal learning. Because humans are the only species in which adults normally play with adults, we can presume that play is equally critical for adult learning in complex situations. If it were not, evolution would have weeded it out. All this leads to the conclusion that new cultures are best learned through intensive representa-tive simulations or immersion methods. The major mode of teaching by instruction in high schools, colleges, and universities is not adequate for the task of culture learning. It is far too simplistic! Its cognitive orientation handicaps students who seriously wish to become internationalized or global-ized.

CAN UNIVERSITIES HELP INTERNATIONALIZE/GLOBALIZE GRADUATES?

As the above thought experiment indicates, internationalization of students and faculty cannot be created by adding new units to courses and shoring up the curriculum with more offerings on international topics. The curricular approach falls far short of the mark as a means for creating internationalization or globalization. The ability to function in another culture is acquired by polyphasic learning in an immersion situation because any target culture consists of a mathematically gigantic set of interactions and processes. The thought experiment laid out above is conservative with respect to the complexity of culture. For example, Vernon Hendrix and I have been working on sets of data from classrooms (Lundy Dobbert and Hendrix, 1993; Hendrix and Lundy Dobbert, 1995) with 14 variables and an average of about six codes per variable, for a possibility of 183,849,716,224 patterns. For this reason, Gibson's fifth model—the model of multiculturalism as normal experience—is the only reasonable solution to globalization, assuming that globalization means the ability to operate without undue stress in some other culture.

My formal definition of globalization/internationalization derives directly from what the thought experiment reveals about culture: A globalized person must (1) speak two to three languages in addition to English at the level of 7 or above on a 10-point scale where zero means no knowledge of the language and 10 refers to native knowledge of the language, and (2) must have resided in at least two non-English speaking countries, in non-Americanized environments, for at least one year each.

To achieve this level of globalization for their students, universities will need to create opportunities for internationalized residencies. To make internationalization and globalization a normal experience, every student and faculty member should be required to do internships in at least two target cultures and live in each for 9 to 12 months or more. They would need to stay long enough to experience culture shock and emerge from it with an acceptance of the target culture. The literature on cultural shock shows that not all persons are capable of doing this. Those lacking the psychological plasticity will harden in their own cultural patterns. Thus, the university's job is to prepare students and faculty prior to their internships.

The type of residencies abroad envisioned here cannot be done via the "college abroad" model. Many students in these programs create small enclaves of U.S. culture abroad and do not venture out into the target culture except for shopping and tourist-type activities. Students must be given real internships; they must be assigned real cultural roles in the target culture and must be supervised by a member of the target culture. Northwestern College in St. Paul, Minnesota, has developed an excellent program for business internships in Japan that could be used as a model (Lunak, 1995).

This type of residency can best be created through quid pro quo international exchanges or through consortia models. At the same time that a student or faculty member from an American university is taking an internship in, say, Mindinao in the Philippines, someone from Mindinao will be taking a residency at the American university. Internships or residencies might also be operated on a consortium model, such as that of the Midwest Universities Consortium for International Activities (MUCIA). This model has two advantages over the quid pro quo model. The first is financial. Students will pay tuition at their own institution. Faculty will be paid at their normal home rate, but will be provided free room and board at their exchange institution. Some modest moneys (perhaps raised through corporate partners) may be needed to create equity for third world residents in the U.S. A second advantage is that the consortium model avoids direct quid pro quo arrangements, which are difficult to make. In either case, both students and faculty will take appropriate roles at the university or college or industry in the target culture. Related visa regulations should permit a maximum 13 months in the country of residency with no exceptions to prevent the use of residencies for immigration.

A third model might be developed using two-year internationalized cohorts. The first year at least 50 percent of an internationalization cohort at the American university would have to be exchange students and faculty from the target nation for the specific linguistic and cultural skills desired by the American students. The setting for the cohort would be built on the well-known Concordia language village model, which provides intensive immersion in a deliberately created environment. The cohort would have be designed to require some types of applied work so that the U.S. students could learn the norms and mores for work in the target culture. This could be most efficiently done by requiring the American cohort members to do all the cooking, cleaning, and basic maintenance of the "village" under the supervision of the international members of the cohort. Lastly, the cohort courses would have to rely almost entirely on peer teaching so that U.S. norms and mores would not dominate the learning structures. Such simulations take advantage of the adult ability to play because, in the sheltered village situation, students and faculty can play with and try out target culture roles, actions, and strategies. During the second year, the international students and the American students and faculty would reverse roles and the American part of the cohort would move to the second culture. To be effective, the "villages" would not permit out-migration except in cases of emergency. Both halves of the cohort would sign a two-year agreement.

Surprisingly, an examination of the costs of optimal globalization for any of the three models (quid pro quo, internship or residency, cultural village), reveals that the human and administrative costs are not as large as might be expected. The three major human costs are the need to learn how to fluently speak one or more languages, the ability to accept uprooting from the culture of origin, and the willingness to be effectively cut off from much of the basic emotional support of home networks. The administrative costs in personnel assigned to globalization, in time, and in moneys to use either the consortium model or the residency model should be manageable. However, it will be necessary to examine some successful or partially successful models. For example, how does St. Olaf College in Northfield, Minnesota, manage to send 55 percent of its students abroad (Rice, 1995)? One could also examine the ways that anthropologists and their students become globalized and internationalized.

In my opinion, the most difficult aspect of the internationalization and globalization of the university will be changing university culture, which now revolves around the presentation and taking of classes. Few internationalization skills can be taught through classes. Nevertheless, the universities can help prepare students and faculty for the experiences that will lead to internationalization and globalization. An important task is teaching beginning language courses. However, this will only be useful if the language is taught intensively using only the target language and only materials (magazines, newspapers, novels) from the language area. Students not yet ready to go abroad on an exchange will also profit from area studies courses, internal intra-university cultural exchanges, and a more internationalized set of course requirements for undergraduates.

According to Yehudi Cohen (1975), all ancient and modern civilizational states (political entities with highly developed cities and multicultural sub-groups) have developed schooling to prepare individuals to work in the boundary regions between such states. Our old-fashioned university methods, inherited from medieval Europe where transportation was difficult and information traveled slowly, are no longer adequate. Not only do we live in a world where the largest Polish city is Chicago, but one where we have multiple methods of communicating with Poland within a one-minute span and can arrive there bodily in 10 to 12 hours. American universities cannot honestly claim to be generally educating students, or faculty, to live in the internationalized, corporate, bureaucratic world of today. As for preparing for next year or the next decade, some believe that our universities and the public school systems that feed them are an endangered species. Let us take heed: In the late 1960s and 1970s, many small colleges disappeared forever. Those who say that universities are on the road to extinction could be right if we do not read the book of the real globalized world and find ourselves a destination in it.

REFERENCES

Cohen, Y. (1975). The state system, schooling, and cognitive and motivational patterns. In N. Shimahara, and A. Scrupski (Eds.), *Social Forces and Schooling*. New York: David McKay.

Gibson, M. (1976). Approaches to multicultural education in the United States: Some concepts and assumptions. *Anthropology and Education Quarterly*, 7, 7-18.

Goodenough, W. (1976). Multiculturalism as the normal human experience. *Council on Anthropology and Education* Newsletter, 4, 4-7.

Hendrix, V. and Lundy Dobbert, M. (1995, April). Describing structure in qualitative data: Explorations in the use of dimensional analysis. Paper presented to the American Educational Association, San Francisco, CA.

Henry, J. (1960). "A cross-cultural outline of education. *Current Anthropology,* 4, 267-305.

Lunak, R. (1995). International business program at Northwestern College: A systems-based explanation. Unpublished manuscript, Department of Educational Policy and Administration, Northwestern College, St. Paul, MN.

Lundy Dobbert, M. and Hendrix, V. (1993, March). Dimensional analysis: Explorations in the use of a mathematical model for describing structure in qualitative data. Paper presented to the Central States Anthropological Society, Beloit, WI.

Miller, B.D. (1979). Culture or culturing. *Cultural and Educational Futures,* 1, 7-12.

Miller, J. G. (1978). *Living systems.* New York: McGraw-Hill.

Pitman, M.A., Eisikovits, R., and Lundy Dobbert, M.(1989). *Culture acquisition: A holistic approach to human learning.* New York: Praeger, pp. 145-68 and 198-212.

Rice, C. (1998). Personal communication.

Spindler, G. (1976). From omnibus to linkages: Cultural transmission models. *Council on Anthropology and Education* Newsletter 5.

Zborowski, M. (1955). The place of book-learning in traditional Jewish culture. In M. Mead, and M. Wolfenstein (Eds.), *Childhood in contemporary cultures.* Chicago: University of Chicago Press.

CHAPTER 4

Global Academies as Strategic Self-Organizing "Think Tanks"

by Arthur M. Harkins

CONCEPTS AND CONCEPTUAL FRAMEWORK

Post-internationalism is to internationalism as internationalism is to nationalism. As internationalism requires nationalism to become a subset of larger processes, post-internationalism is a complex of innovative *global* processes transforming internationalism into a subset of larger processes. Post-internationalism contributes to globalism through measurable empirical manifestations (e.g., global awareness and values, global corporations, and global Internet communities).

Post-internationalism also contributes to globalism through a variety of complex cultural dynamics. These dynamics are largely unpredictable because they are subject to the vagaries of chaotic processes. Cultures emerging from such turbulent conditions may be called post-cultures. Post-cultures make subsets of formerly traditional cultures, including those of national and international origins. Post-internationalism is the *effect* of global post-cultures; it is the envelope created by ever-changing waves or patterns of cultural novelties and their interactions.

Post-cultures are emergent cultures built on the foundations of existing cultures. Post-cultures as processes may be innovated by design or may appear as natural functions of systemic complexity. Post-cultures may reside for long periods of time as personal cultures peculiar to individuals, or they may spread quickly to groups, cohorts, networks, cyber communities, and beyond. Post-cultures may accrete into more stable cultures.

Post-international expressions are functions of post-cultures, and feed back upon post-cultures. Both processes create dynamic emergents that are the result of intentionality and chaotic serendipity.

This chapter explores post-internationalism and post-culture within a larger conceptual framework. The framework is deceptive, in that it appears to represent implied stage theory. A more acceptable approach is to say that the framework offers different organizing principles for human systems design, development, and operation. Systematized information plays a definitive role in every component of this framework.

Our first reason for including these technology-based organizations of human learning and accomplishment is to set a larger context for the discussion of post-internationalism and post-culture. Our second is to warn that sophisticated stakeholders are approaching academies and their services from vantage points characterized as interactive and as mutating ecologies made up of the following "techno-eras":

- **Pre-Agriculture:** Characterized by hunting and gathering. Little formal development of institutionalized role delineations; little accumulation of information outside the human brain.
- **Sedentary Agriculture:** Characterized by farming in one place. Accumulation of stored food permits more formal institutionalized role delineations (farmer, priestess, warrior, etc.). Information is recorded on stone, clay, or parchments.
- **Early Industry:** Characterized by the partial replacement of human muscle power with machines. Necessity for improved record-keeping requires more emphasis on formalized information management and on education.
- **Mid-Industry:** Characterized by the continued development of machines, including better printing presses and book and file production. Increased emphasis upon literacy and numeracy for the growing minority involved in record-keeping, education, and business or government relations. Digital transmissions begin by telegraph.
- **Late Industry:** Characterized by the emergence of typewriters, radio, early television, and automatic conversion of type to digital encoding. Masses of workers are expected to be minimally-to-moderately literate and numerate. Education beyond grammar school becomes de rigeuer; colleges begin to adopt school-to-white-collar-work mission statements.
- **Information:** Characterized by the emergence of the mainframe computer, primitive versions of which become necessary to maintain cost control and reliability in air traffic control, ticket sales, defense communications, and numerous other system contexts. White collar

work involves about two-thirds of the employment force. Educational requirements become high school (mandatory) and two-to-four years of college (mandatory or strongly suggested).

- **Knowledge:** Characterized by the emergence of the personal computer, the Internet, and the intellectual work force. Phrases such as knowledge worker and imagination worker become commonplace. Doubts arise whether traditional college and high school curricula can produce knowledge or imagination workers. International business competition puts strains on countries with low levels of worker quality, and makes their futures look comparatively grim.

- **Affect:** Characterized by recognition that knowledge or imagination workers are emotional entities, whose feelings must be taken into account when organizing real-world and cybernetic businesses, campuses, and relationships. Diversity models begin to replace uniformity models of social and machine systems, and efforts are made to create high-performance collaborative teams made up of diverse persons and skills.

- **Cybercommunity:** Characterized by the emergence of virtual realities to complement empirical realities, and, because of the technologies required, to increase the real and perceived rates of information transmission, with accompanying new pressures on knowledge producers and on affective responses.

- **Cyborg/Chemo/Genetic:** Characterized by emergent experimental modifications to humans that might enable them to work better/faster in cyber communities and in real world teams. Examples of such modifications include implanted transceivers and memory chips, and chemical or genetic modifications to the endocrine and central nervous systems.

- **Comprehension:** Characterized by a rediscovery of wisdom, or the positively synergistic interaction of information, knowledge, and affect. Leading companies develop holistic models of corporate cultures built upon shifting duties, team structures, and high levels of expedient personnel turnovers. Traditional efforts to manage workers shift to managing relationships with increasingly demanding customers.

Limited success may be predicted for those academies and academics who do not understand and heed the importance of shifts away from information-base curricula delivered to passive and powerless clients, and rigid geocentric definitions of community, such as nationalism or nonproductive forms of romantic internationalism.

CONTEMPORARY TRENDS AFFECTING ACADEMIC SERVICE CONTEXTS

The expansion of global information systems is permitting the emergence of learning opportunities that are increasingly independent of time and distance. Independence from cost, already a reality for the privileged, will soon become real for the world's middle classes and later for the masses of workers and their families.

Global information systems are built upon electronic devices (computers, satellites, switches, cables, antennae) and the infrastructures to produce, market, procure, and repair/update these devices.

Global information systems are also built upon infrastructures embedded in education and training, cultures, families, groups, and individuals.

All global information systems feed into the emerging "knowledge industries," which use information as a "raw" resource to be processed into knowledge that can help solve problems, create opportunities, manage change, and create added value.

Examples of knowledge industry growth being supported by global information systems include the following:

- interconnected "intellectual industries"
- electronic networks connecting old and emergent cultures
- world academic services offered by entrepreneurial colleges/universities
- limited automatic translations among languages and dialects
- global role consciousness among technicians/professionals
- tendency of some businesses to seek talent independent of nationality

A shift to information-driven knowledge formulations and applications appears to be a natural future for the academy. Such a shift will quickly separate course-vending from outcome-developing campuses. This future will be different for course-vending campuses in competition with Disney, Industrial Light and Magic, and Microsoft.

In the great research universities, global information systems are stimulating an acute consciousness of familiar problems and dawning new ones. Six examples of this trend include the following:

- Academic institutions can no longer count upon the willingness of stakeholders to support activities that do not return immediate or nearly immediate applied value for dollars and time spent.
- Academic institutions are in growing competition with public and private agencies that duplicate many of their services, and that usually have more interest in returning applied value for dollars provided.

- Internecine competition is growing within higher education and will become a major source of change-forcing functions.
- Academic institutions routinely attempt to delay hard decisions until those decisions are inevitable, thereby reducing short-term risks but increasing mid- and long-term risks to stakeholders and to themselves. Stakeholders increasingly will determine what is timely or tardy, and will judge delivery systems accordingly.
- Academic institutions must learn to reorganize along learning organization principles, designing teams-and-outcomes combinations to meet stakeholder needs.
- Market contexts for academic services are emergingly global. But these are not precisely defined because of the perturbing effects of both planned and chaotic changes. Such changes can emanate from anywhere within networked global information.

Assuming the presence of quality, *timeliness* of applied value will go a long way toward separating winners from losers among the twenty-first century's profit-seeking knowledge industries. This condition will almost certainly apply to the academies, even those that remain partially funded by tax support. Academies aspiring to leadership must recognize that the context of their institutions is increasingly transformative at the post-international and post-cultural levels, and that these trends are just beginning. Indeed, appropriate responses to changing contexts and their constituencies will likely define the future of the academy better than the self-referential planning carried out by administrations or by faculty senates.

TRANSITIONING FROM INFORMATIONAL CURRICULA TO KNOWLEDGE BASE R&D

The most important human resources trend since World War II has been the automation of symbolic labor. Hardware, software, and telecommunications combinations are making this possible on one level, new paradigms of complexity and "intersystems" combinations on another. One obvious intersystems combination is the emergence of human-machine partnerships. Such partnerships share much with ancient human-animal partnerships (e.g., sheep dogs and draft animals).

Work changes are guided by "candidate opportunities" created by the automation or elimination of repetitive symbolic tasks (e.g., keying-in, much office work, most K-12 and higher education lecturing, radio and TV announcements, etc.). This approach is not unlike what has occurred over the past 150 years as symbolic labor has replaced most farm and factory labor.

Standardized testing will be highly responsive to automation, yet it will become a model mechanism for the elimination of traditional faculty teaching positions. Higher education interests will tend to resist the automation of symbolic labor because labor replacements are tending to open in low-wage jobs requiring a minimum of symbolic skills (e.g., clerking, waiting tables), and because labor replacements are developing in mysterious "knowledge work." Knowledge work is not about repetitive jobs, but *contributions* that are creative, individualized, and value-adding.

Curricularly and pedagogically, higher education still admits to little respect for knowledge base curricula. It is still preparing information base graduates who have passed courses. Most such graduates have never heard of the knowledge industries. What they have learned is to suppress innovators within their classrooms, social groups, and employment settings, and to repress their own creative tendencies.

In the United States, public, nonresearch higher education systems must evolve toward post-international knowledge worker preparation. The alternative is to risk shut-down or mergers with public K-12 information/certification utilities.

ONGOING GLOBAL INFORMATION SYSTEMS EFFECTS

Two more important effects of global information systems are the growths in post-international and post-cultural changes. *Post-international* changes are signaled by companies whose capital, personnel, and customers *intentionally* traverse national boundaries at will, creating intentional post-international "corporate cultures." The effects of global information systems already include such new corporate cultures, including *intentional* post-international "personal cultures" that are unique to the individuals who continuously renew them.

Post-cultural changes are signaled by a product of chaos itself: *unintentional* or spontaneous phenomena whose meanings and importances must be invented because these phenomena were not the products of planned changes. Examples include the burgeoning importance of diversity, and the global women's movement. The effects of global information systems already include such spontaneous changes, such as the serendipitous emergence of "situational" personal cultures from the cauldrons of change.

ACADEMIES AND THEIR FUTURE SERVICE RELEVANCY

Academics interested in "international education" or "internationalized curricula" would do well to remind themselves that intentional and spontaneous post-international cultural events are very much underway at the organizational and personal levels. Were academics more inclined toward recognizing, stimulating, and rewarding intentional innovations and spontaneous emergences of cultures at either level, such a reminder would not be required.

But caution is in order, because academics tend to be one or two steps behind human systems changes when recognition of such is inhibited by conventions of decorum and tradition, as it often seems to be. Educational change within the United States itself is inhibited by fussy squeamishness associated with denial or denigration of offending change trends.

In both Japan and the United States, academics are finding that their services are being reassessed along emergent lines of post-modern praxis, which may be thought of as nontraditional intellectual pragmatism. Stakeholders involved in post-modern review of academic services include corporations and governments already operating in emergent post-international situations.

Students are beginning to acknowledge that their professional and social futures will take place in planned *and* chaotically emergent post-international ways. A large minority of students is expecting to be prepared for such futures while still in school.

Academics risk becoming redundant when they harp about the need for including anything that is already present in abundance on and around their campuses. Examples include students from other nations and ubiquitous communications technologies. Today, the phrase "distance learning" is tautological when applied to the service futures of good research campuses.

Academics will need to look to their linguistic or terminological choices because so many of these appear not to reflect the changing conditions and opportunities of the academic context. We are confident that the best of the research universities and scholarly liberal arts schools will make the transition in timely and successful ways.

With this shift comes the expectation that academic institutions will learn to catalyze information into knowledge that *will* improve academic services and that *will* produce better professional knowledge and information workers. This shift will require academies to move from teaching, research, and service missions to research, demonstration, and assessment missions. Teaching will shift to computerized instruction and mentoring. These shifts will result in academies as self-evolving learning organizations, eager to serve the emerging and often barely defined needs of their stakeholders.

Learning organization models offer well-integrated theoretical schema for incorporating the shift from teaching, research, and service into the process of transmuting raw information into knowledge for research, demonstration, and assessment. Timely research, demonstration, and assessment applications will allow academic winners to quickly distance themselves from academic losers.

In the post-international arena, outclassed academies will risk becoming labor pools for knowledge winners, who will drain off their most productive faculty and students and jeopardize their organizational futures. Academic losers may be able to survive by acting as client campuses for improving on intellectual products developed, copyrighted, and Beta-tested on the winners' campuses. Higher education must involve itself energetically in all phases of knowledge, intellect, and practice, including the promotion of collaborative works within stakeholder spheres.

POSSIBLE COMPONENTS OF A MODERN INTERNATIONAL CURRICULUM

"SimWorld"-style global models, requiring the best available software and coaching, might be major components of modern higher education curricula. Students could learn simulated investigative and developmental materials and roles as opposed to using dated resources within romanticized multiculturalist ideologies. (Geographic, language, and related proficiencies in focus populations/areas are conventional and logical components of such a curriculum.)

A curricular component list could contain the following "simulation-friendly" content areas:

- **Theory and practicum in modern and emerging communications systems.** This content acquaints students with the history, present capability, and emerging future of continental and global telecommunications networks.
- **Theory and practicum in creating and sustaining informed, educated, and trained populations.** This writing directs present and projected technologies and software combinations at high "learning refresh rates" and timely applications of symbolic resources in societies and economies of all types. "High learning refresh rates" refers to the shortening times required for modern hardware (HW) and software (SW) combinations to alter their performance capabilities. Some refresh occurs because of human programming; some because HW/SW systems increasingly are able to "teach" themselves new capabilities
- **Roles of computing machines in productivity and the division of labor.** This content extends the present and future content of enterprise and work from the present into the next several decades, and includes projected impacts on labor, skill requirements, and socioeconomic stability/mobility.
- **Simulations in national and international systems and relations.** This content could be taught through disks, CD-ROMs, online, and simulations obtainable from such government departments as state, agriculture, energy and environment, and defense. Many countries'

governments and ministries could also offer highly important resources.

- **Systemic studies of complexity and chaos in national and international entities.** This content refers to modern theories of interactive sociocultural, technological, and environmental systems. One of the technological systems is communications networks.
- **Comparative socioeconomic systems.** This content examines the characteristics of democratic socialism, planned state capitalism, loosely coupled democratic systems, and many other historical, present, and hypothetical forms of "blended" socioeconomic systems.
- **Defense, military alliances, and combat technologies.** This content delineates histories of hot and cold conflicts, including the hardware that was involved in each. It also examines present conflicts and projects future hypothetical conflicts (e.g., terrorism) and the various ways these might be resolved (e.g., nuclear exchanges, mediations, pacts/alliances.)
- **International demographics: cross-national residencies and citizenships.** This content examines historical and contemporary cases of individuals and families routinely living and working in more than one country and looks to the benefits and disadvantages of such demographics. It also demographically projects patterns into the future, and develops hypothetical "best" and "worst" case patterns (e.g., peacemaking co-citizenship, waves of unwanted border-crossings).

These curricular components of a "real-world" global higher education presence are merely suggestive of the strategic and visionary content so often lacking in higher education services.

GLOBAL LEARNING ORGANIZATIONS: VIRTUAL AND REAL SERVICE VENUES

Virtual classrooms and campuses are already here. Virtual classrooms and campuses are matrixed, innovative systems designed to help revitalize imaginatively stagnant and unproductive education professionals, and to help generate an array of alternative future uses for campus resources. One of the main tenets of virtual classrooms and campuses is that humans view their worlds through the lens of more or less conscious conceptual schemes or "paradigms." The conflict between dissimilar paradigms often lies at the heart of change difficulties, and at the heart of innovation itself.

Three paradigms are of most interest here: (1) classic realities, or the "real" worlds that most of our current academic understandings are associated with,

(2) virtual realities, or the technology- and imagination-driven "seeming places" that provide residences for new cyberspace worlds, and (3) liminal realities, or those that connect classic and virtual realities and provide for properly interfaced entities such as virtual classrooms and physical campuses. These environments interleave empirical and virtual resources to add responsiveness, variety, and value to the academic services offered to meet changing stakeholder needs.

From such paradigms, technologies, and changes in mission to reflect stakeholder needs, the best of the higher education industry will set a high performance standard for the future. Even if they earn the label "skunk works," such campuses will have nothing to be ashamed of; indeed, they will be pressed to cope with envy and emulation.

The best of these institutions will have learned to work productively at the edges of many "strange attractor" phenomena, including chaos, indeterminacy, post-internationalism, and post-culture.

BIBLIOGRAPHY

Abernathy, W.J., Clark, K.B., and Kantrow, A. M. (1983). *Industrial renaissance: Producing a competitive future for America.* New York: Basic Books.

Argyris, C. (1982). How learning and reasoning processes affect organizational change. In Goodman and Associates, *Change in Organizations* (pp. 47–86). San Francisco: Jossey-Bass.

————. (1964). *Integrating the individual and the organization.* New York: John Wiley & Sons.

Beer, S. (1979). *The heart of the enterprise.* New York: John Wiley & Sons.

Bell, D. (1973). *The coming of post-industrial society: A venture in social forecasting.* New York: Basic Books.

Bolman, L.G. and Deal, T.E. (1991). *Reframing organizations: Artistry, choice, and leadership.* San Francisco: Jossey-Bass.

Bradford, D.L. and Cohen, A.R. (1994). *Managing for excellence: The guide to developing high performance in contemporary organizations.* New York: John Wiley & Sons.

Briggs, J. and Peat, F.D. (1989). *Turbulent mirror: An illustrated guide to chaos theory and the science of wholeness.* New York: Harper & Row.

Cetron, M. and Davies, O. (1991). *Crystal globe* New York: St. Martin's Press.

Coates, J.F. et. al. (1990). *Future work.* San Francisco: Jossey-Bass.

Cunningham, W.G. and Gresso, D.W. (1993). *Cultural leadership: The culture of excellence in education.* Boston: Allyn and Bacon.

Davidow, W. H. and Malone, M. S. (1992). *The virtual corporation.* New York: HarperCollins.

Deming, W.E. (1986). *Out of the crisis.* Cambridge, MA: MIT Center for Advanced Engineering Study.

Dertouzos, M.L. et al. (1988). *Made in America: Regaining the productive edge.* Cambridge, MA: MIT Press.

DeThomasis, L. et al. (1990). *The transformational organization.* Winona, MN: St. Mary's College.

Drucker, P. (1992). *Managing the future.* New York: Truman Talley Books/Dutton.

————. (1988, January-February). The coming of the new organization. *Harvard Business Review*, 66, 1.

Durkheim, E. (1969). *The division of labor in society*. Translated by G. Simpson. New York: The Free Press.

Eason, K. (1988). *Information technology and organizational change*. London: Tayler and Francis.

Etzioni, A. (1961). *A comparative analysis of complex organizations* New York: The Free Press of Glencoe.

Fjermedal, G. (1986). *The tomorrow makers*. Redmond, WA: Tempus.

Fukuyama, F. (1992). *The end of history and the first man*. New York: The Free Press.

Galbraith, J. (1979). *Designing complex organizations*. Reading, MA: Addison-Wesley.

Gleick, J. (1987). *Chaos: Making a new science*. New York: Viking Penguin.

Hamel, G. and Prahalad, C.K. (1994). *Competing for the future*. Boston: Harvard Business School Press.

Hammer, M. and Champy, J. (1993). *Reengineering the corporation*. New York: Harper Business.

Harkins, A. et al. (1983). *Change and Choice*. Minneapolis: Control Data Press.

Harkins, A. and Maruyma, M. (Eds.). (1978). *Cultures of the future*. The Hague: Mouton.

Harkins, A. and Redd, K. (Eds.).(1980). *Education: A time for decisions*. Washington, DC: World Future Society.

Heifetz, R. A.(1994). *Leadership without easy answers*. Cambridge, MA: Harvard University Press.

Homans, G. C. (1950). *The human group*. New York: Harcourt Brace Jovanovich.

Johnston, R. and Lawrence, P.R. (1988, July-Aug.). Beyond vertical integration—the rise of the value-adding partnership. *Harvard Business Review* 66, 94-101.

Kuhn, T. S. (1970). *The structure of scientific revolutions*. 2nd ed. Chicago: University of Chicago Press.

Lipnack, J. and Stamps, J. (1986). *The networking book: People connecting with people*. New York: Routledge & Kegan Paul.

Masuda, Y. (1980). *The information society as post-industrial society*. Tokyo: Institute for the Information Society; Bethesda, MD: World Future Society.

Michaels, M. (Ed.). (1994). *From chaos to complexity: New tools for a complex world*. Urbana, IL: People Technologies, Inc.

Morgan, G. (1993). *Imaginization: The art of creative management*. Newbury Park, CA: Sage.

Mumford, E. (1983). *Designing human systems*. Manchester, England: Manchester Business School.

Nonaka, I. and Takeuchi, H. (1995). *The knowledge-creating company*. New York: Oxford.

Ohmae, K. (1982). *The mind of the strategist*. New York: McGraw-Hill.

Ouchi, W. G. (1981). *Theory Z: How American business can meet the Japanese challenge*. Reading, MA: Addison-Wesley.

Porter, M. E. (1985). *Competitive advantage: Techniques for analyzing industries and competitors*. New York: The Free Press.

Reich, R. B. (1983). *The next American frontier*. New York: Times Books.

Rorty, R. (1982). *Consequences of pragmatism* (1982). Brighton, United Kingdom: Harvester.

Sakaiya, T. (1991). *The knowledge-value revolution*. New York: Kodansha International.

Schon, D. (1983). *The reflective practitioner*. New York: Basic Books.

Schwartz, P. (1991). *The art of the long view*. New York: Doubleday.

Senge, P. (1990). *The fifth discipline: The art and practice of the learning organization*. New York: Doubleday.

Stacey, R. D. (1992). *Managing the unknowable: Strategic boundaries between order and chaos in organizations*. San Francisco: Jossey-Bass.

Stamps, J. (1980). *Holonomy: A human system theory*. Seaside, CA: Intersystem Publications.

Tapscott, D.(1996). *The digital economy*. New York: McGraw-Hill.

Tilgher, A. (1965). *Homo faber: Work through the ages*. Translated by D. Fisher. Chicago: Regency.

Vaill, P. B. (1989). *Managing as a performing art: New ideas for a world of chaotic change*. San Francisco: Jossey-Bass.

Walton, R. E. (1989). *Up and running: Integrative information technology and the organization*. Boston: Harvard Business School Press.

———. (1988). *Innovating to compete*. San Francisco: Jossey-Bass.

Wheatley, M. J. (1992). *Leadership and the new science*. San Francisco: Berrett-Koehler Publishers, Inc.

Wiener, N. (1954). *The human use of human beings: Cybernetics and society*. Garden City, NY: Doubleday Anchor.

Wooliston, G. (n.d.). *Architecture of critical systems thinking*. United Kingdom: Hull University (School of Management Working Paper).

Zuboff, S. (1988). *In the age of the smart machine: The future of work and power*. New York: Basic Books.

PART 2

· · · · · · · · · · · ·

Multidisciplinary Perspectives on Curricular Change

CHAPTER 5

The Role of Foreign Languages in the Internationalization of the Curriculum

by Michael F. Metcalf

Among the concerns of those who have assessed the need for internationalizing the curricula of our colleges and universities over the last few years has been the status of foreign language learning at both the secondary and postsecondary levels. These concerns have led to the reinstitution of foreign language requirements at a number of institutions, the beefing up of existing language requirements at others, and probing discussions of these issues on a number of other campuses where such changes have yet to be introduced. On balance, foreign language study at the nation's colleges and universities has expanded since the beginning of the 1990s (*Spreading the Word,* 1994), although this expansion has had its ups and downs. The changing international landscape, for example, has contributed to significant declines in the numbers of American students studying Russian; less severe but still important declines in the numbers studying French and German; concomitant increases in the numbers studying Arabic, Chinese, and Japanese; and dramatic increases in the numbers studying Spanish. Both the concerns of reformers and the choices of students have kept considerable attention on language study, posing a number of dilemmas for deans and provosts and a number of challenges for faculty members and language departments.

One of the major changes that has helped to redefine language instruction at many colleges and universities has been the shift in practice from defining the requirements for graduation in terms of the successful completion of a certain number of credit hours in a particular language to requiring the achievement of measurable proficiency in the second language. The experience and practices of the Defense Language Institute and the Foreign Service Institute during the post-1945 period have exercised considerable influence, brokered as they have been through the activities of the American Council of Teachers of Foreign Languages, which has adapted the government language proficiency ratings to the world of language instruction in secondary and postsecondary schools. At the University of Minnesota, for example, students in the College of Liberal Arts have been required since the mid-1980s to pass a language proficiency test to fulfill the graduation requirement in a second language; measurable and demonstrable outcomes have thus become the standards by which students are judged, and this approach has had an important impact on the rigor with which language is taught and learned.

Thanks to the reigning proficiency movement, language teachers at universities, colleges, community colleges, and high schools have banded together in a number of states to develop appropriate standards for the handing off of language learners from high schools to postsecondary institutions. Tackling the age-old problem of varying expectations and requirements across the curricula of both high schools and colleges, these efforts to improve the articulation of language learning across the secondary-postsecondary divide have focused on the levels of proficiency students are expected to achieve during the course of their high school years. The resulting discussions and collaborations between language teachers in the two settings have led to vibrant programs to enhance the pedagogical approaches that teachers in both settings bring to their classrooms, with secondary teachers learning from postsecondary teachers and vice versa.

Aside from reaching consensus on the need for enhanced language learning per se, numerous observers have also agreed that the internationalization of American higher education clearly requires increasing the ability of American students to understand other societies, as well as to understand the interactions among societies and between them and the global phenomena and trends that affect us all. From their beginnings, American colleges and universities have included in their curricula the study of other cultures through literature, language, history, and philosophy. For a long time, however, the focus of these studies was more on the past and what it could teach us than on the present and on the need to understand contemporary cultures and to work with them in attacking the problems and opportunities that face us today and are likely to face us in the future. Similarly, the study of languages at American universities was traditionally linked to the study of literature and history, but a not-so-quiet revolution over the past two and a half decades has transformed much of the language teaching to which our students are exposed.

One of the keys to the transformation of language pedagogy is the growing emphasis placed by language teachers on developing students' communicative skills in regard to speaking and understanding spoken language; another key is the use, from the outset, of authentic texts rather than of texts developed specifically for pedagogical purposes. As Merle Krueger and Frank Ryan (1993) of Brown University have pointed out, "The emphasis upon 'communicative competence' has served to differentiate use-oriented, student-centered, context-embedded instruction from what was perceived as an inordinate concern with formal structures and grammatical rules, presented with minimal attention to communicative function and drilled without reference to discernibly meaningful contexts" (p. 4). Much has been learned in this area from innovative approaches to teaching English as a second language that are used in the United States and in other English-speaking countries, where the pressures on ESL teachers to develop communicative skills and the ease of using authentic texts from everyday life have given them both the reason and the opportunity to develop effective new pedagogical strategies. Moreover, the emphasis on communicative skills and authentic texts in the teaching of second languages has also brought about something of a decentering of literature and literary texts in language teaching. Such texts are still used, of course, but a wide variety of other texts, ranging from advertisements to newspaper articles and Web sites maintained by organizations overseas, have entered the language classroom.

At a growing number of institutions over the past few years, the trend toward diversification of texts in the language curriculum has been wedded to conscious attempts to bring the use of second languages into the study of disciplines ranging from cultural studies and geography to environmental sciences and sociology. Taken together, these attempts to incorporate the foreign language knowledge and abilities of students and faculty into the exploration of a large number of disciplines have developed into a national movement known variously as Foreign Languages Across the Curriculum (FLAC) or simply Languages Across the Curriculum (LAC). Many such experiments have been conducted in the humanities, the social sciences, and the natural sciences; in some of the nation's professional schools, the practice has also spread to the study of law and management. The number of such experiments has grown to such an extent that practitioners of LAC have joined together to present the field through a useful Web site on the subject maintained by Brown University's Center for Language Studies <www.language.brown.edu/LAC>.

The promise of wedding the study and use of languages other than English to the study of a broad range of subject matter that readily lends itself to enhancement through the use of texts not available in English has made such inherent good sense that a number of federal agencies and private foundations have responded positively to requests that they fund such projects. Institutions ranging from small liberal arts colleges to large public research universities have implemented the LAC concept in a variety of ways. Some of these attempts have proven more productive and viable than others, but all these attempts have brought new excitement and meaning to the role of languages in the life of the undergraduate. Earlham College (Jurasek, 1993), St. Olaf College (Anderson, Allen, and Narváez, 1993) and several other liberal arts colleges (see *Spreading the Word II*, 1996, pp. 43-45, for a partial list) have undertaken a variety of strategies to bring the use of foreign languages into other areas of the liberal arts by interjecting analyzes of brief foreign language texts into the regular curriculum, by systematically discussing the problems of translation, or by offering discussion sections attached to English-language courses but using texts in a second language and discussing those texts in the target language. Special discussion sections conducted in a second language have been implemented at large universities such as the University of Kansas (Weidner, 1994) and the University of Minnesota. Minnesota has gone even further by offering immersion terms that give students the chance to do all their academic work involving two or more disciplines in the large enrollment languages of Spanish, French, and German (Metcalf, 1994). At the University of Rhode Island, a highly successful program involving a double major in German and engineering has made it possible for students to marry theory and practice through engineering internships with German firms working in New England and with both the German-based parents of those firms and U.S. firms operating in Germany (Grandin, 1993). Parallel programs in French and engineering and in Spanish and engineering have subsequently been launched at Rhode Island, while the University of Connecticut has emulated Rhode Island's original German and engineering program.

Similar, yet somewhat different, LAC efforts have been implemented at Binghamton University in the State University of New York system, where international students have been mobilized to serve as language resource specialists in selecting, reading, and discussing texts in their native languages with students taking course work ranging from international business to environmental studies, political science, and philosophy. Between 1991 and 1996, 1,323 Binghamton students availed themselves of the opportunity to work with language resource specialists in 11 languages while taking course work under 17 different course designators ranging from accounting to women's studies (Straight, 1997, pp. 16-19). The practice of LAC at Binghamton has varied from language to language and from discipline to discipline, but the experience has ranged over a sufficient number of fields to merit a closer look.

Commenting on his use of LAC in a U.S. immigration history course at Binghamton, Thomas Dublin reports that 30 of 80 students enrolled in the course signed up for LAC study sections in six languages, although the numbers signing up for Russian and Italian were too small to justify study groups in those languages. Such groups were, however, organized in Korean, Spanish, French, and Chinese, and the texts they read in those languages both enhanced students' learning in the course and animated their contributions to the regular discussion groups on the readings assigned in English (Dublin, 1997). History, of course, is a discipline in which foreign languages have traditionally been mobilized in the service of research, but the Binghamton program has also reached into the natural sciences and the study of international business. In the natural sciences, Peter Knuepfer found the use of LAC to be beneficial in three of his courses on environmental sciences. He noted that "access to another language can supply the student of environmental sciences with unique perspectives on global, regional, and local environmental issues that are inaccessible to those who cannot read in a language other than English" (Knuepfer and Carabajal, 1997, pp. 58-59). Knuepfer had channeled this activity "especially by using texts that present a developing-world perspective on environmental issues that [the students'] textbooks cover from a developed-world point of view" (p. 60). Binghamton's George Westacott found LAC so important that he initially made it mandatory for students in his introduction to international business course, although he has since retreated from that position. He explains his enthusiasm for LAC by pointing out that "cross-cultural managerial experience is becoming a requirement for top American corporate positions in the 1990s," many of which have gone to European expatriates and to Americans with overseas experiences in their companies; moreover, Westacott points out that the "cross-cultural experience and knowledge of students and managers with second languages strongly drives our belief in the necessity of at least one second language to escape the box of one's own culture" (Westacott, 1997, p. 70).

Despite its growth in the academy, the practice of LAC faces a number of problems in our discipline-bound colleges and universities, where the reluctance of disciplinary departments to take ownership for the concept has been increased by the inability or unwillingness of collegiate administrators to fund sufficiently or consistently an innovative activity that lies at the boundaries between disciplines. Such growth pains should not, however, be seen as insurmountable impediments to the ultimate success of LAC. Instead, they should be viewed as serious challenges to the creativity of deans and departments to move beyond the received notions and practices of the past to devise college-based or trans-departmental mechanisms for assuring the survival of a set of practices that inextricably link the study of second languages and the command of those languages to the exploration of business practices and the economy, history, politics, and sociology of other societies in ways that are informed by a deeper penetration of the understandings that emerge from a nuanced and sophisticated reading of language.

Deans and provosts interested in exploring Languages Across the Curriculum as a set of principles and practices for possible adoption by and adaptation to their campuses need to keep a number of practical considerations in mind if they hope to achieve a lasting impact and realize LAC's full potential. First, they should realize that LAC requires a certain level of investment in the training of its practitioners, in the preparation of teaching materials, and in the delivery of instruction either by the regular faculty or by graduate teaching assistants. Many models can be used, ranging from the extra discussion section conducted by a graduate student who is a native or near-native speaker of the language to the similar discussion section taught by a regular faculty member and the full-credit course offered entirely in the second language. For obvious reasons, the full history course taught entirely in French is unlikely to enroll anywhere near as many students as that same course offered in English, so administrators must face head-on the competing values of high student credit hour ratios and the enhanced learning experience offered by a full course taught in the student's second language. Indeed, many institutions may conclude that the more elaborate forms of LAC are simply beyond their reach, yet they too can find approaches to LAC that are based more on the inclusion of opportunities for students to use foreign language texts and sources in their regular course work than on the staging of special classroom opportunities led by faculty or graduate students. Whichever pedagogical models are chosen to introduce LAC, deans and provosts should recognize the real costs (however modest) involved and find the resources to meet those costs on an ongoing basis. Better not to start LAC than to rely on faculty volunteerism or external grants in the early years, only to discontinue the activity through lack of support once the volunteers tire or the grants end.

Changes in the world of language instruction and the application of foreign languages to the learning situation in disciplines outside the traditional sphere of languages and literature have raised the legitimate hopes of many advocates of internationalization for a real breakthrough in American higher education for both language acquisition and internationalization. Writing in his capacity as a mentor in the American Council on Education's program to publicize promising developments in undergraduate foreign language education, Richard Jurasek (1996) has set forth a powerful argument for the value of languages across the curriculum to a liberal education.

> From the student perspective, FLAC programming has refreshing concreteness. FLAC learners live the life of the mind *they* have chosen. That is, they use the FL skills *they* have developed to enrich and enliven their own curricular world. . . . From the institutional perspective, . . . because FLAC certifies language proficiency in real world ways, it enables the institution to demonstrate that claimed programmatic learning outcomes actually can be achieved in a consistent manner. And what better way can an institution demonstrate that the internationalization of the curriculum has been realized at the classroom and syllabus level? (p. 28)

FLAC is a new kind of connected knowing that helps make attainable a measure of wholeness in the world of undergraduate learning.

Thomas Adams (1996) of the National Endowment for the Humanities has gone further in pointing out the special role played by LAC programs in promoting internationalization.

> While many institutions announce intentions to internationalize the curriculum, espousing the objectives of cultural awareness, multiculturalism, and global savoir faire, institutions with LAC programs have breathed life into those phrases by establishing coherent and sustained opportunities for learning. Scaling the language barrier has become a collaborative enterprise that brings faculty members and students together, promoting reflection on good practice in teaching and stimulating a highly creative process of curriculum building with culture and language at its core. (pp. 17-18)

The prospects for the internationalization of our college and university curricula are certainly enhanced by recent developments in language pedagogy, collaborative approaches to that pedagogy by secondary and postsecondary faculty working together, and the promise and practice of Languages Across the Curriculum. While the contributions of language teachers and practitioners of LAC are not sufficient in and of themselves to bring about the revolution in internationalization that many envision as essential to our success as educators in the late twentieth and early twenty-first centuries, they can together contribute some of the most powerful components of internationalization imaginable. For as systems of representation and of understanding, languages provide us with prisms on reality that deeply influence our concepts of life and beauty, as well as our understanding of how to negotiate an agreement or to explain a complicated phenomenon in the natural sciences. If each of our students becomes sufficiently proficient in a second language to read and appreciate materials in that language that are linked to his or her major field of study—and if we provide students the encouragement and the opportunity to use such materials in their studies and help them contextualize those materials—then we will be approaching the level of internationalization of our students' experience that will place them on a par with their peers at the most internationalized universities in other parts of the world.

In mobilizing the new approaches to language teaching and the new uses of languages across the curriculum to further the agenda of internationalizing the curriculum, we must remember and continue to pursue a more traditional strategy toward the same end. Study abroad has long been appreciated as an essential element in any program that promotes internationalization. We must continue efforts to send increasing numbers of U.S. students abroad to hone their language skills, as well as to expose themselves to the life-transforming experience of immersion—or at least partial immersion—in another culture. Herein lies neither a contradiction nor a conflict. The new approaches to language teaching through the emphasis on communicative skills and the use of authentic texts can and should be wedded with study abroad, and U.S. institutions offering courses abroad as part of their study abroad programs should give serious consideration to incorporating into them elements of LAC that would be both facilitated and enhanced by the venues in which those courses are taught.

REFERENCES

Adams, T. H. (1996). Languages across the curriculum: Taking stock. *ADFL Bulletin, 28,*1 9-19.

Anderson, K.O., Allen, W., and Narváez, L. (1993). The applied foreign language component in the humanities and the sciences. In Merle Krueger and Frank Ryan (Eds.), *Language and content: Discipline- and content-based approaches to language study.* (pp. 103–13) Lexington, MA: D. C. Heath.

Dublin, T. (1997). Foreign Languages and the teaching of United States immigration History (LxC in History 264: Immigration and Ethnicity in U.S. History). In Virginia M. Fichera and H. Stephen Straight (Eds.), *Using languages across the curriculum (translation perspectives X)* (pp. 49–55). Binghamton: Center for Research in Translation, State University of New York at Binghamton.

Grandin, J. M. (1993). The University of Rhode Island's international engineering program. In Merle Krueger and Frank Ryan (Eds.), *Language and content: Discipline- and content-based approaches to language study* (pp. 130–37). Lexington, MA: D.C. Heath.

Jurasek, R. (1996). Languages across the curriculum across the country. In *Spreading the word II: Promising developments for undergraduate foreign language Instruction—A report on a mentoring and dissemination project of the American Council on Education to improve the teaching of undergraduate foreign languages* (pp. 27–33). Washington: American Council on Education.

————. (1993). Foreign languages across the curriculum: A case history from Earlham College and a generic rationale. In Merle Krueger and Frank Ryan (Eds.), *Language and content: Discipline- and content-based approaches to language study* (pp. 85–102). Lexington, MA: D. C. Heath.

Knuepfer, P. L. K. and Carabajal, C.C. (1997). Use of languages across the curriculum in the environmental sciences (LxC in Environmental Studies 101, 201, and 320). In Virginia M. Fichera and H. Stephen Straight (Eds.), *Using languages across the curriculum (Translation Perspectives X)* (pp. 57–67). Binghamton: Center for Research in Translation, State University of New York at Binghamton.

Krueger, M. and Ryan, F. (1993). Resituating foreign languages in the curriculum. In Merle Krueger and Frank Ryan (Eds.), *Language and content: Discipline- and content-based approaches to language study* (pp. 3–24). Lexington, MA: D. C. Heath.

Metcalf, M.F. (1994). FLAC and FLIP at Minnesota: Bringing foreign languages into the broader curriculum. *International Education Forum, 14,* 105-12.

Spreading the word: Improving the way we teach foreign languages—A report on a mentoring and dissemination project of the American Council on Education to improve undergraduate foreign instruction. (1994). Washington, DC: American Council on Education.

Spreading the word II: Promising developments for undergraduate foreign language instruction—A report on a mentoring and dissemination project of the American Council on Education to improve the teaching of undergraduate foreign languages. (1996). Washington, DC: American Council on Education.

Straight, H. S. (1997). Language resource specialists as agents of curricular internationalization (An overview and evaluation of Binghamton University's LxC Program). In Virginia M. Fichera and H. Stephen Straight (Eds.), *Using languages across the curriculum (Translation Perspectives X)* (pp. 11–39). Binghamton: Center for Research in Translation, State University of New York at Binghamton.

Weidner, T. (1994). Language across the curriculum: The University of Kansas experience. *International Education Forum*, 14, 91-104.

Westacott, G.H. (1997). International business and languages across the curriculum (LxC in IBUS 520: Introduction to International Business). In Virginia M. Fichera and H. Stephen Straight (Eds.) *Using languages across the curriculum (Translation Perspectives X)* (pp. 69–79). Binghamton: Center for Research in Translation, State University of New York at Binghamton.

CHAPTER 6

Teaching about Cognition and Cognitive Development
How to Internationalize the Topic

by Herbert L. Pick, Jr.

INTRODUCTION

How do people classify or categorize things? Many psychologists interested in thinking processes have considered this question a central aspect of cognitive behavior. One of the most obvious, simplest, and straightforward ways of finding out about this process has been to ask people to sort sets of objects. For example, suppose I ask you to sort the following objects by putting all objects that go together in separate piles: potato, pencil, shoe, hat, piece of paper, scarf, apple, knife, eraser, onion, screwdriver, chisel. Most of us would put the potato, apple, onion in one pile, the shoe, hat, scarf in another, and so on. If asked why, we would say that we were putting all the edible items together, the clothing items together, the tools together, and so on. We would be forming some sort of functional taxonomic organization. Researchers concerned with cognitive development have found that young children behave differently. Children form smaller groups with a more thematic basis. They might put the knife and apple together because the knife is used to cut an apple, the shoe with the potato because when you go to the store to buy potatoes, you put on your shoes.

Would people from other cultures classify things the same way we do? This has been a question of great interest to cross-cultural psychologists and cognitive anthropologists, because it potentially sheds light on whether or not there are cognitive universals. During the first two-thirds of this century, researchers investigating this kind of behavior in "underdeveloped" cultures reported that adults categorized objects the way children in Western "developed" countries do. However, Glick (1975) reported a particularly illuminating and instructive observation. He and his colleagues were studying the sorting behavior of Kpelle adults in the standard way. One subject kept sorting in the thematic way described above. When asked why he sorted in this way, he explained thematically that the knife cut the fruit and ultimately commented that this is the way a wise person would do it. The researcher finally asked how a fool would do it and the subject responded with the taxonomic sorting of Western adults.

Besides the embarrassing indication of the egocentrism of earlier Western researchers, an obvious lesson in this incident is that more than one principle of categorization is ordinarily available to people, and that the preferred principle may be a matter of culture, or possibly context within a culture. More generally, such examples as this, as well as the impact on Western cognitive psychology of a Soviet/Russian theoretical approach (not to mention more thoughtful analyses by cognitive researchers), has suggested that the demands of all human cultures are sufficiently complex that the members of all cultures are constantly engaged in complex problem solving and formally abstract thinking processes. This perspective then has led cross-cultural-minded cognitive researchers to change the focus of their questions. They are now trying to understand the nature of problems that people in any culture are trying to solve and how they go about solving those problems. This, in turn, leads to trying to understand whether and how cultural practices support such solutions.

HOW CULTURAL PRACTICES INFLUENCE COGNITIVE PROCESSES: COGNITION IN SOUTH SEA ISLANDERS' NAVIGATION

The inhabitants of Micronesia in the South Pacific make impressive trips in outrigger canoes across wide stretches of ocean and out of sight of land, often for many days. They accomplish these trips using none of the navigation instruments that would be an absolute necessity for Western travelers. How do they do this? Their system of navigation has been carefully examined by a number of anthropologists who were experienced sailors themselves (e.g., Gladwin, 1970; Hutchins, 1995; Hutchins and Hinton, 1984).

These trips are undertaken sometimes for a functional purpose, sometimes more or less as a lark. They are guided by expert navigators, who have high prestige in this culture. But what is it that these navigators know and how do they use this knowledge to guide these voyages? Two requirements for successful accomplishment of such voyages are (1) maintaining a particular course and (2) keeping track of one's location in the open sea out of sight of land.

For our understanding, how they maintain a particular course is relatively easy to grasp. One basis is a form of celestial navigation. They know that particular stars always rise and set in the same directions, forming a kind of sidereal compass. For any given direction, a series of stars may rise one after another throughout the night giving constant information for that direction. These stars then follow each other along the same trajectory across the night sky in what is called a star path or linear constellation. Of course, even the South Pacific is sometimes cloudy, and there must be alternative ways to maintain a straight course. The navigators also resort to knowledge about the characteristic direction of wave trains in this region of ocean. Three main wave trains differ in amplitude and frequency and the direction from which they come. By maintaining a constant angle of the boat to one or more of these wave trains (or the wind which is producing them), it is possible to maintain a steady course in the absence of celestial information.

Navigators know what direction to go to get to their destination because they have laboriously memorized a set of sailing instructions for going from every (important) island to every other island in their region. Compare this to how our navigators know how to go from here to there. They pull out a chart of the region and plot out the direction lines on the chart. This method may seem simpler, but it depends on a huge technological infrastructure to make charts available to sailors; it also requires instruments to plot courses on charts, ample storage space for the charts, and a table for studying charts. The Micronesian solution trades off the navigator's mental effort in learning and recalling against the work of map making and building of ships with necessary space and facilities.

Knowing where one is along the journey might not be absolutely necessary to reach the original destination (if one were able to simply keep sailing in the correct direction). However, knowing where one is would be essential if a storm had blown the boat off its original course or if one decided to change one's destination in the middle of the trip. Some information about location is available in the sailing directions the navigators have learned. For example, the directions will include information about color changes in the water as the routes pass over reefs of various depths, or information about changes in wind as the route passes in the lee of islands that are too far away to be visible yet still disturb the wind flow.

Even though Western navigators might not be so sensitive to the direction of combinations of wave trains or subtle changes of water color, we can readily conceive of people guiding themselves by attending to such information. We have all become more or less attentive or sensitive to differing kinds of information. However, the way Micronesian navigators keep track of where they are in the sense of conceptualizing their journey is particularly intriguing to us because it is very different from the way we do it. From their sailing instructions, they know that going from Island A to Island B requires passing (usually without seeing) Islands, C, D, and E. They conceptualize their journey by visualizing themselves sitting in a stationary boat as these other Islands move back past them until they reach their destination. Thus, for example, in the beginning of their journey they would be able to say that Island C is ahead and to the right of them (in the direction of the rising of some particular star). As they progress towards B, Island C moves back so it is 90 degrees to the side and then still further back so it is at some angle behind them and at a still greater angle when they reach their destination. Thus the conceptualized movement of these islands can serve as a reference for keeping track of how they are progressing. Remarkably, if no convenient real island is available, they use an imaginary island called Etak. Because all movement is relative, it is perfectly consistent for them to conceptualize the trip with a stationary boat and the world moving past it. It is a logically equivalent way of thinking about what is going on. Of course, to us it seems bizarre.

But it may not be so strange to conceptualize the trip this way. If we asked a Western navigator how we were progressing along a trip, he or she would again pull out the chart and say something about moving along a line from Point A to Point B, indicating with a finger or pencil some intermediate point as our present location. Obviously, the navigator does not mean that we are literally at that place on the chart, or that we are literally moving along a line on the chart. The chart is just a convenient way for us to conceptualize the trip. But what makes the moving world and stationary boat a convenient way for the Micronesian navigators to conceptualize their trip? Hutchins and Hinton (1984) have suggested a plausible hypothesis.

Their hypothesis starts with a geometric fact—when an observer moves in relation to an object the relative direction of the object changes. For example, the direction of objects ahead and to the right of our direction of movement will gradually change to being directly to our side, i.e., an example of motion parallax. The rate of this change in direction depends on the velocity of the movement and the distance between the observer and the object, i.e., rate of change is roughly proportional to the velocity/distance. When viewing the stars that are often the main "landmarks" Micronesian navigators steer by, there is no change of direction, i.e., the rate of change of direction is, as the following equation shows, zero:

$$\text{velocity/distance} = 0$$

The only way this equation could be true is if the relative velocity between the stars and the observer (in this case the boat) was 0 or if the distance were infinite. An argument can be made that the distance of the stars is not registered, perceptually at least, as infinite, so the relative velocity between boat and stars must be 0. Given such constraints, it is easier to conceive of the boat and the stars as stationary and attribute movement to the rest of the (unseen) world. Thus the Etak system of the Micronesian navigators not only makes logical sense in terms of motion between boat and world being completely relative, it also makes psychological sense in that it accords with much of the evidence of the senses that is available to the navigators.

The Micronesian navigation system illustrates two ways in which cognition may differ across cultures. One is related to the kinds of information or cues to which the members of a culture are disposed to attend. The other is related to the ways the members of a culture conceptualize aspects of the world, the kind of mental models with which they operate. What about cultural experience leads to differences in how people attend? The physical ecology of the South Pacific constrains and affords the possibility of using certain kinds of information and no doubt this is crucial in determining how the navigators attend. But more relevant to cultural influences on thinking is the possibility that language may influence our attention and thinking.

Language and Cognition

The most far reaching proposal that language structures our cognition is known as the Sapir-Whorf hypothesis of linguistic relativity. Edward Sapir was a linguist, a student of the anthropologist Franz Boas, and Benjamin Lee Whorf, a chemical engineer by training and a fire insurance inspector by profession, took courses with Sapir. The hypothesis, developed by Whorf (1956), suggests that language structures our thinking and hence speakers of different languages conceive and even perceive the world differently.

At the level of perception, this idea was proposed and tested with respect to lexicons of different languages. The extreme form of the idea was that if a language didn't have specific words for the items of a domain, speakers of that language wouldn't differentiate among the items. One of the earliest examples involved the fact that Eskimos had a number of different words for snow that specify different forms of this substance, although all these forms are encompassed by the single English term. (This was before the increased popularity of skiing in the English-speaking world.) Perhaps the most systematically investigated example of this idea was in the domain of color perception (Brown and Lenneberg, 1954; Berlin and Kay, 1969; Rosch, 1973).

Languages across the world differ markedly on how finely they cut up the color spectrum. Some languages seem to have only two divisions that separate all colors into light and dark categories. Other languages have an even finer breakdown of colors than English. If the extreme form of the Sapir-Whorf hypothesis held, it would predict that monolingual speakers of a language would only be able to perceive colors for which their language had a word. The systematic research both within our own culture (Brown and Lenneberg, 1954) and across cultures (Rosch, 1973) decisively refuted this prediction. Members of any culture are able to differentiate and perceive far more colors than they have simple names for. The best that might be saved for the Sapir-Whorf hypothesis is that the more a task depends on remembering or classifying colors (as opposed to discriminating among them), the more likely it is to reflect the influence of the existence of names for the colors.

Evidence like this, particularly with respect to the part of cognition that is relevant to perception, generally discredited the Sapir-Whorf hypothesis. However, even for perception, something like linguistic determinism seems to occur in one domain. This is the domain of the phonetics of speech perception. Different languages of the world cut up the speech/sound system differently. An example familiar to many English speakers is the confusion native Japanese speakers have with /r/ and /l/. These two sounds are often confused in the speech production of a native Japanese speaker who is learning English. Besides confusing the sounds in their own speech, most Japanese native speakers are also unable to hear the difference between the two sounds when an English speaker pronounces them. English speakers have an exactly analogous confusion with respect to a phonemic distinction in the Thai language. Thai distinguishes among some speech sounds along a so-called dimension of voicing, the same dimension along which our /p/ and /b/ sounds are distinguished. However, Thai speakers divide this dimension into three categories: (1) a prevoiced /b/, (2) something like our /b/, and (3) something like our /p/. Most native English-speaking adults simply are unable to hear the difference between the Thai prevoiced /b/ and the Thai /b/, a difference as clear to a Thai speaker as the difference between /b/ and /p/ is to us. What is even more startling is the fact that our children as infants in the first year of life can make this discrimination! We, as adults, presumably as a function of our linguistic experience, have lost this ability! We can only recover this sensitivity with extraordinary difficulty (Strange and Jenkins, 1978).

Admittedly, this domain of phonetics of speech perception is a very particularistic one by which to assert the viability of the Sapir-Whorf hypothesis. Nevertheless, perhaps the Sapir-Whorf hypothesis was discredited too soon. A somewhat weaker form of the Sapir-Whorf hypothesis may be viable in a different cognitive domain, one which may be more relevant to thinking than perception, the domain of categorizing and classifying.

The idea here is that languages may cut up our world differently, not only by having different names, but in even more subtle ways by requiring a speaker to make distinctions in some languages but not in others or perhaps by masking some distinctions in one language that are easily made in another. Thus one of Sapir's original observations was that English speakers must pay attention to time when speaking to use the proper tense of the verb whereas this is not required in some other languages (Pinker, 1994).

Recently, Sera (1992; Sera, Reittinger, Pintado, 1991) began a systematic study of the possible influence on fundamental aspects of classification of a linguistic distinction in Spanish that is not made in the same way in English. This distinction concerns the two forms of the verb *to be*, the Spanish copulas *ser* and *estar*. One general semantic distinction between them is that ser is used in connection with permanent characteristics and estar in relation to temporary characteristics. Thus "apples are round" would be said with a form of ser if roundness were considered an essential property of apples while "apples are dirty" would be said with a form of estar if the dirtiness were considered a temporary or incidental characteristic of apples. Of course, "Mary is a woman" would employ a form of ser. However, this characterization of the meaning has some complications. A main one involves the use of the two forms of *to be* in the specification of locatives with objects and events. Sentences like "Minnesota is in North America" use a form of estar, while "the graduation is in Northrop Hall" uses a form of ser. This apparent violation of the permanent/temporary rule could be subsumed under that first characterization by considering that location of objects is ordinarily an incidental or transitory property; even if Minnesota were somehow transplanted to the South Pacific, we would still call it Minnesota. On the other hand, an event is often defined by its location and if the graduation were in Kennedy High School, it would be another event, hence the form of ser.

Sera's research supports the linguists' description of the use of the ser/estar distinction. Sera (1992) found that the distribution of use of the two copulas generally conforms to the linguistic analysis. In addition, she demonstrated that the use of the different forms of the copula in describing objects makes a difference in how the objects are categorized. In general, Spanish as well as English speakers will categorize novel objects on the basis of shape rather than size, color, or texture if there is no linguistic description of the object. However, for Spanish speakers, if the object is described in terms of its size, color, or texture using a form of *ser*, that property will be used in categorizing the object. For example, if the description is "this gidget is (ser) red," the gidget will be categorized on the basis of color in subsequent sorting tasks. Describing it as red using the form of estar affects categorization behavior no more than not describing its properties at all. Furthermore, use of the relevant form of the verb *to be* for English speakers has no effect on subsequent categorizing behavior. "The use of *ser* to describe an attribute seems to imply to speakers of Spanish that the attribute should weigh heavily in the definition of the category while the use of *estar* seems to carry no such implication." (Sera, 1992, pp. 418-19.)

Sera has been particularly interested in how the acquisition of such linguistic distinctions in children affects the kind of distinctions children typically make in the world. In fact, examining the relation in children between linguistic distinctions and real world distinctions, such as in categorizing behavior, may be a sensitive way of demonstrating such influences. This sensitivity would arise because children's categorical behavior is in the process of development and perhaps can be more easily biased in one direction or another. A related but slightly different example of how such linguistic influences might work is in the domain of children distinguishing between real and apparent properties of objects (Sera, Bales, and Pintado, 1997). Under some circumstances, young children have difficulty distinguishing between the superficial appearance of an object and its real properties. If, for example, a three-year-old views a white object through a red filter, he or she may say that it is really red (even if the child has just seen that it is white). Or, if children observe an object through a magnifying glass they may say that it is its magnified size even if they had just seen its undistorted size. A year or so later, children have no difficulty distinguishing verbally between such apparent and real properties. Sera and her colleagues found that Spanish children will make this distinction correctly earlier in age in the case of real properties if the question is posed to them using the ser form of the copula. A Spanish-speaking child looking through a red filter at an object will more likely respond to the question "What is (ser) the color of this object really?" with the correct color than if they were asked the same question using the form of the verb estar or than would an English-speaking child just using the form of the verb to be. The linguistic distinction that the Spanish children are acquiring seems to help them focus on the real and apparent physical properties.

The main message of this section of the chapter is that the ordinary day-to-day problems of any nation or culture are interestingly complex and involve complex cognitive processes in their solution. The solutions of different cultures and nations to similar problems may involve different cognitive processes and these different cognitive processes may be supported by different cultural artifacts. One approach to making this realistic for students is to identify interesting examples where this has happened or could happen. An instructor could do this by consulting some of the bibliographic references in this chapter; for instance, see particularly Hutchins (1995).

An interesting exercise or research project for students would be to ask them to identify complex day-to-day tasks that would seem to require abstract and complex thinking. Examples of such tasks might be construction, conflict resolution, child rearing, agricultural practices, family economic planning, etc. The assignment would ask students to think about these tasks analytically and suggest the kinds of abstract thinking that might be involved in their solutions. The assignment would conclude with library research on how the task is actually carried out in a particular culture and how the members of that culture learn to accomplish the task. It would be particularly interesting to compare two cultures, e.g., ours and another, in relation to how similar tasks are accomplished.

IMPORTING THEORETICAL APPROACHES FROM OTHER CULTURES: VYGOTSKY'S SOCIOCULTURAL THEORY

A second major way of internationalizing the study of cognition and cognitive development is the introduction into courses of theoretical approaches originating in different nations and cultures. Three Russian scientists have had a major influence on Western, particularly American, cognitive psychology. Ivan Pavlov is most widely known to the lay public. However, with the rise of the anti-behaviorist flavor of modern cognitive psychology, Pavlov's impact has been essentially lost. A much more interesting figure is Nicolai Bernshtein, an anti-Pavlovian, activity physiologist. His theoretical approach makes motor physiology a fascinating cognitive problem. Although his major research was conducted between 1930 and 1960, his ideas are currently stimulating much research on cognitive aspects of motor control. The ideas of Lev Vygotsky, the third scientist, a Russian psychologist, will be used to illustrate the importing of theoretical approaches.

Vygotsky's influential research was carried out in a short career between 1920 and 1935 when he died of tuberculosis. Even in that short period it became obvious that Vygotsky was a superb scholar of the stature of Piaget. Given the political climate of the times, it is not surprising that he was a Marxist-oriented psychologist. At that time, many Soviet psychologists were striving to accommodate their theoretical perspectives to the Marxist point of view. However, their accommodations seemed to be very crude, almost characterizations of Marxist materialism. Vygotsky elaborated a more subtle perspective, which captured some of the flavor of the dialectical materialist position, but was certainly less doctrinaire and was exceedingly profound.

His perspective has been termed a sociocultural approach to psychology. An emphasis in his approach that is crucial is that human cognitive development occurs in a social context and the social aspects of the process are primary and the individual psychological developments are derivative. This is fundamentally different from much of Western psychology where the individual's development is primary and is overlaid onto social processes. Vygotsky begins by acknowledging that as biological organisms humans share with animals a set of "natural" cognitive functions, such as perception, memory, learning, etc. However, there is rapid development of strictly human "higher" mental functions that are essentially similar processes but are critically elaborated to involve the possibility of voluntary control and reflection about the processes themselves. According to Vygotsky, the development of these higher mental functions is completely dependent on the social context and social interaction. Indeed, the higher mental functions exist first in social interaction and then get internalized and become part of an individual's psyche (or psychology). In Vygotsky's terms, every higher mental function develops first on a social plane and then on an individual plane.

Zone of Proximal Development

The influence of the social context in this development can be subtle, as when parents guide their children, not only about how to do or think about things, but about what things are relevant to do or think about. Naturally, the process of this guidance is especially important in Vygotsky's view. He suggested that advances in cognitive development occur when a more knowledgeable peer or older person guides a child to act or think just beyond his or her current level of functioning. Vygotsky developed this idea with a concept called "zone of proximal development."

The zone of proximal development refers to the range between the cognitive level at which a child is able to function completely independently and the maximal level at which the child is able to function with the structured help of a knowledgeable expert. Help within that range will facilitate cognitive advance. If help is provided at the level the child is already functioning, the child won't improve in cognitive function and might even be frustrated. Conversely, if help is provided beyond this zone of proximal development, the child is incapable of benefiting from it.

To take this concept seriously and use it for designing educational practice is difficult work. Before introducing expert guidance, a great deal of preliminary work must be done to define for any given child what the zone is so that appropriate help can be constructed. A number of American psychologists have carried out this labor intensive procedure with some success (e.g., Brown and Ferrara, 1985).

Vygotsky was extremely critical of Western intelligence testing, trying to characterize the cognitive level of a child by momentary performance on some test assessment. He introduced the idea of the zone of proximal development as a much better alternative procedure for assessing the cognitive level of a child. Seeing how the child is capable of advancing in the zone of proximal development would be a more valid *dynamic* assessment of a child's cognitive functioning and has been carried out with some success both in the West and in Russia. However, the use of the zone of proximal development for assessment is also a laborious activity.

Vygotsky and Language as a Cultural Tool

Vygotsky considered certain aspects of the acquisition of language to be among the clearer examples of development from the social plane to the individual psychological plane. He focused on the egocentric speech in which many young children engage. Piaget had observed this phenomenon and concluded that this talking to themselves for the benefit of themselves was just another reflection of children's general egocentrism. They would eventually grow out of that as they learned to take another's perspective. However, Vygotsky's observations of this phenomenon led him to an almost completely opposite interpretation. He saw speech developing initially in social interaction between child and adult and being used for communication, starting with such gestures as pointing and developing into verbal signs. After this initial stage, children would begin to vocalize for themselves in trying to guide their own behavior. Gradually these overt vocalizations became abbreviated and eventually dropped out as speech became completely internalized. Thus language developed first in the process of and as a means for social regulation and then moved towards self-regulation and self-planning. Alexander Luria (1961), a famous Soviet neuropsychologist, described a series of experiments where he demonstrated this transition (although subsequent researchers have had difficulty replicating his results, the experiments vividly illustrate the idea).

Language also exemplified for Vygotsky how cognitive function is mediated by the use of tools. This idea possibly originates in a Marxist perspective about the means of production determining the human state. Vygotsky conceived of tools as mediating between the natural elementary functions and higher mental functions. These might be real physical tools, but Vygotsky was more interested in mediation by psychological tools, and language and other symbolic representational systems were for him prime examples of psychological tools. He considered symbolic systems such as language as mediating a human's own psychological processes.

An excellent example of what Vygotsky had in mind comes from a study by Miller and Stigler (1987) comparing the early counting behavior of Chinese and American school children. They noted that the Chinese word names in the Chinese numbering system are more regular than English. In particular, the Chinese don't have special names for the second decade of numbers, such as we have for eleven and twelve and for the formation of the rest of the decade (thirteen, fourteen, etc.). Unlike the Chinese, we form this decade differently from the way we form the higher decades (twenty-one, twenty-two, etc.). In Chinese, the decades are formed by specifying the number of tens and then the number of units, so, for example, *eleven* would be equivalent to *ten-one*, and *twenty-seven* would be specified as *two-ten-seven*, etc. This sort of analysis suggested that in learning to count English-speaking children might initially make more errors with the teens simply because there were more number names to keep in mind, and more errors as they went from one higher decade to the next, as when children say *thirty-eleven* for *forty-one*. Miller and Stigler asked American and Chinese beginning elementary school children to count as high as they could and to enumerate sets of objects. The found that Chinese students generally made fewer errors overall than the American children, and the pattern of errors was as predicted. Interestingly, the only place the Chinese children had any difficulty at all was at the transition between decades when they had to remember both to increment the *tens* and reset the *units*.

Stigler (1984) provides another arithmetic example of the importance of cultural tools in the performance of cognitive processes. Stigler studied the performance of mental arithmetic by abacus users. In the abacus, each decade of numbers is represented by a column of count markers, the positions of which specify how many of that decade are present. Thus, 30 would be represented by moving three count markers at the bottom of the tens column up to a new position. However, when one gets to five (50) and above, a five marker at the top of that column is moved to a new position, and the markers at the bottom of the column are reset. This is equivalent to representing numbers above four (five, six, seven, etc) as five plus zero, five plus one, five plus two, and so forth. Stigler examined the mental arithmetic of expert child abacus users in Japan and found that many of their errors involved being off by the amount of five, as if they were working out their problems on a mental abacus and forgetting to move the fives marker. This contrasted sharply with American children who rarely made that kind of error when doing mental arithmetic. Overall, the abacus users were much better at mental arithmetic, but the errors they did make were often sensible in terms of abacus operations.

CONCLUSIONS

This last example of the influence of a cultural tool on children's mental processes illustrates exactly what Vygotsky was trying to assert. More generally he felt the whole social and cultural context constrains and guides an individual's cognition. It facilitates some kinds of thinking and interferes with some kinds of thinking in ways that have been suggested above. The importance of this world view is just beginning to be realized in American cognitive psychology and it is manifest in a variety of terms that cognitive psychologists are beginning to use to describe cognition as it naturally occurs: *situated cognition, shared cognition, distributed cognition*. These terms emphasize the contextual dependence of cognition and the constraining effect of cultural artifacts on our cognition. They also emphasize that cognition is usually a social process as a whole with various kinds of divisions of labor that are unlike what happens in the traditional psychological laboratory.

One reason a perspective like Vygotsky's can have an impact on our cognitive psychology is that he and Soviet/Russian psychology were concerned with the same kind of problems that we are. A more radically different perspective might shake up our thinking even more but would have much less chance to have an impact because it would be hard to see its relevance to issues of concern to us.

A second message of the chapter is that the distinctive theories of cognition and cognitive development can arise from the different psychological traditions of different countries. This was exemplified by the sociocultural theory of the Russian psychologist, Vygotsky. An interesting class discussion question would be why such a theory would develop in that country. And then more generally, what kinds of national or cultural characteristics would influence the kinds of psychological theories developed and accepted? While this might require specialized knowledge of other specific countries, the question can be asked about the United States, thus illustrating the idea that having an international slant in our courses can help us learn more about ourselves.

REFERENCES

Berk, L.A. and Winsler, A. (1995). *Scaffolding children's learning: Vygotsky and early childhood education*. Washington, D.C.: National Association for the Education of Young Children.

Berlin, B. and Kay, P. (1969). *Basic color terms: Their universality and evolution*. Berkeley, CA: University of California Press.

Brown, A. L. and Ferrara, R. A. (1985). Diagnosing zones of proximal development. In J. Wertsch, (Ed.) *Culture, communication, and cognition: Vygotskian perspectives* (pp. 273–305). New York: Cambridge University Press.

Brown, R. W. and Lenneberg, E. H. (1954). A study in language and cognition. *Journal of Abnormal and Social Psychology, 49*, 454–62.

Gladwin, T. (1970) *East is a big bird*. Cambridge, MA: Harvard University Press.

Glick, J. (1975). Cognitive development in cross-cultural perspective. In F. D. Horowitz (Ed.). *Child Development Research IV*. Chicago: University of Chicago Press. (pp. 595–653).

Hutchins, E. (1995). *Cognition in the wild*. Cambridge, MA: MIT Press.

Hutchins, E. and Hinton, G. E. (1984). Why the islands move. *Perception, 13*, 629–32.

Kozulin, A. (1990). *Vygotsky's psychology: A biography of ideas*. Cambridge, MA: Harvard University Press.

Luria, A. R. (1961). *The role of speech in the regulation of normal and abnormal behavior*. New York: Pergamon.

Miller, K. and Stigler, J. W. (1987). Counting in Chinese: Cultural variation in a basic cognitive skill. *Cognitive Development, 2* 279–305.

Pinker, S. (1994). *The language instinct: How the mind creates language*. New York: William Morrow and Company.

Rosch, E. (1973). On the internal structure of perceptual and sementic categories. In T. Moore (Ed.). *Cognitive Development and the Acquisition of Language.* New York: Academic Press.

Sera, M. D. (1992). To be or to be: Use and acquisition of the Spanish copulas. *Journal of Memory and Language, 31,* 408–27.

Sera, M. D., Bales, D. W., and Pintado, J. C. (1997). *Ser* helps Spanish speakers identify "real" properties. *Child Development,* 68, 820–31.

Sera, M. D., Reittinger, E. L., and Pintado, J. C. (1991). Developing definitions of objects and events in English and Spanish speakers. *Cognitive Development,* 6, 1999–42.

Stigler, J. W. (1984). "Mental abacus:" The effect of abacus training on Chinese children's mental calculation. *Cognitive Psychology,* 16, 145–76.

Strange, W. and Jenkins, J. J. (1978). Role of linguistic experience in the perception of speech. In R. D. Walk and H. L. Pick, Jr. (Eds.), *Perception and Experience.* Plenum Press: New York.

Vygotsky, L. (1987, 1993). *The collected works of L. S. Vygotsky. Vols 1 and 2.* (R. W. Rieber and A. S. Carton, Eds.). New York: Plenum.

———. (1981). The genesis of higher mental functions. In J. V. Wertsch (Ed.). *The concept of activity in Soviet psychology.* (pp. 144–88). Armonk, NY: Sharpe.

———. (1978). *Mind in society: The development of higher psychological processes.* Cambridge, MA: Harvard University Press.

Whorf, B. L. (1956). *Language, thought, and reality.* New York: Wiley.

CHAPTER 7

Internationalization through Networking and Curricular Infusion

by John J. Cogan

I have been involved in several attempts over my university career to "internationalize" the curriculum; all have had some success but none to the extent that we would have liked. I am hopeful that the current effort at my institution, the University of Minnesota, Twin Cities, to redefine what international education should be at the university in the next decade will lead to further successes. For until we truly "internationalize" the university curriculum, all our other efforts will be secondary. Students and faculty must see themselves connected both personally and professionally to the wider world if they are to be active players in it in the coming century.

The title of this chapter reflects my attempt to move this concept forward into practice. I have always supported the infusion of new material into existing courses over the development of new offerings. The last thing I believe we should be aiming for is a set of new offerings on the "internationalization" of the curriculum. We need to strengthen and revitalize existing courses with the infusion of new material. We need to do it; not talk about it.

By infusion, I mean the integration of examples of research and scholarly work into assigned course work. These include the assigned readings, the illustrations I use in my class lectures, my experiences from working in other nations, and the use of course assignments. To each course I teach, I bring my work in the area of international education, both in the United States and abroad, over the past 28 years. I have been deeply involved in activities in this area at both the collegiate and all-university levels as well as abroad. I have used these experiences to broaden my own vision about international education and I have sought to pass this experience on to my students.

INTERNATIONAL EXCHANGES AND NETWORKING

Several specific areas of work are central to the infusion approach. The first comes out of my own research interests and projects with others abroad. I shall say more about these later in the chapter. The second comes from my involvement in the several educational exchange agreements the University of Minnesota's College of Education and Human Development (CEHD) has made with sister institutions abroad. I was very much involved in establishing each of these agreements and actually negotiated several. I strongly believe that our faculty and students must connect in meaningful ways with their counterparts in other parts of the world and must, whenever possible, actually study and work together. Over the 15+ years they have been in force, these exchanges have provided opportunities for students and faculty to meet and to engage in scholarship and intellectual inquiry. These relationships allow Minnesota students and faculty to link with their counterparts at the partner institutions. Financial aid is seldom available; the exchanges merely provide access. For several of our M.A. students in Comparative and International Development Education, these exchanges have been the difference in finishing a thesis project. Others have actually undertaken periods of study abroad, some for as short as a term and others for as long as two years. Faculty have benefited from study visits to meet with colleagues, participation in exchange seminar visits and collaboration in research projects. Connecting people in the academy is a primary goal of these exchange agreements and history shows that once the linkage is made things begin to happen.

Before I discuss the infusion of my work into my courses, I want to describe the evolution of this network of agreements that the College of Education and Human Development has with partner institutions in other parts of the world. Because these exchange agreements have resulted in so much of the material I have put back into my courses, I believe they deserve special mention herein. They have significantly impacted my own scholarship as well as my instructional skills.

The College has developed study and exchange agreements with York University (United Kingdom), University of Amsterdam (Netherlands), Hiroshima University (Japan), Chulalongkorn University (Thailand), Sukhothai Thammathirat Open University (Thailand), and Beijing Normal University (China). Some agreements are more active than others at any given point in time but all have contributed to the process of internationalization. At least half of these agreements came about as a result of University of Minnesota alumni being in prominent positions in the partner institution. I emphasize this because international alumni are a great reservoir of goodwill that goes largely untapped but that could be used much more effectively with a little effort. International alumni represent an enormous opportunity missed.

About 12 years ago, I worked closely with colleagues in the Centre for Global Education at the University of York in England. The actual exchange agreement had been concluded earlier by then Dean William Gardner and Professor Ian Lister at York. Dr. David Selby, director of the Centre, who has since moved to Canada, and his colleagues had visited the college to examine our work in the Global Education Center. We found mutual interests and made a return visit to York. As a result, I became aware of a wide variety of quality global education materials being produced in Great Britain to which I had absolutely no access in the United States due to copyright conventions or lack of an American partner publishing house. The discovery of these materials greatly enriched what I could do in my own courses. I was also able to watch David Selby and his colleague Graham Pike work with English teachers in courses and see some of the different instructional approaches being used. These, where applicable, I brought back to this side of the Atlantic. Finally, I was also able to engage with classroom teachers regarding their beliefs about the need for instruction in this area, how they defined global education, the specific foci they took, and the outcomes they expected.

In the course of these observations and conversations, I concluded that the approach to global education in England and Wales differed in several substantial ways from American practice. First, their emphasis was far more on process than content. In the United States, we believed that teachers, and those studying to be teachers, lacked the requisite content knowledge background to work with students in this area. We did not have nearly the same concern about their instructional capacities. The same area of practice took very different approaches in the two nations.

Second, I realized that whereas we in the United States take a holistic approach to global education, the British are much more focused upon specific issues, such as human rights, anti-racism, anti-sexism, and development education. The British organize themselves around specific issues, and focus their activities in this area rather than in a more general approach to global issues that embody many or all of these areas in a single issue. This too was most informative.

Also during that return visit, we began to explore the possibility of a summer study seminar for teachers from Minnesota to visit York to learn more about global education as practiced in England and Wales. If we could get teachers moving back and forth between the two nations to work with each other and to see how global education was practiced, they would be enriched and would continue to find ways to connect with one another. We began this effort with just 10 teachers in a successful seminar at York. The next summer we had hoped to have a similar group of English teachers come to the U.S., but the sudden fall of the British pound against the dollar precluded that. However, David Selby and Graham Pike came to conduct a workshop for 35 Minnesota teachers that in part served the same purpose.

This exchange went on for several years and included a student teaching experience in England with Selby and Pike for a handful of our students in schools focused on global education. The exchange ultimately broke down when our two colleagues in York moved to Toronto, Canada, but the learning it engendered remains to this day in how and what I teach.

The York experience is simply one case example of how these exchange agreements led to collaborative efforts that ultimately strengthened the curriculum at both institutions. We incorporated elements of what they were doing in their courses into our courses, including readings and materials not available on this side of the Atlantic. They did the same. Teachers corresponded about their practice; some even went back and forth between the two countries on individual study visits, including an English primary school head teacher who spent an entire year with us under a Rotary International Fellowship.

Many other illustrative cases can be cited from these exchange agreements, such as the similar set of exchange visits with colleagues in social studies/global education at Sukkhothai Thammathirat Open University (STOU) in Thailand. Once again we conducted a set of seminars for each other's institutions. These successful seminars led to a joint study of global education practices in Thailand. Our Thai colleagues were interested in developing a database of global education practice in schools across their country as a benchmark from which to begin developing some coursework. I worked with them in developing instrumentation that we pilot tested with some teachers in the metropolitan Bangkok area. We then refined the questionnaire based upon this feedback and selected the sample for the nationwide effort. In this case, we were not conducting a joint study of practices in our own respective nations; rather, I served as a consultant to improve research practice. This successful effort for the Thais led to the development of an entire course of study at STOU in this area.

This experience caused me to reflect upon my assumptions as I went into a consultant relationship. I was forced to reassess how I approached the task, what biases I brought to it, how I could best serve those with whom I was working, and when and how to recognize situations where they knew far better than I what they needed. They simply needed affirmation from someone outside their own circle that the path they were following was on the mark. The experience was humbling for me in many ways and dramatically impacted the remainder of my work in such circumstances.

Another Thai example, from Chulalongkorn University, the premier institution of higher learning in the country, is a three-week consultancy undertaken by Professor Fred Finley and myself. This effort led to a master's degree in global environmental education and the establishment of a curriculum center in this area to serve teachers and schools in the metropolitan Bangkok region. Under the auspices of the USIA Academic Specialist Program, which brings visiting scholars to an institution to do a specific set of tasks, Professor Finley and I were able to achieve the above results in a relatively short time period. The dean of the Faculty of Education at Chulalongkorn had to make application to the cultural attache in the U.S. embassy for our services. Once approved, we were contacted by a USIA official in Washington, D.C., about the opportunity, our interest in it, and when we would be able to go for a three-week period. This successful venture would never have come about without first having the educational exchange agreement in place between the two faculties. The kinds of experiences we gained as a result of this work have gone directly into our own coursework. Our work at Chula caused us to rethink our own curriculum in this area and we subsequently revised an existing global education course into an expanded and enriched global-environmental education course that has been offered several times with great success. This course has indirectly led to yet another exchange agreement that I shall discuss later in the chapter.

Another example comes from Japan and the linkage with the Hiroshima University Faculty of Education. I take particular pride in this exchange agreement because I personally negotiated it. I had been a Senior Fulbright Researcher at Hiroshima in 1982-83 and had forged a good working relationship with colleagues there. Upon returning to Minnesota, I suggested that there might be a good opportunity for an exchange agreement with the Hiroshima Faculty of Education, generally regarded as the premier education faculty in the country. I knew this would take time to negotiate because Hiroshima had never before negotiated an agreement between faculties, but only at the university level. I cautioned administrators here that we would have to be patient, that this could take as long as two years to develop. I was off by only four months.

In the end, the Japanese saw the merit and benefits in such an agreement and the first document was signed. The Hiroshima faculty immediately and successfully applied for funds from the Ministry of Education for joint research projects between the two institutions. The two faculties then engaged in a joint study of teacher education programs and made exchange visits of faculty researchers in the process. This project lasted for three years.

Following this successful joint study project, we decided to expand this area of interest to a wider audience. A consortium of Japanese and U.S. faculties of education came together in 1987 to form JUSTEC, the Japan-U.S. Teacher

Education Consortium, which still exists. These 20 institutions, 10 from each nation, meet annually to share the results of their joint research and make plans for new activities in the coming year. The collaboration has resulted in journal publications, seminars, and even a book.

Hiroshima has since expanded the initial agreement into other areas, such as the annual exchange of two students from each institution to the other for a period of six to nine months. The two deans have wisely chosen to avoid many of the pitfalls of typical exchange agreements by having the exchange students register for any credit desired in their own institutions before beginning the program. The students also agree with a mentor at their home university about what the nature of their study project will be and about how it will be assessed once they return. Thus, the students exchange more like visiting scholars than credit-seeking, tuition-paying students. They sit in on courses of interest to them and have access to libraries without all the red tape that usually accompanies such exchanges.

Finally, the capstone of this exchange agreement activity is the nine-nation Citizenship Education Policy Study (CEPS) which I have just finished. This project came out of a series of discussions with colleagues from several of the exchange partner institutions over a two-year period. These discussions related to the changing nature of citizenship education programming needs in the partner countries over the early part of the next century. The result was a coming together of four of the exchange partners to form an international research consortium network to undertake this study. The partners were the University of Minnesota (Project Secretariat), the University of Amsterdam (Netherlands), Chulalongkorn University (Thailand), and Hiroshima University (Japan). Having worked strictly on a bilateral basis for a number of years, the members agreed to merge their individual capacities into a much larger project of an international nature in which all four institutions would play a major role. The CEPS project provided the perfect avenue to test this networking idea.

I shall not go into any detail about the CEPS project here other than to say it has been a monumental learning and collaborative working experience. We began very tentatively, for, although we were all linked with one another through separate exchange agreements, this was the first time we had attempted a collaboration. The first two years were difficult in that trust had to be established and working relationships defined. There was a particular concern about the North Americans and Europeans taking over the research activity and both of these teams as well as the Japanese and Thais worked hard to ensure that this did not happen. The result was many long and intense discussions regarding terminology, concepts, research methods to be employed, and working habits. In the end, however, the experiment has been a tremendous success. We have now completed the various project reports and book on this nine-nation study. It is entitled *Citizenship for the 21st Century: An International Perspective on Education* (Cogan and Derricott, 1988). We are already discussing the next project(s) this network might undertake to keep the momentum going.

The final exchange agreement, alluded to earlier, came about two years ago with Linkoping Universities in Sweden. This agreement took us to a new level in that it was concluded at the all-university level but focused specific attention upon the work in environmental education of the Colleges of Natural Resources and Education and Human Development at the University of Minnesota. These two colleges had worked together over a year-long period to forge a cross-collegiate relationship in this area. Further, the work culminated in the establishment of the Center for Environmental Learning and Leadership (CELL), which was charged with developing graduate degree programs and curricula and with extending its work throughout the state and region through the Minnesota Extension Service and environmental educators throughout the state.

The groundwork for this agreement was laid through exchange visits between the faculties at Linkoping and Minnesota. The agreement was signed by the presidents of the respective institutions in Sweden in late August 1995. It has already resulted in a cooperative summer institute for teachers from both nations held in Minnesota during the summer of 1996 as well as several individual faculty colaborations.

This long description of the various exchange agreements has been a necessary introduction to the main topic of this chapter. Without it, the rest of what I have to say will make little sense.

CURRICULAR INFUSION

To internationalize courses which, in this instance, are a part of the overall curriculum, I have brought to bear upon them the lessons I have learned in the course of my consulting work, my studies, and my research. Four courses that have been substantially impacted by my work abroad will illustrate how the process of infusion works. I shall describe below the measures I have taken to "internationalize" them through infusion. These are not particularly novel ideas and it amazes me that they are not taken up by colleagues more often. They only require a little thought when putting together the course syllabus. Of course, one must first have the experiential base.

The four courses include the following:

1. CI 5730 Social Studies for the Elementary and Middle School Inservice Teacher

2. CI 5747 Global Environmental Education (jointly taught with a science educator specializing in environmental studies)
3. EdPA 5131 Comparative Education
4. EdPA 5605 Research Topics in International Development Education

I have tried to internationalize each of these courses in several ways: (1) through the kinds of readings assigned, (2) through the kinds of assignments given, and (3) through the kinds of examples I use in my lectures. This process is somewhat easier for the latter three courses because they lend themselves more naturally to international topics and issues.

The CI 5730 course is designed specifically for American elementary and middle school teachers, but I believe they also need a sense of what teachers in other parts of the world are doing in this area of the curriculum, whether similar to or different from their practice. One of the things I try to do in this offering in particular is to bring in readings from outside the normal framework for this course. I use children's literature a great deal because I think in helps to bridge cultures and because it paves the way for a more interdisciplinary offering. I do not assign typical methods books for this course. Rather, I choose literature, both children's and adult, which exposes the teachers to a broader view of the world through the eyes of those living it. I assign from four to six paperback books for the teachers to read over the term and then give them specific writing assignments to get them to reflect cross-culturally on the readings. They are asked not only to critique and reflect upon what they have learned from these readings, but also on how they would use them in their own classroom instruction. This makes the transition from the theoretical conceptualization to the praxis. The feedback from students at the end of the term has been overwhelmingly positive. Indeed, they want to know how and where they can obtain lists of books like these to use in their own classes to help their students understand the universal values and attitudes we hold as well as the unique differences we embody. Having anticipated this, I have a bibliography of books ready for them.

I have expanded on this concept by asking my students to bring in and share books of a multicultural, cross-cultural, international nature with their peers. They are required to bring a minimum of five of these books and to be prepared not only to summarize the book for others not familiar with it but to share how they use the book with their own students.

In other courses, I have required students to compare current issues in the United States with similar issues in other nations in other parts of the world. In the Comparative Education course, for example, I typically require that students choose for their major paper some topic or issue with global implications that is of interest to them. The student make-up in this particular course makes this rather easy because it is a broad mixture of American and international students. The discussions throughout the quarter are greatly enriched by this mix and the students often choose topics for their papers that arise out of the classroom dialogue. I require the social studies students to do likewise in the major work for that course. They must choose an instructional model topic that is international in character. They can select a local issue or topic but they must show how it is manifested internationally. Most of the time this comes naturally to them, though I occasionally have to sit down and discuss possible implications with them. In the end, they all come up with global course projects.

Where I am able to use my study and research abroad most directly is in the examples I cite in lectures in the various courses. The examples range from discussions of the National Curriculum in England and Wales with respect to the social subjects and how they are taught and assessed there as opposed to practice here, to the use of my own research in examples for the Comparative Education and the Research Topics courses. I find in each instance that students are interested that their professor has actually conducted research or studied abroad. They tend to think of us simply as instructors and are always amazed that we have actually done the kinds of things academicians really do. They are also eager to learn of the practices of others, that others face the same challenges and are likewise concerned about their subjects and how they convey the material to students. They are similarly surprised that teachers and educators the world over are facing the same kinds of problems and issues in their daily teaching and work schedules. This realization seems to greatly relieve them—they are not in this alone.

Students are particularly interested in the kinds of problems and issues one faces in conducting research abroad. I use these experiences especially in the Research Topics course where I walk them through a case study of the study I carried out in Japan under the Fulbright fellowship. I include everything from the scholarly issues, to getting things wrapped up here before one leaves, to getting settled in the host country. I emphasize that it takes at least three times as long for me to do research abroad as it does here simply because of the many cultural hurdles and nuances I must confront. But I also emphasize that it is just these issues that make the work so much more interesting.

In each of the courses, I am able to draw upon the kinds of experiences I have had working with colleagues from the exchange partner institutions. These experiences have been invaluable. For example, in the CI 5747 Global Environmental Education course, I use the work I did with Selby and Pike at the University of York in the Centre for Global Education as well as the consulting work I did with colleagues at Chulalongkorn University. In this instance, I am also able to draw upon experiences in meeting and working with United Nations officials from several of the regional offices in Bangkok. The UN has a major presence in Thailand and Bangkok serves as the South-

Southeast Asian Regional Centre for most of its agencies. So whereas the UN is sometimes a distant abstraction to our teachers, I am able to share how it plays an important role directly in the lives of people in this part of the world.

Sometimes internationalization is as simple as capitalizing upon an opportunity. For example, in November 1995, my CEPS project was to have a steering committee meeting in Chicago in conjunction with the National Council for the Social Studies annual meeting; a number of us from the project were to make presentations. It occurred to me that all these persons would have to transfer through Minneapolis by air on their way to Chicago—we had a golden opportunity before us. Why not arrange for these scholars to come several days early and stop over in the Twin Cities to meet with colleagues with whom they might have common interests and to attend a seminar on educational reforms taking place in the respective nations. This idea meant changing some flight schedules, getting some modest financial support from the College and the Department of Educational Policy and Administration, finding a large enough venue, and doing some publicity. We did it; nearly 100 people showed up to listen to and dialogue with these scholars. Some simple foresight and a little extra effort gave both the students and faculty who attended and the scholars who presented something to remember. It was so simple; that's the point. And yet these scholars could just as easily have transited Minneapolis on the way to Chicago and no one would have known the better.

One other thing I have learned to do over the years in internationalizing my courses is to use the talent pool represented by the students in the course as a resource. In the EdPA courses in particular, I am able to draw upon a rich base of students from other parts of the world, and upon U.S. students who have spent time working or studying abroad. Each year we have Peace Corps Volunteer returnees in our courses as well as those who have lived abroad with families, have worked in other parts of the world either as teachers or in other kinds of labor, and who have much to share with their colleagues here.

Finally, I'm suggesting eight starting points for internationalizing courses through infusion. These are not inclusive, only representative.

- Assessing individual course syllabi in terms of possibilities for internationalization
- Rethinking course goals in terms of internationalization (e.g., how can course objectives be more inclusive to incorporate local through global issues?)
- Examining the kinds of reading assigned to students for a course, both books and journal readings, that reflect diverse points of view on topics/issues/content being read and discussed
- Rethinking assignments so that they allow for and encourage (perhaps even force) students (both American and international) and the

faculty members to think beyond national borders

- Using the representative diversity of the student demographics in the classroom as a teaching tool; allowing the students to use their own experiences to dialogue about the multiple perspectives on the various content topics and issues under discussion
- Using one's own research, study abroad, and international consulting and conference attendance as a faculty member to enrich and enliven a course
- Inviting visiting international faculty members as guest speakers or panelists to provide a wealth of information to students about another culture
- Capitalizing upon the opportunities of an international nature at the institution and taking advantage of related opportunities

CONCLUSION

As I said at the outset, I have said nothing particularly new or earthshaking in this chapter. Curricular infusion does require some international experience so that one's assumptions about the world and the way in which we do things are challenged. I find this to be an ongoing part of my work. It gives life to what I do.

Indeed, during a recent term break, a British colleague and I spent several days working with a Hungarian educator and his colleagues. We had met him at a meeting in Amsterdam in November 1992 while doing a workshop on school reform and teacher innovation. This work was a result of a lunch-time conversation with this Hungarian educator, who was worried about teachers in his nation. They would now have to move from a highly centralized system of school organization to one where teachers would have to make most of the decisions for themselves. Over the past three-and-a-half years, we have maintained contact, met several times, worked with him and his colleagues on the conduct of a survey designed to get at teachers' beliefs about change and innovation, found some modest funding to support the work, and brought all together in a workshop in Budapest. Many barriers might have prevented this at many stages. But there was a will here that kept all of us going. I cannot tell you how rewarding it is to work with people who are so dedicated and so eager to implement change. We have told them they don't really need our input any longer but they will not let go because we have formed a personal bond. We like each other and working together is a joy. Before we left, our Hungarian colleague was already designing the next stages of this project so we can continue to meet and collaborate. I only wish more of my colleagues here could see the forest for the trees and understand that there is so much more outside the national borders of the United States. They are prisoners in their own house and I pity them for all they have missed.

What I have gained from my work, more than anything else, is the friendship and mutual respect of colleagues the world over. I could not possibly put a price upon this. It is one of those intangibles that means much and yet has no value outside of those who experience it, except, in this case, for the students with whom I work here at the university. They gain a richness that simply would not be there without my experiences. It is the greatest gift I could possibly give to them.

REFERENCE

Cogan, J.J. and Derricott, R. (Eds.). (1998). *Citizenship for the 21st century: An international perspective on education*. London: Kogan-Page.

CHAPTER

Mind Opening through Music
An Internationalized Music Curriculum

by C. Victor Fung

One of the major goals in internationalizing a curriculum is to broaden students' views and perspectives in an area of study. For an effective education in today's global society, this mind-opening process seems indispensable. The contemporary world is a world of diversity, openness, new possibilities, and inventions. The last decade has seen countless numbers of devices, concepts, and theories with the prefix "multi-," from multimedia computer to multinational business, multicultural education, and multiple intelligences. All these new devices, concepts, and theories require an open mind to understand how they operate. One also needs an effective broad-based education to survive within the practices of these devices, concepts, and theories. To open one's mind through music using an internationalized curriculum, one should be aware of some universal issues, some nonuniversal issues, and some empirical evidence relevant to open-mindedness and attitudes towards music.

UNIVERSAL ISSUES

A likely answer to the question "Do you like music?" is "Yeah, I like music." This response suggests that most people have positive attitudes toward certain types of music. This common positive affection makes music a marvelous tool for a mind-opening experience.

Although a liking for certain types of music seems to be a universal phenomenon, the universality of music should not be overstated. To simply say that music is a universal language is no different from saying all humans must eat. B. Nettl (1983, Nettl et al., 1997), a renowned ethnomusicologist, suggests that there are universals and nonuniversals of music. The musical universals are easily recognized, e.g., all societies have something that sounds to us like music. Virtually everywhere, music is presented in units that can be identified as songs or pieces with more or less marked beginnings and endings. There is some redundancy, some repetition, balanced by some variety articulated through rhythmic, melodic textural means. There is a level of simplicity and levels of complexity. In addition, all human beings can sing, and there is always meaning or intention behind each song. Also, all human beings are capable of remembering a tune, and all cultures use music to transform an ordinary experience, like a ritual, concert, or festival. Moreover, the function of music everywhere is to accomplish something. It often reinforces boundaries between social groups in a society and therefore creates a specific musical emblem of identity for each group. The major function of music in many cultures is essentially educational. Music teaches people important things about their own culture.

NONUNIVERSAL ISSUES

We often easily overlook the fact that each type of music is based on a different system and philosophy. Musical meaning, sounds, singing qualities, instruments, and other rituals cannot be categorized under one concept by all societies. The foundations of musical structure and aesthetics in each type of music are fundamentally different, that is, nonuniversal. All musics have a unique history and virtually all cultures have unique musical instruments. These musical nonuniversals constitute the core of mind-opening experience through music. The role of musical universals, however, is to keep some paths to mind-opening readily available. Musical universals may allow connections between the music a student likes and the student's mind-opening experience in music.

Anthropologist A. P. Merriam (1964) proposed a model in the study of music where sound, conception, and behavior were equally weighted and closely related. According to Merriam, sound had a structure that cannot exist independently of human beings. Therefore, music was the product of human behavior. Conception of music must come before a specific behavior that would in turn produce the sound. Without concepts of music, behavior could not occur, and without behavior, music could not be produced. Conceptualization was the stage where musical values were found, and these values filter upward through the system to affect the music. This simple model offered a broad perspective in the study of music. It gave an integrated understanding of the human phenomenon of "music." This model was enlightening because music scholars had been largely focused on the study of sound alone. Based on Merriam's model, I would like to raise several fundamental and nonuniversal issues in music that make mind-opening possible.

First, music may be considered as a product-process continuum, depending on the cultural context. For example, musical experiences in the Western-art tradition tend to be product oriented. All kinds of audio and video recordings and concerts are products that listeners or consumers enjoy. Activities such as recruitment of performers, rehearsal, promotion, and financing are centered around the products. In contrast, some other cultures, such as most of those in Africa, consider societal participation a primary criterion for musical success. The process of improvisation is the key to musical activities. Most African music is not meant to be reproduced outside of its context.

Second, music reflects social and cultural beliefs. A Chinese proverb says, "When one listens to the music, one can tell whether the leader of the society is doing a good job." Music is not simply the special type of sound from a given area. It is often aesthetically and philosophically expressing, in sound, the important issues and concerns of the society. Studying the music of various world cultures may allow opportunities to study different social and cultural beliefs.

Third, different musical traditions may operate under different social organizational structures. Music making in the Western-art tradition is usually hierarchical or individual but rarely communal. A symphony orchestra, for example, operates under a tightly structured hierarchy. Even performers playing the same instrument must sit in designated seats. For example, a second-chair violinist cannot sit on the first chair. Each individual performer is also capable of performing a rich solo repertoire. Furthermore, each performer must practice individually before he or she can come together with the others to play as an orchestra. In contrast, Indonesian gamelan music operates on a communal system. One cannot practice gamelan music individually. Mature gamelan musicians should be able to rotate seats and play any instrument in the group.

Fourth, music is transmitted by notation or by oral tradition. Music notation is often claimed to be one of the most invincible achievements in Western-art music. Western-art music notation is in many ways far more sophisticated than many other music notation systems in the world, but this achievement has inhibited the experience of oral tradition, which is essential to such musical traditions as the Native American. When music is transmitted from one generation to another through oral tradition, the music encourages immediate and long-term musical memory. It also heightens the spirit of an individual with a unique identity specific to the receiver. Many non-Western-art musical traditions (e.g., Native American and African) have kept their music alive without any written notation for many centuries and generations.

Fifth, the function of music varies from one culture to another. Most Westerners use music to entertain and to relax. Others may use music to validate social institutions and religious rituals, to bring stability and continuity of culture, to provide symbolic representation, or to integrate people into the society. By learning various musical functions, students will have a broadened idea about what music may do for the human race.

Sixth, music has various elements (time, pitch, timbre, and loudness) and certain music may emphasize some of these elements while others may not. Johann Sebastian Bach was known as "the father of music" because of his contributions to establishing the Western tonal system and functional harmony. However, he confined his rhythmic structure in two, three, or four beats. His music did not have the interlocking rhythmic pattern that is common in many examples of African music. Bach never used the seven-, nine-, or eleven-beat cycles common in many Middle Eastern pieces. By being exposed to a wide array of musical elements, students may become more open-minded in seeing the range of musical possibilities and the limitless boundaries of musical sound.

These are only six of the preliminary issues reflecting musical nonuniversals. If one teaches only Western-art music, for example, students will likely miss the idea of music being a process, a communal activity, or a part of oral tradition. Three basic rationales were established to internationalize music curricula (Fung, 1995b). The social rationale proves that an internationalized (or multicultural) music curriculum develops multicultural awareness, understanding, and tolerance. It also promotes a deeper understanding and acceptance of people from other cultures, cultivates open-mindedness and unbiased thinking, and eradicates racial resentments. The musical rationale suggests that an internationalized music curriculum can provide opportunities to study musical concepts and reinforce the knowledge of musical elements; refine aural skills, critical thinking, and psychomotor development; increase tolerance of unfamiliar music; and develop more sensitive perceptions of familiar music. The global rationale requires a complete person in the modern world to be sensitive to cultures in a global context and to be educated on how to interact appropriately. An internationalized music curriculum is a tool for developing this global understanding. All three rationales pertain to the nature of American society and other international communities, the wide spectrum of musical elements available in the world, and the global society that brings people closer than ever.

EMPIRICAL EVIDENCE

Mind-opening through music occurs when one sees the various definitions, values, functions, and contexts of music. Some empirical findings support the idea that more open-minded people are more receptive to unfamiliar music and to music from various cultures. Using the *Dogmatism Scale* devised by Rokeach (1954, 1960), Soh (1972) found that close-minded people significantly preferred conventional Western-art music (Brahms symphony and serenade) when compared to the preferences of open-minded people. Mikol (1960) found that open-minded people had significantly more positive attitudes towards unconventional musical pieces (Schönberg quartet). Although there were inconsistencies within and among the findings of Soh and Mikol, open-mindedness seemed to play a role in people's attitudes toward unfamiliar music. Brim (1978), studying responses to excerpts from classical, rock, jazz, mariachi, march, oriental, and country-western styles, found that open-minded people preferred both low and high numbers of musical selections, while close-minded people had a consistently moderate number of preferences (i.e., a curvilinear relationship).

Using musical excerpts from Africa, China, India, Indonesia, Japan, Korea, the Middle East, and Thailand, Fung (1994) found that preferences for musical excerpts were significantly related to a student's multicultural attitudes. Students who were more willing to tolerate people who differed from themselves tended to prefer musical excerpts from various cultures. Multicultural attitudes explained about 19 percent of the variance in world music preference.

AN INTERNATIONALIZED CURRICULUM

When an instructor decides to include many kinds of music from the world in the curriculum, one of the first concerns is likely to be the organization of the course. Three common basic approaches exist for organizing a world music course (Fung 1995a): (1) cultural-geographical, (2) musical, and (3) topical. Although these three approaches are distinct, most instructors combine them in practice. In the cultural-geographical approach, an instructor organizes world musical materials according to the original sources of the materials and each source is unique to a culture or to a geographic region. For example, course topics may include Native American music, Latin American music, Japanese gagaku music, or Hindustani sitar music. I believe that most college world music courses are organized in this manner because it is the easiest way to organize a world music course, given the distinct cultural and musical stylistic differences among various world musical cultures, and because many world music curricula are driven by available texts. Most of the common standard world music texts (e.g., May, 1980; Nettl, et al., 1997; Titon, 1996) are organized in compartmentalized specialists' style. Each chapter was written by an area specialist(s). This is an advantage for the course in that the musical and cultural information about each cultural area is based on the specialist's years of research. However, the students may not be able to connect these cultural-geographical regions and make sense of how music is related to humankind.

The musical approach is found less frequently at the college level than at the grade levels. With this approach, an instructor focuses on teaching such musical concepts as duple time, syncopation, polyphony, pentatonic scale, and hocket. As these musical concepts are being addressed, the instructor may use music from any of the world cultures. Especially for nonmusic majors, explanations on and activities about these musical concepts are extremely helpful. For music majors, the use of these musical terms may help them associate world musics with "the music" that they already know. However, this approach often has little concern about culture and contexts.

The least common approach in organizing a college world music course is the topical approach. With this approach, an instructor organizes the curriculum according to such selected topics as healing, lullabies, entertainment, gender roles, and social hierarchies. These topics usually have a social significance. Again, the instructor may use a palette of musical examples from any world culture. This approach can minimize ethnocentrism. Students may be able to make connections among various cultures easier. Some scholars may prefer this approach over the others, but it is extremely difficult to implement because no available text at the college level is organized in such a manner. As far as can be determined, only one text is available at the high school level (Fowler, 1994). Therefore, if this approach is being used at the college level, the instructor has to create and organize his or her own material.

Although most instructors combine these approaches in practice, one of these approaches must serve as the backbone of the curriculum. It is not necessarily bad to follow the layout of a text as the backbone of the curriculum, but currently available world music texts are obviously fond of the cultural-geographical approach. If scholars have recognized the value of the topical approach, scholars must collaborate to create materials based on this approach.

Several curricular recommendations are worth considering. Music instructors should use a combination of cultural-geographical, musical, and topical approaches in the curriculum. The balance among the three approaches should be based on objectives set forth by the institution and the instructor. Instructors may start with the music that students are familiar with. Students should recognize the limitations of musical universals. Instructors may prepare students to investigate and understand the musical nonuniversals using a wide range of musical examples. In the mind-opening process, instructors should consider using a range of devices and activities (e.g., audio and video experiences, passive listening, observing live musical events, active music making, oral discussion, and writing). Given the rich audio-visual elements to be covered in world musics, multimedia devices could be put to good use in instruction.

Mind-opening through music is a multinational and multicultural enterprise. Students may come to understand cultural differences around the globe. Internationalizing the music curriculum is a recent trend. Institutions are becoming aware of, valuing, and practicing it more vigorously than ever. The trend is still growing rapidly with a parallel movement in musical materials available in the market. To internationalize the music curricula throughout the nation, continuous effort is needed at all levels from instructors, administrators, professional organizations, and the publishing industry.

REFERENCES

Brim, R. (1978). The effect of personality variables, dogmatism and repression sensitization upon response to music. *Journal of Music Therapy*, 15(2), 74-87.

Fowler, C. (1994). *Music! Its role and importance in our lives.* New York: Glencoe.

Fung, C. V. (1995a). Approaches in world music curriculum. *Social Science SRIG Newsletter* (Spring 1995): 3.

————— (1995b). Rationales for teaching world musics. *Music Educators Journal*, 82(1), 36-40.

————— (1994). Undergraduate nonmusic majors' world music preference and multicultural attitudes. *Journal of Research in Music Education*, 42(1), 45-57.

May, E. (Ed.). (1980). *Musics of many cultures.* Berkeley, CA: University of California Press.

Merriam, A. P. (1964). *The anthropology of music.* Evanston, IL: Northwestern University Press.

Mikol, B. (1960). The enjoyment of new musical systems. In M. Rokeach, *The open and closed mind* (pp. 270-84). New York: Basic Books.

Nettl, B. (1983). *The Study of ethnomusicology.* Urbana, IL: University of Illinois Press.

Nettl, B. et al. (1997). *Excursions in world music.* Englewood Cliffs, NJ: Prentice-Hall.

Rokeach, M. (1960). *The open and closed mind.* New York: Basic Books.

—————. (1954). The nature and meaning of dogmatism. *Psychological Review*, 61, 194-204.

Soh, K.C. (1972). Dogmatism, training and enjoyment of Western classical music. *Psychologia*, 15(1), 59-64.

Titon, J. T. (Ed.). (1996). *Worlds of music.* 3rd ed. New York: Schirmer Books.

CHAPTER

Internationalization of Course Work in Soil Science and Agronomy

by Peter Graham

T he soil is basic to the progress of humanity. It is the medium in which crop plants are grown, and its physical and chemical properties contribute to the vigor of that growth, and to final crop yield. To quote from The Cockle Bur, cited by Hartel (1998): "Whatever our accomplishments, our sophistication, our artistic pretensions, we owe our very existence to a six-inch layer of top soil and the fact that it rains." Improving the soil can lead to enhanced crop production, or to a more stable and environmentally gentle production system. Conversely, misuse of the soil can result in progressive erosion and soil loss, and to lowered soil fertility and crop yield. Soils differ in both their inherent fertility and their fragility under pressure, influencing the extent to which they can be exploited without degradation. To determine how best to use a particular soil, the soil scientist must understand the structure and chemistry of the soil, the factors that affected the genesis of that soil, the biological processes affecting soil nutrient balance, and the availability of nutrients needed for crop growth.

The related discipline of agronomy (from the Greek *agros*, or field) considers the management of crops or pastures under field conditions, and encompasses topics as different as plant spacing to maximize light interception, irrigation practices, land preparation, and the control of pests and disease. The training needed by graduates in these two fields is changing as we approach the twenty-first century. One example of this is the increasing need to consider environmental issues, such as the accumulation of pesticides or fertilizer nitrogen in the groundwater, the retention of wetlands as a means of groundwater filtration, or the use of recycled biosolids as a form of low-grade fertilizer. Equally important is the increasing need for an international per-spective in our instruction. In this chapter, I will look at agriculture in Latin America to try to justify the need for such a perspective and to provide examples of how we might improve on current course offerings.

AGRICULTURE IN THE TWENTY-FIRST CENTURY

Two factors, population increases and enhanced regional trade, are likely to affect the agriculture of Western Hemisphere countries in the early part of the next century. The population of Latin America is projected to rise from 448 million in 1990 to about 750 million by the year 2020 (Parikh, 1994), and in several Central American countries, population increases have already exceeded 3 percent per year in each of the last three decades. A doubling of food demand by the year 2020 is not unlikely for a number of countries in this region (Ruttan, 1994). In a similar situation in the 1960s, the "Green Revolu-tion" brought about dramatic increases in cereal grain yields across much of the third world, with a number of third-world countries achieving self-suffi-ciency in grain production for the first time in many years. A similar revolution will be needed to significantly improve crop production in the Western Hemisphere over the next 30 years, but, for the following reasons, is likely to be much more difficult to achieve (Ruttan, 1994):

- close to 85 percent of the food produced in the region is grown on small or medium-sized (1 to 5 hectares) holdings, or by the consumers themselves
- many small farmers can neither afford, nor readily obtain, the technical inputs needed for high yield
- improved crop production in the region will need to be achieved without further significant depletion of fossil fuel reserves, and with an eye to limiting the potential for further pollution or land degrada-tion
- support for research and development, high during the initial years of the Green Revolution, has declined (Eicher, 1994), with increased support now needed simply to maintain existing yield levels (Plucknett and Smith, 1986)

Although Asia faces a similar problem, the approaches taken in Asia and Latin America are likely to be different. In Asia, where the area available for an extension of agricultural production is limited and the cost of extending irrigation systems is high, further intensification of agriculture will be essential for enhanced crop production. In contrast, intensification of agriculture in a number of Latin American countries is likely to be balanced, perhaps even overshadowed, by an expansion of agriculture into new and often somewhat fragile ecosystems. These systems include more than 500 million hectares of under-utilized land in the "cerrados" of Brazil and the "llanos" of Colombia, as well as some forest boundary and high elevation locations.

Enhanced agricultural research capacity will be needed to make such an expansion work. Ruttan (1994) has already suggested that the poorer countries of the tropics and subtropics will need enhanced research capacity and greater training opportunities if they are to take advantage of recent advances in such fields as molecular genetics. Eicher (1994) notes that Argentina, Brazil, and Mexico currently employ two-thirds of the region's agricultural research workers, with some countries in the region devoting less than 1 percent of their GNP to agricultural research. Where is the enhanced agricultural research capacity needed to improve crop yields in the region likely to come from? Eicher (1994) believes that a major change will be in the privatization of research, with multinational firms "aggressive in conventional plant breeding and seed sales in the third world." I have two sons and both were recruited out of graduate school by the same seed company. I am sure that this was at least in part because they were bilingual, at home with the customs of Latin America, and somewhat familiar with its agriculture. Further trade agreements, for example, the expansion of the NAFTA agreement to include Argentina, Uruguay, and Chile, will increase opportunities in the region, and result in increased international employment for U.S. graduates in agricultural extension, education, and research. One area where this is already being seen is in significant funding for environmental and ecological health issues in the area along the U.S.-Mexican border (Reed, 1995).

For American graduates to play a role in the expansion of agriculture throughout this region, they will need a clear understanding of crop production practices in these countries, and an awareness of how such practices might influence the quality of products for export. Combined, these changes are likely to mean that our future graduates in areas such as soil science and agronomy will need a markedly different education from what they currently receive.

An additional reason why soils and agronomy courses should be more international in content is that international students make up a significant proportion of the undergraduate and graduate students attending my institution, the University of Minnesota, and other American universities. They contribute significantly to the ambiance of a university as a learning and research center. Further, a number of these students are supported by their governments, and constitute a significant source of revenue for universities. As alternate quality venues for higher education become available in Latin America, we risk losing these students if the material covered in our courses is not relevant to the situation in their own countries or, in the case of graduate students, does not improve significantly upon what they have already been taught.

A Mexican graduate student commented recently that many of his colleagues preferred to study in Europe because the graduate degree there is usually by research and thesis only. This made me think that when an American student is admitted to the graduate program, we will usually accept at face value the courses he or she has taken somewhere else. By contrast, we will often not even consider the courses the foreign student took before coming to the U.S., and in most cases have only a poor understanding of the quality of his or her institution and needs. The U.S. is not unique in this, but often the education provided for such students is not even user friendly. Rather than using these people as a resource for obtaining information about other agricultural systems and practices, we try to press them into our mold. The projects they write on and the literature searches they undertake thus often have little relevance to production conditions and practices in their own country.

INTERNATIONALIZING COURSE OFFERINGS IN SOIL SCIENCE AND AGRONOMY

If it is desirable that both U.S. and foreign students be exposed to a more internationally oriented coverage of the fields of soil science and agronomy, how could such information to be packaged to excite student interest?

An Undergraduate or Graduate Minor in International Agriculture

I believe that a student must first know his or her discipline, then learn how to apply it in an international context. Despite that, agricultural and forestry colleges need to include undergraduate and graduate minors in international agriculture in their curriculum. An undergraduate minor exists in the College of Agriculture at the University of Minnesota, but currently has few teeth. It requires 30 credits, including 14 credits in unspecified courses outside the major; 10 credits in the language, culture, geography, or history of a specified region, a 5 credit research project; and a seminar on international agriculture. How could this minor be strengthened? One possibility would be that it include a required period of study abroad. To do this, the university would need to develop interchange programs with universities in Latin America and strengthen the infrastructure needed to support study abroad. In the universities with which we sign collaborative agreements, we would need to identify, approve, and promote suitable courses for study by our students. Interchange programs to Latin America would require students to achieve some level of language competency before going abroad. While at the host university, they would be expected to undertake one or more of the approved courses, and develop and write upon a project relating to some aspect of local agriculture. A number of universities in this region, for example the Escuela Panamericana in Honduras, require that students participate in "on farm" operations, an additional benefit for U.S. students with an urban background.

No currently existing graduate minor in international agriculture is appropriate to soil science and agronomy students. In forestry, Peace Corps activities can sometimes be tailored to satisfy research requirements for the M.S. degree, and a similar program is needed for soil science and agronomy. Some soil science and agronomy students at Minnesota have the opportunity to undertake "sandwich" degrees, first completing all their coursework at Minnesota, then working on a research program at some foreign location. Such research activities are most commonly tied to a specific research project, for example, the USAID Bean/Cowpea CRSP project in Ecuador, and then integrated into a larger activity. Sandwich degrees are likely to become more common as countries lacking graduate programs in agriculture fund graduate education for their young scientists in the U.S., but expect them to undertake research projects in their own country. Such students are also likely to have a special interest in the development of a graduate minor in international agriculture. Despite strong foreign-student involvement, such a minor would need to include language competency, the study abroad of research topics tied to the major, and the inclusion of specified "international" courses in the graduate coursework program.

Designated "International" Courses

A second suggested change in the undergraduate minor is the inclusion of specified "international" courses in a student's case load. In a number of areas of soil science and agronomy, what happens in other regions of the world is so different from what we conventionally teach in the U.S. that separate packaging and presentation is warranted. Examples of such "international" courses might include "Tropical Crops and Pastures," "Germplasm Diversity and Property Rights," "Tropical Soils," "Tropical Forests and Ecosystems," and "Disease and Insect Pests of Tropical Crops and Pastures." I will discuss here only four possible "international" courses in the soil science/agronomy area. After years of living in Latin America, I would sell my soul for a good mango, papaya, or passion fruit, or even for frozen cassava to French fry. They are available in the Twin Cities, but usually one must tell the check-out clerk at the supermarket what they are so they can be rung up. I am equally surprised when I must explain to my students that sugar cane is planted using "setts" rather than seeds, and that these setts carry nitrogen-fixing bacteria that will reduce the need for nitrogen fertilization in this crop; or that day length and temperature have a profound effect on the flowering of a number of crop species, so that many short-day bean varieties fail to flower in Minnesota.

Obviously, many crop species used in Latin America, and the systems under which they are grown, are very different from agriculture in the American Midwest. A course discussing these differences is important, and a description of unfamiliar crop species and their culture, as well as of the different systems used to produce more familiar crops, should have considerable interest for students. Because some of the examples used in one of the courses I teach involve plant species unknown to the students, I have always held a taste-testing during the course. It is both popular with the students, and an aid to their memory. Something similar—perhaps of different ways to prepare corn, or of ways to combine corn and beans in a single dish—would make a nice complement to a course on tropical crops and production systems.

Many of the crop species important in U.S. agriculture are not indigenous to this country—soybeans originated in China, peanuts and beans in South America, and clovers and medics in the region bordering the Mediterranean. The introduction of such species into U.S. agriculture is the result of extensive collection, evaluation, and selection in the National Plant Germplasm System (National Research Council, 1991). Other "soybeans" remain to be discovered. For example, crops such as pop beans or fruits such as cherimoya, which are little known in the U.S., were popular in the agriculture of the Incas (National Research Council, 1989). The legume *Leucaena leucocephala* or *huaje,* is so important in Mexico that the state named Oaxaca means "land of the huajes." This rapidly growing tree species provides pods for human consumption, high-nitrogen foliage for animal feed and green manure, and timber for construction and burning.

Appreciation for biodiversity and the loss of species following rainforest logging has increased in recent years and has been accompanied by concerns for the property rights to indigenous species (Crucible Group, 1994). In some cases, this concern has resulted in ill feeling among Latin Americans at the collection by outsiders of potentially important native species. For example, a plant called "uña de gato," used for a long time in the folk medicine of the Andean region of Latin America, is now on sale in the U.S. at over $12 a bottle as an arthritis remedy. A course that considered introduction success stories from the past, and examined some current needs in U.S. agricultural production, would be a fascinating and widely relevant offering. Such a course could characterize a number of species having potential for the U.S., show how these species are used in their center of origin, and examine all aspects of germplasm property rights issues.

The characteristics of a particular soil are determined by five major factors: (1) the nature of the parent rock material from which it was formed, (2) environmental conditions (particularly temperature and rainfall), (3) biological forces, (particularly type of vegetation cover), (4) topography, and (5) the time over which these forces have been acting. While no two soils are likely to be exactly the same (Wild, 1988), differences in the forces affecting tropical soil formation and those operating in the northern U.S. guarantee very different end products. American students, particularly those concerned with sustainable agricultural production, could learn a lot from the approaches adopted in the agricultural development of Latin America and other regions of the tropics, as well as from a consideration of the fragility of tropical ecosystems and of what is needed to maintain them. The development of a formal course in tropical soils would be an essential part of the internationalization of our class offerings.

One of the major differences between crop production in the tropics and subtropics and in Minnesota is in relation to disease and insect pests. I work with beans, a crop that can be essentially wiped out by at least 10 different plant diseases and insect pests of the tropics and subtopics. Even when the grain has been harvested, the farmer must sell it quickly or risk major loss through attack by seed weevils. Such epiphytotic diseases are much less common in Minnesota.

A course that examines the reasons for this difference between world regions would illustrate many of the principles of pathogen and pest dynamics.

INTERNATIONAL EXAMPLES IN NORMAL COURSE OFFERINGS

International, rather than local, examples can provide a nice break in virtually any course, especially if accompanied by colorful slides. I spend one period in my soil biology class having the students apply the principles of legume inoculation to the development of an inoculant industry for a country such as Ecuador. Other Latin American examples discussed in that course include the following:

- Initial problems in establishing legumes on the acid soils of the Brazilian cerrado
- Soil problems resulting from deforestation in the Amazon rain forest
- The role of soil- and plant-associated microorganisms in reducing the evolution of methane, a gas important in global warming, from flooded soils and rice paddies
- The use of termite nests as a low-cost fertilizer in the tropics

These examples have been gleaned from extensive travel in the region, and through the ability to read journal articles in Spanish and Portuguese. How can such Latin American exposure be extended to others? Increased opportunity for study abroad will open the way to such experiences for many American students. Faculty exchanges associated with a study abroad program, or service on the committee of a student undertaking a "sandwich" research program will also provide experience. And such experience can also lead to research collaboration and further interaction in the region.

Faculty mentoring, in the form of support for young faculty to accompany others with more experience of the region on project travel, would also enhance the international competence of our faculty. One additional possibility might be to encourage sabbatical leave programs to the more prestigious institutions in this region. Most faculty now take sabbatical leaves to other U.S. institutions or to Europe. They could be encouraged to take a sabbatical leave in Latin America by such premiums as additional travel support, start-up funding for collaborative research activities, or the opportunity to attend international conferences in the region.

LONG DISTANCE EDUCATION

Advances in long distance education are currently used to support out-state locations and nonconventional students. They could equally well be used to provide continuing education for foreign alumni, and to enhance international enrollments. A considerable foreign market for American courses could be developed, particularly at the graduate level and in countries lacking graduate programs of their own. In the past, students in such countries have been forced to seek conventional M.S. or Ph.D. degrees in Brazil, Mexico, Costa Rica, Argentina, the U.S., or Europe. However, such formal education can only satisfy a fraction of the need for graduate training. I am involved in a project that aims in part to provide research training for agricultural scientists in several of the smaller Latin American countries. At a recent meeting, one of the participants commented that after 15 years we could still fit all the students we had trained using the M.S./Ph.D. model into a single room. Certainly the type of training we have done is not likely to benefit the extension workers or government officials in these countries who are charged with bringing new technologies to the farmers.

The international centers with their emphasis on shorter term traineeships, workshops emphasizing specific themes, and documentation support have done a better job, but still rarely reach beyond the national research program or local research station. Graduate training of foreign nationals in the U.S. is often achieved at great cost and personal hardship, and can be plagued with study and social problems, of which language is not the least.

For the first couple of years I worked in Colombia, it was so tiring to follow conversations in Spanish that by the afternoon it was easier to accept a point than to query it. Most of us know students whose grades reflect their knowledge of English, rather than their ability; and of thesis research undertaken that has no relevance in the student's own country. Why not formalize a relationship with selected sister institutions in Latin America and teach core programs through long distance education, supported by e-mail services in English and Spanish? Grades in the core courses could then be used as the basis for acceptance into American graduate programs, with students undertaking thesis research in their own countries, and with international committees. This system would permit greater numbers of foreign students to receive training, but would minimize cost and hardship to them and still generate revenue for the American institution.

To my knowledge, I am the only biological scientist writing for this volume. Similarly, it is uncommon, at least on my campus, to find collaboration between specialists in education policy and administration and those working in the fields of agronony and soil science. That is a great pity because the agricultural sciences would make an ideal model on which to test new approaches to international education and education theory.

CONCLUSION

My initial graduate experience was in a narrow area of bacterial taxonomy. I was theoretically, rather than practically, oriented, and limited in the teaching and research I could do. Latin America changed that by showing me the benefits of multidisciplinary research and by opening my eyes to new research problems. The time I spent in Latin America provided me with the breadth and experience I needed to be a more effective teacher and researcher. Internationalization of our courses in soil science and agronomy, particularly in relation to Latin America, could provide some of the same perspective to our students, and enhance their capability and competitiveness. It could also be a mechanism by which American universities enter a new market at a time of reduced state support.

REFERENCES

Crucible Group. (1994). *Gente, plantas and patentes.* CIID, Canada Publishers, p. 106.

Eicher, C.K. (1994). Building productive national and international research systems. In:V. W. Ruttan (Ed.), *Agriculture, environment and health.* Minneapolis: University of Minnesota Press, pp. 77-103.

Hartel, P. G. (1998). The soil habitat. In: D.S. Sylvia et al (Eds.) *Principals and applications of soil microbiology.* Englewood Cliffs, NJ: Prentice Hall, pp. 21–43.

National Research Council. (1991). *Managing global genetic resources.* Washington, DC: National Academy Press, p. 170.

————. (1989). *Lost crops of the Incas.* Washington, DC: National Academy Press, pp. 415.

Parikh, K.S. (1994). Agricultural and food systems scenarios for the 21st century. In V.W. Ruttan (Ed.), *Agriculture, environment and health.* Minneapolis: University of Minnesota Press, p. 26-47.

Plucknett, D.H. and Smith, N.J.H. (1986). Sustaining agricultural yields. *BioScience* 36, 40-
    45.
Reed, P. (1995). NAFTA and transboundary environmental and ecological health issues.
    Environmental Toxicology and Chemistry 14, 361-62.
Ruttan, V.W. (1994). Sustainable agricultural growth. In V. W. Ruttan (Ed.), *Agriculture,
    environment and health,* Minneapolis: University of Minnesota Press, pp. 3-20.
Wild, A. (Ed.). (1988). Russell's soil conditions and plant growth. 11th ed. *Longman
    Scientific,* Avon, p. 991.

CHAPTER 10

Explaining Ourselves through Others' Cultural Visions

A Mini Course on America

by Harvey B. Sarles

INTRODUCTION

Globalizing or internationalizing American universities may take many different paths, from studying other languages and cultures, to studying geography or political economy, or studying abroad. Involving students in the actual lives and experiences of other peoples is necessary and important.

Involving U.S. students with international students in a *Mini Course on America* is an engaging and interesting path to pursuing this study. In this setting, one can meet others and gain a strong sense of their understanding of the United States and the various experiences that inform their thinking.

The idea of this course came from my experiences in the late 1970s and early 1980s when I taught a course on American life and culture to newly arrived foreign Fulbright Graduate Fellows. These students had come to the University of Minnesota for three weeks of pre-academic orientation prior to going to the various universities where they would be studying for a year in various fields. Most interesting and challenging for me were the vast differences in the students' experience and orientation to the United States. Their vastly differing backgrounds and knowledge required differences in explanations and interpretations in my own critical thinking and presentations. My training, orientation, and experience as an anthropological linguist were important in developing and teaching this course.

Including U.S. students in this course on American life would help the goals of internationalization and globalization. The expected results would instantly multiply, for both groups need to deepen and broaden their knowledge of American culture. U.S. students have been socialized to their own culture by osmosis as well as by education, although studies indicate they have great cognitive gaps in understanding their own country. U.S. students also need to know about the vastly different ways in which people of different cultures interpret their own life experiences, and those of others. In our interdependent world, U.S. students will increasingly work with other people. To facilitate successful interactions and mutual understanding, U.S. students will need a deeper awareness of who they are, and who others are.

International students acquire knowledge of life in the United States from formal education, and from the media and other informal means of learning. In some respects, they probably "know" more about the U.S. than their U.S. counterparts because people learn about their own cultures differently from the way they learn about others. However, other media often inform international students as much by prejudice and politics as by pedagogy.

People learn cultures in different ways, depending upon where they stand in relation to that culture. International students learn about American culture in the "etic" way, standing outside looking in, while U.S. students learn the "emic" way, standing inside looking out. Since etic learning is always the entry point to another culture, the two groups can learn how to switch from the etic to the emic and vice versa. The learning goals are thus reversed; international students will eventually learn emically (how Americans view themselves), and U.S. students will learn etically (how others see us from outside the culture).

Such cognitive shifts can have the following enormous consequences.

1. The knowledge gained is different, so students learn a great deal more (emically and etically) at the same time.
2. Students know both of these knowledges.
3. Such shifting of frames is an important intellectual skill that is the basis of another intellectual competence, comparative thinking. Both frames enable the two groups of students to "translate" themselves to others, a skill that is gaining significance in the light of increasing interactions among people globally.
4. Both groups also learn to think in interdisciplinary terms because the ideas and information they receive transcend narrowly defined disciplinary knowledge.
5. The proximity of the two groups, engaged in academic discourse—the principal learning method—increases personal participation in learning that leads to a sharing of concepts and experiences. Students who

are personally involved with people of other cultures are more likely to keep up their interest in those countries and in their relations with the U.S.

6. The course challenges the stereotypical thinking about international students having one common perspective, while U.S. students have another. Both groups may have diverse views.

7. Both groups will learn to communicate cross-culturally in an environment that is conducive to searching for meanings, clarifying concepts and relating them to cultural variables, and learning how to phrase questions and formulate responses. Communicating cross-culturally reduces uncertainties arising out of cultural differences and facilitates discussions even of controversial and emotionally loaded issues within the framework of academic discourse.

8. Both groups will gain new knowledge and information that will challenge the attributions they have made about each other prior to such experiences. The new attributions are likely to be more positive and emphatic, thus contributing to the general goal of international education, which is to create a better mutual understanding between peoples— a goal often neglected in the face of pressure to concentrate on narrower disciplinary goals.

9. Understanding one culture in the context of this course also produces "culture general" knowledge that can be applied to studying other cultures. In times of increasing interdependence, such a pedagogically difficult skill is essential. In traditional instruction, each of the above mentioned goals may require a separate course.

10. People tend to think of themselves as being "unique." However, being unique means not being comparable to others, yet, paradoxically, distinguishing ourselves from others in such a way already assumes a comparative judgment about the basis for such uniqueness. Making assumptions about uniqueness and comparability explicit is a major educational method of this proposed Mini Course, thus making the course an educational bargain in which students can learn multiple goals all at the same time.

The following conceptual outline is based on the issues and understandings that international students traditionally associate with their conceptions of the United States. While most of the following topics are also taught by other disciplines, often in a developmental mode, as for example in history, here the sequence of themes represents a cluster composed of issues that our experiences identified as being most misunderstood by and puzzling to others, and most difficult for U.S. students to explain about themselves.

This course goes out of its way to avoid advocating any one perspective, to avoid taking a defensive tone about the criticism others make of the U.S., and to avoid taking its own critical stance toward the U.S. The primary effort is to explain why we are what we are, and the primary method is open discourse and critical knowledge.

If there is any bias to this course, it is that all countries, nations, and peoples need to be understood the way they are, and that such understanding should be mutual, reciprocal, and generic of all international educational exchange programs.

The Mini Course occupies some 15 hours of time spread over 10 class sessions, which are described in more detail below.

DAY 1

My experiences with the Fulbright Orientation Centers suggest that there is a desirable sequence of topics for each session, beginning with the rather neutral approaches stemming from physical, economic, and human geography. The focus is on the vastness and the economic, social, and political diversity of the U.S., which strikes visiting international students immediately on arrival. If they arrive in the Twin Cities, they see a fairly large city located seven hours by car from Chicago, nine from Saint Louis, and three days from Seattle.

Minnesota is about the size of Great Britain, with 4.5 million persons to Great Britain's 70 million. Outside the Twin Cities area, the state is a vast emptiness with mile after mile of grain fields, forests, and lakes. To the west are real mountains; to the East, high hills, the Great Lakes, rivers, and oceans. We examine prevailing winds, where it is wet and dry, and where coal, oil, and other natural resources are found. Most Americans live in cities, mostly in the Northeast and on the West Coast. Students often ask "What is the Sun Belt"? and "Why do people live in the Frost Belt"? Some even ask "What is frost?"

This exercise includes the use of relief maps as visual devices to keep the *picture* of the United States in front of the students' eyes, to help them get accustomed to American English pronunciations of places, to develop a holistic vision of the U.S., and to begin to query and fill-in details of where different cities and regions are located. It is important to raise questions of why particular cities are located where they are; how they support themselves; how goods, food, minerals, and manufactured goods move; where various high-tech firms are; and where the military is located.

The demographics of the United States need to be considered next, especially the age, gender, and ethnic distributions of the present population, which tell a story of the formative experiences of people. Here we consider also the baby boom, the aging of the population—including the professoriate—and the coloration of North America and the recent immigrations.

Finally, we return to Minneapolis and St. Paul and discuss how these cities work. The Yellow Pages alone can explain a great deal about the categories and particulars of a mid to large U.S. American metropolitan area, surrounded as it is by inner and outer ringed suburbs and ex-urban rural areas. Students need to understand both differences and similarities of living, outlook, and experience, and how the freeways and the rise of the suburbs contributed to the consequent move toward conservatism.

This exercise problematizes the United States in a way strange to American students, who have taken geographic America for granted. They can begin to see anew through the questions and issues that arise in this discussion.

DAY 2

On Day 2 we address American federalism and "constitutionalism." We read the Declaration of Independence and the U.S. Constitution and discuss the social contract theory that led to the American Revolution. We include a lesson on the history of ideas that characterize Western thinking, from Plato to the present, and from Judeo-Christian thought to the Catholic Church, the Reformation, Humanism, John Locke, and the American Founding Fathers.

Since most national constitutions are statements of ideals and hopes, it is important to state that the U.S. Constitution is *the* foundation of U.S. law, and that Americans seem to *believe* in it at a deep level. Reading the Declaration of Independence reminds students that the U.S. began as a revolt against Great Britain. The Declaration points out the French Enlightenment philosophical-political history from which the United States derived its ideas—a sense of egalitarianism accompanied by a parallel notion of individual excellence (Gardner, 1961).

A reading of the Constitution informs students how the U.S. government is elected, what it consists of, what is the make-up and power of Congress, the executive branch, and the Supreme Court. Although this document is the law of the land, the international students wonder about political parties, which are mentioned nowhere, but are part of the informal convention. They are puzzled by the concepts of "checks and balances" and the separation of church and state; they wonder also about the actual power of the executive and the effect of television and the market economy on the president. Intense questions concerning the nature of American citizenship introduce questions about African-American slavery, the treatment of American Indians, and how the country was settled.

The importance of the Supreme Court as the arbiter of constitutionality raises questions about the nature of the law, how laws are interpreted, and how they are revised and enforced. Students are perplexed about political control of the military and wonder about other matters—e.g., the status of Puerto

Rico, for whom Americans actually vote, how local government works, how many levels of government exist, and the role of the media.

Students soon discover that the U.S. news media has little apparent concern with international news. I relate this to the vastness of the country, to the distance from international borders, and to the history of settling this country. Still, most international students are amazed that we do not get the BBC here, and that there is little sense about the Voice of America. Since the teacher's job is to get them to enter into an understanding of how Americans live their lives, it is important to neither defend nor attack Americans on any of these issues, but repeatedly to describe us as we are, what we know, and why. In this context, it is also important to point out that no living American has known war domestically, the last domestic conflict being the Civil War. Again, U.S. students gain a new perspective on their country in the context of international students' questions.

DAY 3

What is the role of government in the lives of people? We begin by examining the executive branch of the federal government. Describing the various offices of the cabinet gives shape to the business and concerns of the government. Most questions are about the Departments of State and Defense, specifically directed at the ways ambassadors get appointed and how diplomatic personnel are trained. Other questions ask how the military is organized, how free the states are in the national scheme of things, whether the states compete with one another, and how free is movement between states. We discuss current conservative *attacks* on federalism, and what this might mean. U.S. students relate to how different are the concerns of international students, especially with respect to cabinet positions and issues.

Students are also curious about how much average U.S. citizens know about their government and its programs, including welfare, medical care for the poor, and drug regulation. Questions also arise about the allopathic nature of U.S. medicine, which is oriented to the use of drugs to cure pathology, and about the current rise of alternative medicine. We also discuss problems with federalism and property rights, and the role of government in preserving national parks. Interest in indigenous peoples brings up the Bureau of Indian Affairs (BIA), the dual citizenship of Indians, treaties and battles with the Indians, and gambling casinos.

We also take up the Bill of Rights and its major proponents, such as the American Civil Liberties Union. The First Amendment deserves special attention particularly in the areas of freedom of religion and separation of church and state, but also as it regards academic freedom at universities. This

American concern with religion and especially its entry into politics spills over into the continuing debate about abortion.

Discussing Amendments 13 to 15 reminds us that the U.S. abandoned legal slavery only 130 years ago. The prohibition era and its place in twentieth-century history brings us to the question of how societies regulate alcohol and drugs, and what happens when regulations and enforcement do not work.

We conclude this session by discussing universal suffrage, how recent it was (1920), and American feminism. This discussion provides the opportunity to talk about family life, women's work, family care, divorce, and the current debate about multiculturalism, postmodernism, and political correctness. This discussion is useful for U.S. students to review their own thinking on these important issues.

DAY 4

On Day 4 we consider the history, settlement, and immigration of the American population. We describe North America prior to Europeans—the similarities and differences in language, culture, and philosophy of the indigenous peoples. We also discuss why an urban Indian slum exists near the University of Minnesota, the reasons for reservations, the success of a few Indians, Wounded Knee, the role of the BIA, and how knowledge of Indian values influences ideas about ecology.

The international picture of the United States is substantially white and middle-class, but the actuality is different, so we discuss who is here, how they got here, what the Americanization process has included, how it has varied over time, and current pressures to limit immigration. American immigration history (Jones, 1960) has its colonial beginning in Puritan New England, so it is important to state how the U.S. has seen itself as a place for religious outcasts seeking a new Eden, a place of opportunity and a place to worship freely.

The question of who we are has stressed English roots. The language is English, with current emphasis on Spanish in Florida and the Southwest. But the U.S. remains Anglophile in outlook and retains a sense that immigrants will *assimilate* to a majority model. Several waves of immigration filled the land from the East Coast westward, and later up the Mississippi. Students ask "How was the land secured?" We are to a great extent a land of *peasant* origin, a notion that remains important to gain a sense for why there is virtually no *intellectual class* in this country, contrasted with most other countries.

American immigration has been slow, with occasional waves and bursts, especially now. These patterns affect economic development and determine how ethnicity reigns in many cities. Even with this vast pluralism there is a kind of *glue* that holds the U.S. together and gives people a shared sense of what it is to be an American. Immigration has been able to provide a cut-off from prior history that has allowed the U.S. to avoid the regionalism or tribalism that plagues many nations. However, recent cycles of racism and splinterism appear to drive much of the political debate (Lipset, 1969).

Today's topic includes discussion about how the entrepreneurial-individual spirit of the American people affects the economy, how and why most of the corporations were controlled by WASPS (and what are WASPS), and how many immigrants succeeded in moving from menial jobs in the first generation into the middle class within one or two generations by becoming educated and garnering funds. The exceptions are the Native Americans and most African Americans and Hispanics, who have remained a kind of permanent *underclass*. This fact helps explain some of the tension between U.S. minorities and the immigrant minority. Finally, I ask students to consider whether the U.S. (and the world) can become colorblind.

DAY 5

The fifth day examines relationships between individuals and organizations, as well as social class, religion, and ethnicity. Most social relations in the U.S. are *negotiable*, with few clear-cut rules for how to deal with relationships. The U.S. appears to be very *informal*. Difficulties over whether to call someone by their title or first name are common. Many international students learn about social rules only after they have violated them.

American social classes are complex. The U.S., because of fortunate geography, history, natural resources, and an entrepreneurial spirit animated by an ongoing sense of opportunity, is very wealthy. We have an abundance of goods and foods. Even though 90 percent of the wealth is owned or controlled by some 10 percent of the people, there remains a great deal of money and ability to obtain goods.

The U.S. economy seems to move in a cyclical fashion. Although we are presently in an era of continuing growth, the changing nature of work and the move from a manufacturing to a global service economy are causing some dislocation and a sense that the future is *unscripted*, especially for students (Sarles, 1993).

The general abundance of goods and opportunities for the vast middle class tends to obscure the fact that there are also great pockets of poverty, and that only some of it has to do with a *lower class*. Social class in the U.S. is mixed with color, ethnicity, location, and history. Many Americans even deny that class, per se, exists here.

How we fare has much to do with where people settle and how well opportunities are identified and used. Most of the wealth and power resides in White America, until recently in the hands of Anglo-Saxon Protestants, but increasingly open to others, especially of European descent, a fairly fluid situation.

The U.S. has a kind of Protestant individualistic outlook divided into many denominations that dominate in different places, depending on ethnic settlement patterns, or as the result of the Civil War, which created two sets of Churches (North and South). The U.S. is currently experiencing a new awakening of religious fervor that is being organized into a political force known as the "religious right." The Roman Catholic Church tends to dominate some urban areas, and has been shaped historically by the great influx of Irish and South Germans last century who settled in northern cities, and who were joined later by French, Italian, and Hispanic Catholics. Jews have moved into the mainstream since World War II, and have been successful in education and small businesses. The position of the Jews in the history of Christianity and the Holocaust in Germany begins to explain the relationship between the U.S., Israel, and the other nations of the Middle East, relationships complicated by the increasing Muslim population.

In summary, this day deals with social class as money, material wealth, housing, cars, sense of style, and choice of schools, as well as why there are poor people in the rich U.S., what the "American dream" is, and how it may be changing.

DAY 6

Day 6 is devoted to the media and its role in providing Americans with information and experiences. I recall teaching this course to newly arrived Fulbright Fellows during the Reagan era; they had a sense of tragicomedy that an actor could be president. This criticism became a metaphor for the U.S. as a market economy.

Beginning about 1950, television became dominant in bringing information to Americans. By 1968, each presidential candidate had hired a media representative to make him look good on television. As important has been the shift of where people are during the evening: at home, alone, or with a few others, each receiving television images. Americans have narrowed their outlooks as well as their circles of acquaintances and interactions with television, and it is obvious that there is little international news on major stations during the prime time. News readers are high-paid actors who engage in little or no analysis. What is "news" in the U.S. has to do with what is not *boring*. Unlike radio and print, television requires frequent changes of image, and passive audiences. This has the effect of making most Americans more reactive and less analytic or critical.

How does television work? The weekly Nielsen ratings show which programs and which networks were rated highest the previous week and how this translates into commerce and money for particular advertising slots on these programs. Isn't there a restriction on the amount of advertising? Yes, by audience reaction. Thus the marketing advertisers try to give the public what it *wants*, and try to persuade the public to want what they are selling.

The difficulty is that issues of politics, economy, justice, international relationships, war, and crime are presented on television in a way similar to advertising commercials. Do television and the market economy tend to shorten and redo our sense of history? It has seemed increasingly easy to live only in the brief present. We seem to lack deep appreciation for our own history as well as an understanding of the histories of other peoples (including our minorities) and what their histories may mean to them.

As the students begin to understand how ratings, advertising, and commercials work, it is important to introduce the opposite types of programs, such as *All Things Considered*, the *Lehrer News Hour*, *Nightline*, or the History or Discovery channels, and how these are funded. Other media, such as radio, newspapers, magazines, and the Internet, need to be discussed as critically as television.

This is a good time to reconsider the claim that there is no particular intellectual class in the U.S., and to put into perspective the existence of many publications that are read by the intellectually active public. In addition, many media are circulated by professional, artistic, humanistic, and cultural associations, and the impact of several important "think tanks" can be compared with similar institutions in other parts of the world.

Students, American and foreign, need to peruse the diverse media with critical care to understand how Americans get information—both in content and form.

DAY 7

Day 7 analyzes current debates between science and the humanities, and the relationship between politics and religion. The class will also discuss critical attacks upon scientific thinking by postmodernism. Common issues are a return to texts and narratives and a critique of positivistic science and objectivism. In the first case, there are two attacks, one primarily philosophical, with conservatives wishing for a return to Platonic and other canonical texts, and the second a critique that science is a form of politics rather than intellectualism. In the religious context, the return is to texts, especially the New Testament.

Most international students are less interested in the debate between science and humanities and more interested in and surprised by the rise of religious thought in the U.S. The religious right is having an important impact upon politics, a fact of American life that seems peculiar to non-Americans, who associate the U.S. more with secular capitalism than with any underlying urge to religion. To address this movement, I approach fundamentalist Christianity via scientific creationism, basing the discussion on the text by Henry Morris (1974). The entrance of religion into politics is a recent phenomenon in the U.S., and a dominant force in the U.S. in spite of the severe doubts of international students.

The discussion begins with the Old and New Testaments because creationism is a reinterpretation of the Old Testament Book of Genesis through New Testament concerns. Historically, this can be traced to the time of Christ, then to St. Augustine, who had wed Greek Platonic ideas with the New Testament. The current fundamentalism derives from that history and is being fueled by the approach of the year 2000 as a millennial time, possibly setting off a messianic urge in many people.

This fundamentalism can be discussed as a literal interpretation of particular Biblical texts: a literal 24-hour, six-day Creation, including the notion of the eating of the apple of the Tree of Knowledge as the fall to earth, and life as a sin for disobeying God. Scientific creationists are asking the primary question of "Why Existence?" and responding that humans are particularly perverse (Morris, 1974).

The discussion of fundamentalism is followed by consideration of evolutionism vs. special creation and of secular humanism. Questions are also raised about what is meant by absolute morality and the basic sinfulness of humans, about the differences between creationism and science, and about why the two ideas seem to argue past one another. How have these ideas gained power recently? It is primarily because of the notion of fairness (Nelkin, 1977), by which apparent opposites are held equivalent by Americans, with the urge to hear both sides equally and fairly. Additional explanations point out that fundamentalism tends to dispense with any concept of history, that it is affecting the educational process and schooling in the U.S., and that its political form could move us toward theocracy.

This powerful lesson expresses clearly the divergence of opinion and outlook in the U.S., and stimulates a huge range of reaction and questions. Most of the American students also find this discussion stimulating.

DAY 8

On Day 8, we discuss Cold War politics and foreign relations. It is useful to rethink our relationship with the former Soviet Union: e.g., how we had demonized Communists, derived a sense of our identity from this opposition, and how this era defined the ways in which the U.S. has thought about its foreign-global policies. A good deal of American character, certainly as Americans face the rest of the world, may be discerned within this history.

Rearming the U.S. and the antagonism between the U.S. and the Soviet Union is traceable to World War II. In the U.S., World War II is remembered as a good war, with clear enemies out to destroy us and dominate the world. The war carried us out of an economic depression and united us against an evil foreign enemy.

The American people, especially those over 60, who dominated this country until recently, were powerfully propagandized against our enemies during World War II. They tended to search for black-white issues to distinguish a moral view of the U.S. compared to evil outsiders. After that war, we depicted the Soviet Union as inheriting the evil Nazi character. Much of our foreign policy has been dominated, especially in the 1950s through the 1980s, by fighting a war—sometimes vague, sometimes actual—between the U.S. and World Communism.

Because a dominant world power has to deal with all the nations and interests in the world, it must have some sense of active policy toward all. We had tended to opt for supporting what we perceived as stable governments. When there arose a problematic situation, support was extended to non-democratic governments if they were anti-Communist.

Preoccupation with our own cause made it difficult to understand the Soviets in terms of their own significant history—coming out of an era of church-supported royal despotism and sustaining huge losses in World War II. Generally, American policy is primarily directed internally, toward its domestic economy, sensing that we are the strongest world power. Recent American hegemony in the world is perceived as being more natural than cyclical, and is reacted to as needing to be defended more than studied and understood. Recent lack of support and interest in foreign studies and foreign languages underlies this outlook.

To be fair, there are purposeful groups of people who work to reverse this historical trend, who want to move toward global cooperation and respect. Nevertheless, the legacy of the Cold War has left us with various foreign policy problems—e.g., questions of world debt, Third World policy, and the paradox of a world economic-political order at odds with a U.S. that tends to isolate itself.

The U.S. is vast and self-contained. Our traveling habits abroad tend to keep us in cities or the resorts of other countries, not with the peoples or roots of other nations. Our sense of history, always short, seems to prevent us from understanding how other peoples are affected by the way they perceive and understand their history.

This session ends with the events following the fall of the Soviet Union in 1989 and why the CIA and leading American scholars of the Soviet Union effectively failed to predict the Soviet self-destruction. Finally, we return to the U.S. State Department, its thinking and policies and the sense that the

U.S. still distinguishes sharply between domestic and foreign policy. Domestic policy is being dominated by the political economy of the world and tends still to overlook issues of culture, language, ethnicity, and nationalism.

DAY 9

Day 9 looks into the life experience of Americans as a number of defining events. Less involved in history than most, Americans create "folk chronologies." For those over 70, the Great Depression remains powerful—e.g., the National Labor Relations Act has determined the nature of work relations in the U.S. and the role of the labor union movement weakened as we shifted from manufacturing to a service economy. Social Security ended the fear of poverty in old age, and is now up for national discussion.

World War II affected us powerfully as a popular war with clear enemies. After World War II, we emerged as a powerful nation. Having a sense of the U.S. as providential, we carried our moral outlook to the world. Seeking evil enemies, we found them in the Soviets. Older Americans remember Senator Joseph McCarthy's efforts to ferret out domestic Communists in the 1950s.

That decade also saw the virtual end of epidemics with the development of penicillin, the Salk vaccine for polio, and antibiotics. Advances in medical technology have created a rapidly increasing older population. The early 1950s introduced television, which had a privatizing-isolating influence on American life. Between TV, computers, the Internet, and a love affair with the automobile, Americans are thoroughly enmeshed with technology. Through the 1970s, Americans experienced a different sense of war; Korea and Vietnam have given young Americans a distrust of the idea of war.

The Interstate Highway System enabled suburbs and movements of people from rural to urban areas, and promoted a migration of African-American southerners to northern cities, resulting in a tension between minority cities and suburban white populations. This development, as well as other changes in the climate of minority-majority relations, led to a civil rights era in the 1960s and an ongoing debate on racial questions and relations.

In 1957, vast governmental funding for a space program followed the launching of *Sputnik*. With an expanding baby boom population, the U.S. economy improved, higher education expanded, jet planes entered commercial aviation, and the world became smaller.

The 1960s began by electing a Catholic president, enfranchising minorities, especially African Americans, and unleashing forces that spread to the handicapped and women. The most tragically memorable day in many Americans' lives was November 22, 1963, when President John Kennedy was assassinated. President Lyndon B. Johnson set-off a dramatic program of civil rights domestically, and an expansion of our involvement in Southeast Asia internationally. By 1968, with the assassinations of Robert Kennedy and Martin Luther King, Jr., the mood of Americans turned toward radical solutions, especially in urban areas. This led to a massive affirmative action program, which is now in a period of reaction.

In 1973, the Supreme Court permitted abortion on demand. Occurring in the context of the civil rights movement, this decision has created many new styles of life: e.g., entry of women into the workforce, a rise in divorce, and a large change in the relations between the sexes. It also caused sizable reactions, especially a religious-political response to abortion.

This chronology awakens both international and American students to the importance of considering the folk chronologies in understanding various outlooks of the U.S. population.

DAY 10

The last day of the course considers the integration of a vast amount of information into a thoughtful understanding of the U.S. and its people. Questions on most students' minds include questions of the family, divorce, and questions about values and morality. Has industrialization and progress fueled the current sense of great change? What caused what Lasch (1979) called "narcissism," a concern with individual development, freedom, and self-actualization that manifested itself in the 1960s?

Even after 10 days of this course, we expect that most of the international students cannot understand how little Americans know about themselves, about U.S. foreign policy, and about the rest of the world. We discuss again how most Americans had peasant roots, looking to the U.S. as the promised land. Yet they are impressed by how hard-working Americans seem to be, trying to succeed and to be engaged in doing.

They are impressed by how well the Twin Cities seem to work, the cleanliness, beauty, apparent lack of large slums, and the hum of the streets and of downtown Minneapolis. The musical performances at the lakes and in the parks are lovely and mellow. The buses run mostly on time, the telephones connect, the Internet is easy to access; technology is everywhere and most of it works well. The American love affair with the automobile overwhelms, but there are few traffic jams, the streets are not too dirty, and the poor mostly stay at home. The Twin Cities are a good place to begin, but this is a fairly wealthy place, and all is not so well in many other places.

CONCLUSION

The course attempts to paint the study of the U.S. with a broad brush, as a short-cut that penetrates who we are and how we live and think. The broad brush requires both a higher level of abstraction and dealing with specific issues. People from other countries do not organize their views according to the neat disciplinary categories into which our educational system is organized, but analyze things the way information from the environment hits them. The themes include everything that is on the minds of students, U.S. and foreign. We need to study and reflect, and we need perspectives as others see us. But we need them not only in terms of what international students thought we were from afar, but also in terms of who and how we are to ourselves and in comparison with others.

In an interdependent world, Americans will be interacting increasingly with individuals from other countries, and to be effective in such interactions will need three skills that this Mini Course will help them acquire.

1. The ability to communicate cross-culturally on sensitive issues.
2. The ability to use cultural knowledge.
3. The ability to use foreign nationals as cultural resources.

What is most important about the U.S. and its people changes, and it is our task to study us well, to analyze us critically both in our terms, and in terms of others. For us to know others, we must also attempt to understand them. Understanding other cultures and peoples is another important intellectual skill that this course hopes to produce. There is much we do not know, and other people will write the outline of this course differently. What we do know is that this course will help teach students to think globally, synoptically, to translate continually, and to get us as far as possible into the nature of American culture as it interacts with the world.

REFERENCES

Auletta, K. (1982). *The underclass.* New York: Vintage Books.

Gardner, J.W. (1961). *Excellence, can we be equal and excellent too?* New York: Harper & Row.

Jones, M.A. (1960). *American immigration.* Chicago: University of Chicago Press.

Lasch, C. (1979). *The culture of narcissism.* New York: Norton.

Lipset, S.M. (1969). *Prejudice and politics in the American past and present.* In C. Glock and E. Siegelman (Eds.). *Prejudice U.S.A.* New York: Praeger, pp. 17-69.

Metzger, W.P. (1955). *Academic freedom in age of the university.* New York: Columbia University Press.

Morris, H.M. (1974). *Scientific creationism.* San Diego: Creation-Life Publishers.

Nelkin, D. (1977). *Science textbook controversies and the politics of equal time.* Cambridge, MA: MIT Press.

Sarles, H.B. (1993). *Teaching as dialogue: a teacher's study.* Latham, MD: University Press of America.

CHAPTER 11

Curriculum by Bytes—Using Technology to Enhance International Education

by R. Michael Philson

I n 1913, while discussing the future effects of the newly invented motion picture on education, Thomas Edison remarked

> Books will soon be obsolete in the schools. . . . Our school system will be completely changed in the next ten years. (Gagne, 1987, p. 13)

In 1890, T.C. Mendenhall, the retiring president of the American Association for the Advancement of Science, told an AAAS meeting that

> Time and space are practically annihilated . . . and scores of things which only a few years ago would have been pronounced impossible are being accomplished daily. (Marvin, 1988, p. 206)

Although both these quotes were first voiced over 80 years ago, either one might well have been spoken in the 1990s to describe recent advances in technology. These quotes illustrate three important points often neglected in today's fascination with the rapid development of electronic technologies: (1) dramatic change is not limited to recent years; (2) predictions about the future are difficult, if not impossible, to make accurately; and (3) traditional institutions are often remarkably slow to respond and change, much less adapt, to technological change.

Change magazine, a well-known publication of higher education, dedicated its entire March/April 1996 issue to the challenges of "teaching and learning in the computer age." The focus was understandable, for the use of computers, in particular the Internet and the World Wide Web, has grown exponentially.

Less than four years ago, the World Wide Web had fewer than 400 sites. Now, thousands are added daily (Green, 1996). The July/August 1997 issue of *Change* included an essay in which Sir John Daniel, vice-chancellor of the British Open University, argued that technology may be the answer to the crises in higher education arising out of the issues of access, cost, and flexibility (Daniel, 1997).

Today, academic journals and other publications often include regular articles on recent developments in information technology. In *The Chronicle of Higher Education*, for example, one of the seven major news sections now focuses exclusively on information technology. Many journals and publications discuss how technology, in particular computer-mediated communication (CMC), is being used in traditional classroom settings and for distance education delivery.

Given the recognized ability of technology to transcend many of the traditional barriers of both space and time, the marriage of international education and information technologies would seem a natural union, providing educators with opportunities for collaboration with colleagues and access to resources never before available. Many faculty and institutions are taking advantage of the new media. The University of California-Irvine, for example, is working with the Institute of Multimedia in Chiba, Japan, to offer UCI students Japanese language and culture electronically. Lehigh University is using computer conferencing to organize international group projects for management students in Korea, Egypt, Finland, and the United States.

C. T. Clotfelter (1996) suggests that electronic communication will make faculty more outward-looking. "An increase in national and international exchange of ideas seems a likely result of these advances" (p. 260). However, just as some faculty and administrators find it difficult to incorporate international perspectives into their classes and institutions, some educators are more willing and able than others to exploit the opportunities provided by emerging technologies. This chapter examines the interface between campus efforts at internationalization and the use of information technologies in higher education.

ASYNCHRONOUS TYPES OF EDUCATIONAL COMPUTER-MEDIATED COMMUNICATION (CMC)

E-Mail

Electronic mail is probably used more widely in higher education today than any other form of CMC. Many faculty in countries around the world have become comfortable with the use of e-mail as a means of communicating not only with individual students or groups of students, but also with other faculty and researchers in other countries. The United States has clearly been a leader in providing national access. Lewis (1996) noted that 50 percent of American schools were connected to the Internet in 1995. The number of subscribers signing on with a multitude of Internet service providers (ISPs) is growing daily; America Online alone serves over eight million customers ("AT&T," 1997). One 1994 survey found that 86 percent of U.S. colleges and universities were connected to an Internet network (Miech, Nave, and Mosteller, 1995). Another annual survey of computer use in higher education found one in four courses now using electronic mail. Over half of all faculty and almost one-third of all students have their own computers (DeLoughry, 1996). Forrester Researcher predicts that within five years half the U.S. population will be using e-mail regularly ("Our love affair," 1997).

A question just as important, however, is how great the usage is outside the U.S. In some cases, connections are clearly more extensive than in the U.S. In terms of overall percentages, Japan is even more connected than the United States, with 18 percent of households online compared to the national U.S. rate of 16 percent ("Net gains," 1997). Even countries not typically thought of as leaders in Internet connectivity are rapidly expanding their capabilities. According to Negroponte (1995), "the fastest growing number of Internet hosts (percent change) in the third quarter of 1994 were Argentina, Iran, Peru, Egypt, the Philippines, the Russian federation, Slovenia, and Indonesia (in that order). . . . The Internet is not North American anymore" (p. 182).

Reuters reports that use in Latin America is growing at a rate of about 1000 percent annually, and usage in China is expected to surge from current estimates of around 100,000 to over a million users by the year 2000. Less than three years ago, China had only 1,700 users ("Net use growing," 1996). The director of Microsoft's division in Latin America concurs about the tremendous increase in connections overseas, noting that usage in Argentina rose from 5,000 in 1995 to 50,000 in 1996, and Peru has been seeing an increase of 15-20 percent every month ("Internet's popularity," 1996).

These statistics paint an optimistic picture. Couch (1996) asserts that "Access to telephonic networks is approaching universality, as on a worldwide basis there exists almost one telephone for each adult" (p. 165). Couch believes that this is particularly true for academic collaboration, noting that "Telecommunication networks have rendered proximity almost irrelevant for the formation of sustained association. . . . Among scholars, e-mail correspondents are replacing departmental colleagues" (p. 172).

Mansell and Silverstone (1996) analyze the same data and arrive at different conclusions. In their book, published the same year as Couch's, they reflect that "Any assumption of the homogeneity and ubiquity of the information and communication revolution is seriously flawed" (p. 223). They point out that even after several generations of electronic communication, large areas of the world still have telephone and television rates in the single figures. For example, the average rate of telephone penetration ranges from almost 50 percent of the total population to less than 1 percent, depending on the economic status of the country. Television reception in North America is close to 50 percent, while the rate in Africa drops to less than 4 percent

Neither of these views is necessarily inaccurate, and they do not actually contradict each other. The pattern of the spread of information technologies is actually similar to that of other technologies in the past. The telegraph, telephone, and television also experienced rapid, but uneven, growth, with early users being understandably distributed among those most able to afford and use the technology.

Asychronous modes of communication such as e-mail allow participants to send or receive messages at any time of the day or night. This ability clearly has tremendous value when working with students or faculty in different countries and different time zones. It eliminates the need for the members of a course or research team to "meet" at the same time. Location also becomes less important, because the participants need not communicate from any particular location, such as a classroom, lecture hall, or laboratory. Admittedly, a large percentage of the average population in many countries may not yet have access, but reports indicate that institutions of higher education are being connected to national and international networks. One source lists 4,488 ISPs around the world, with virtually every country included (The List, 1997).

In addition to these time and space advantages, the limited time-delay feature of the technology provides another benefit that can be particularly valuable for international participants. The vast majority of online communications are conducted in English. Although non-native English speakers face clear obstacles when using English, asynchronous communication allows time for composition and reflection (and thus self-editing) before sending messages over electronic networks.

The most common use of e-mail is implied in the name—as an electronic alternative to traditional postal systems. Advantages to this form of communication include both cost and time considerations. For most people in most countries, the cost of using e-mail to communicate is less (often much less) than that of using regular postal systems or regular long-distance telephone lines. These savings are possible because the majority of connections to the Internet are made with a local call to a regional ISP. Even more significant than the cost savings, however, is the time element involved. Transmission of e-mail messages around the world is almost instantaneous, and virtually all software programs enable the user to save and store messages for later use. Another significant advantage of e-mail is the ability to "broadcast" the same message to many recipients in different locations at the same time, with no increase in cost or time. This capability has been amply exploited through the development of different "listserv" discussion groups, allowing groups of individuals sharing a common interest to establish their own communication network. The number of such electronic forums now exceeds 6,000 (Rojo, 1995).

Computer Conferencing

Closely related to e-mail, computer conferencing extends the capabilities of that medium to include a more media-rich environment, providing not only access to a wider range of information but also increased communication features. The ability that computer conferencing offers to share files and graphics makes peer editing and collaboration more extensive than is possible using just e-mail. Another common feature of such systems is the ability to set up and manage a number of different sub-conferences on themes or topics of interest to the members of the group. It is also possible to "personalize" the structure of the conference discussions, so that a record is kept for each individual. Of course, just as in e-mail, computer conferencing also allows archiving of material for convenient future access.

SYNCHRONOUS TYPES OF COMPUTER-MEDIATED COMMUNICATION (CMC)

Although the advantages just discussed suggest a strong preference for asynchronous communication among international educators, some interesting collaborations are now occurring over synchronous electronic networks. Synchronous communication modes typically include IRCs, MUDs, MOOs, WOOs, and MAUDs. IRC refers to Internet Relay Chat, a form of real-time conversation among participants online. The real "meat" of synchronous communication comes with MUDs, MOOs, WOOs, and MAUDs. MUD stands for Multi-User Domain (or Dungeon or Dialogue), which first became known through role-playing games high school and college students played on their computers. MOOs are MUD-Object Oriented, and carry the ability to interact even further by strengthening the ability of the participants to create and manipulate environments and objects. This ability not only allows participants to conduct real-time conversations with others over their computers, but also provides them with the tools to literally create their own cyberspace environments. One of the older and better known MOOs, Diversity University, as well as many of the more recent efforts, is organized much like traditional university campuses, with a graphical layout indicating separate rooms for student centers, libraries, faculty offices, and other standard campus features. WOOs are often described as Web MOOs that incorporate the graphic capabilities of the World Wide Web with the interactive communication capabilities of MOOs.

Most computer conferencing systems, while known primarily for their asynchronous applications, also allow participation in synchronous collaborative projects in which the distributed members work together in real-time editing and reviewing of common documents, as well as carrying on extended conversations online.

All these acronyms incorporate one important element in any discussion on instructional processes involved in online curricula—the capability for real-time interaction. For someone who has never participated in a MOO session before, it is difficult to understand both the technical aspects of manipulating the environment and the affective impact of such an exercise on the participants. One student in an online course bringing together faculty in different countries to study the process of teaching online expressed it this way:

> In contrast to the "traditional" focus on computers and other technologies in terms of informational access, it seems to me that many of the significant educational implications relate to the very "interactivity" of CMC programs. What is immediately striking when you "experiment" with such programs is the dramatic affective and motivational implications for learning which they encourage: the seductive sense of global community, the opening up of new worlds of possibility, and the pure pleasure of "learning" new skills and knowledge in a meaningful and/or playful context. (C. Richards, personal communication, April 15, 1996)

Clearly, the emerging electronic information technologies differ from face-to-face (f2f) communication in many respects, and attempt to mimic it in others. Some research has been conducted to examine both the advantages and disadvantages of such technologies. Some of the possibilities have already been alluded to above. Some consistent research findings have begun to emerge in studies focusing on group work via electronic media. Bikson and Eveland (1990) found that using computers to communicate helped reduce social barriers and broaden leadership roles. "Electronically supported groups develop a richer communication structure with less hierarchical differentiation, broader participation, and more fluctuating and situational leadership structures." (p. 285). McGrath (1990) also found that computer communication resulted in more equal (less hierarchical) distribution among participants than f2f. Sproul and Kiesler (1993) conducted studies at Carnegie Mellon University and found that computer communication not only resulted in more participation than f2f, but also produced more proposals for action.

Not all research has been so clearly positive, however. The Sproul and Kiesler studies had predicted that CMC would improve group decision-making because it was largely based on plain text (thus presumably more purely intellectual) and was less affected by social skills. Although participation and action proposals increased from CMC, so did the amount of "flaming" (critical, personal attacks in rude language) and the length of time needed to make decisions. Krauss and Fussell (1990) noted that the absence of visual information "reduces the richness of social cues available to the participants, increasing the social distance that separates them and causing them to adhere closely to prescribed task roles" (p. 143). The absence of certain sensory inputs also affects the temporal component of messages. Written computer communication has been found to be less orderly, with less pressure on the recipient to respond, fewer constraints on the length and number of messages, and less requirement for connectedness between messages (McGrath, 1990, p. 52).

Baldwin and Austin (1995) studied 15 collaborative teams and discovered some results directly relevant to the issue of international faculty collaboration. They found that "close proximity . . . helped start many of the collaborations but was not necessary to maintain them" (p. 53). Proximity was just one of six factors identified as being important in determining how collaborators define their work and the process of communication that they follow. Of course, in the context of international education, the element of proximity is especially appropriate, and Austin and Baldwin note that distance between collaborators results in a greater need for more structured conversations to account for the loss of f2f contextual cues (p. 62).

Research, therefore, suggests the existence of both positive and negative outcomes associated with electronic communication in an international context. Before considering media factors that limit the extent to which international educators are able to use such media, it might be constructive to first review some current examples of how institutions and faculty are using the technologies.

EXAMPLES OF EMERGING TECHNOLOGIES IN AN INTERNATIONAL CONTEXT

Numerous examples exist to illustrate the use of satellites, the Internet, and the World Wide Web in higher education instruction around the world, including organizations collaborating internationally. Certain "administrative" approaches come to mind immediately—statistical databases to track students and their progress; Web pages to introduce study abroad options, including detailed information on coursework and living situations; the use of e-mail to receive and submit assignments, as well as communicate with individual tutors; online applications providing convenience while saving time. While not ignoring the importance of such uses of the technology, this discussion takes a somewhat different approach. At the risk of oversimplifying the situation, two broad categories of usage seem to encompass the majority of applications—courses offered over the Internet and the World Wide Web, focusing primarily on students; and research collaboration, focusing primarily on faculty. This chapter touches briefly on the first category, but most of the discussion concerns faculty collaboration.

Online Courses

The number of courses offered electronically is increasing rapidly. Not only are individual faculty preparing and delivering such courses, but also entire units in an institution are being established to offer online alternatives. The New School of Social Research, for example, promotes its DIAL courses (Distance Instruction for Adult Learners), taught using computer conferencing. In addition, complete degree programs are now available in a growing range of disciplines. Perhaps the best-known provider is the University of Phoenix, an accredited institution in the U.S. offering online undergraduate and graduate degrees. In Canada, Athabasca University is a well-established virtual campus serving thousands of students in Canada and overseas. The "traditional" universities are even beginning to offer complete degree programs online, such as Drexel University (M.S. in Information Systems), University of Illinois (M.S. in Library and Information Science), and East Carolina University (M.S. in Industrial Technology).

In many cases, the leaders in the development of international education links are new, private, nonprofit organizations. Examples include brokers such as the Globewide Network Academy and the Electronic University Network, which help link students with institutions offering courses online, as well as organizations that develop their own courses.

Although the technology enables institutions to expand their curricular offerings to prospective students around the world, few of the traditional higher education providers seem to be making conscious efforts to either market their courses overseas or to use the potential of the media to internationalize their curriculum. One of the recent exceptions is MUCIA Global, the Midwest Universities Consortium for International Activities, an organization begun in the summer of 1996 by the Big 10 universities in the U.S. as a for-profit entity to provide distance learning to Asia via the Internet and the Web.

International Collaboration

The World Wide Web was actually created—in 1989 by Tim Berners-Lee of CERN—for the purpose of facilitating collaboration among high energy physicists. This section of the chapter will examine several international collaboration programs in depth, and complement the discussion with a table identifying selected elements of some other experiments in international collaboration and communication. The programs chosen for in-depth review include an experimental course by the Association of International University Presidents, seminars run by a virtual organization, a scientific colloboratory headquartered at the University of Michigan at Ann Arbor, and a series of academic listservs.

Table 1 lists 10 organizations that involve faculty collaborating with colleagues in other countries. (Many other examples could have been included, but space limitations prevent a more complete list.) Looking through the list of examples provided in the table, some common patterns emerge. First, many of the examples reflect collaboration between the science disciplines. Second, many of the organizations operate primarily on a regional basis. Third, although almost all areas of the world are covered by these regional groups, the strongest alliances seem to be those bringing together faculty and institutions in the European countries. Mason (1993) introduces even more such regional European networks in his article on computer conferencing in Europe. He identifies the following as major efforts: COMET, encouraging collaboration between universities and industry to improve training; DELTA, focusing on the development of European learning in general; JANUS, one of the DELTA projects focusing on creating a network for European distance education; PLUTO, linking individuals and institutions involved in teacher training; and ELNET, joining higher education institutions in England, France, and Germany to develop curriculum for business and language studies.

The four examples discussed in greater depth below indicate a wide range of approaches to the use of electronic communication by international educators.

Worldwide Course on Economic Development. In August 1993, Dr. Donald Gerth, president-elect of the International Association of University Presidents, met with Maurice Harari, John Brownell, David Outcalt, and Beverly Gerth to discuss plans for their upcoming conference. The group decided to develop a project that would illustrate how the Internet could be used at their member institutions. The project involved the development and teaching of a course in economic development, created by Dr. Outcalt, professor of economic development and former chancellor of the University of Wisconsin-Green Bay. The course model was approved in the summer of 1994, and the pilot project was offered in Fall 1995. The medium used was asynchronous electronic mail with a listserv, with critiques and dialogues taking place across many time zones. Faculty in 11 universities in 7 countries on 5 continents participated in the project. Electronic communication was in English. During the period of the course, a total of 682 messages were sent by 102 active subscribers to the listserv, including 76 messages led by faculty.

At the conclusion of the course, formative and summative evaluations of the project were conducted by faculty from the University of California-Santa Barbara. Their findings supported many of the advantages of the technologies

TABLE 1

EXAMPLES OF INTERNATIONAL FACULTY COLLABORATION USING INFORMATION TECHNOLOGIES

Organization	Technology	Participants	Purpose of Organization
Australian Academic and Research Network (AARNet)	Internet	U.S., Japan, Australia	To link universities for research purposes
Consortium for Upper-Level Physics Software (CUPS)	Internet/WWW	27 physicists in different countries	To develop software
Cooperative Program for Operational Meteorology Education and Training (COMET)	videoconference	Professionals and researchers from 18 countries	To assess use of technology to promote education and training
Electronic Networks and Information Sharing (ENIS)	Internet	European countries	To promote electronic networking
Professional and Academic Channel for Europe 2000 (EuroPACE)	Internet	Universities in 20 countries and 11 research institutions	To provide means for collaboration in research
Global Alliance for Transnational Education (GATE)	Internet	Database for about 50 countries	To provide global education resource
The Gravity Society	Internet	U.S., Italy, Russia, Finland	To bring together physics researchers
International Education and Resource Network (I*EARN)	Internet	New Zealand-based, 1000 schools in 20 countries	To develop international curriculum projects
Joint ATM Experiment on European Services (JAMES)	Internet	Europe	To encourage interconnections among countries
Trans-European Research and Education Networking Association (TERENA)	Internet	38 member countries	To promote international research networking

identified earlier, but also raised questions about others. On the one hand, the report found increased faculty contact with colleagues in institutions around the world, and claimed that non-native English speakers improved their English language skills. In spite of this, however, participation rates on the academic listserv were "heavily dominated" by native English speakers. This finding seems to contradict earlier reports suggesting that the unique nature of the Internet would "level-out" the playing field for non-native speakers, since they would have ample time to compose and edit their messages before posting them.

Another beneficial effect noted by the evaluators was an increase in faculty pedagogical skills, including technical skills in using e-mail and the World Wide Web. Faculty attitudes toward using the technology were also positive. "All faculty who responded viewed the course as a success…." The report also noted that the faculty "have spent more time talking with colleagues, both local and international, about the content and methodology of this course than is typical for their courses."

Quipunet—A Virtual Organization. Begun from a debate on a Peruvian listserv, Quipunet was born in cyberspace in June 1995. The original purpose of the organization, to help unite Peruvians through the sharing of knowledge and resources, has since grown to encompass a wider international focus. In 1995, Quipunet offered its first seminar, dealing with the Kobe, Japan, earthquake; 160 representatives from 16 different countries attended the sessions. Their second seminar, offered in conjunction with the UN International Decade for Natural Disaster Reduction (UN-IDNDR), focused on solutions for cities at risk and attracted over 450 participants from 56 countries.

The organization of the seminars themselves vividly illustrates the ability of the technology to facilitate international collaboration. For example, the third seminar, which began while this chapter was being written, was created through the following shared efforts:

- an officer of the group in Ecuador obtained a contract from UN-IDNDR in Geneva
- this officer then hired webmasters in Australia, Peru, and the United States
- the webmasters performed their work at San Francisco State University, home of the group's server and of two other participants
- a staff member in Costa Rica assumed responsibility for the "customers"
- publicity was delegated to another member in Peru
- translation was provided by groups in both the U.S. and Peru

All this activity took place completely online. Details on the current seminar, which has attracted over 600 people from 60 different countries, can be found at the Quipunet Web pages at http://www.quipu.net:1997 (M. Davies, personal communication, September 20, 1997).

Quipunet illustrates how a small, private, nonprofit organization can successfully bring together representatives of higher education, government agencies at all levels, and private citizens to provide education and resources.

UARC—Scientific Collaboration at a Distance. One highly developed network to foster collaboration at a distance is the Upper Atmospheric Research Collaboratory (UARC), a collection of space physicists working together to analyze data from instruments in Greenland. A half-dozen instruments send data on the Internet to scientists at 10 different sites. The system allows access to not only archival data, but also to real-time data. The scientists can build multiple "windows" on their individual computers with separate areas for viewing real-time data, for accessing archived data, and for communicating real-time with colleagues using a "chat" function. Current participants in the program include sites in Michigan, Massachusetts, and Maryland in the U.S., and single sites in Greenland and Norway. The Collaboratory has been funded by the National Science Foundation (NSF) since its beginning in 1992.

UARC is unique in the amount of research conducted on the program that has focused specifically on the use of the technology to facilitate communication among the scientists at the different locations. Thomas Finholt and Gary Olson of the University of Michigan, where the project is based, have studied the development of UARC, using the increasingly common notion of a "Collaboratory." Their studies confirm many of the earlier findings regarding computer-mediated-communication—the increased opportunities afforded researchers to have access to colleagues worldwide and to share scarce, expensive resources is tempered somewhat by the recognition that such long-distance communication requires more structured dialogue, including conscious efforts to establish common understandings about the data being discussed.

Studies of the UARC program have taken advantage of computer technology to examine the interaction patterns among scientists and staff at the different sites. Because all the communications were maintained in a time-dated log in the computers, it was possible to determine the originators and recipients of messages, as well as the content of the messages. Analysis of the communication patterns showed that individual scientists were specific about whom they communicated with, the general tendency being to contact those who had diverse expertise to complement one's own knowledge (Finholt, 1997). Details on UARC can be found on the organization's Web pages at http://http2.sils.umich.edu/UARC/Labtocollab.html.

The studies conducted thus far on UARC suggest that the technology itself facilitates research into the processes of communication and collaboration among geographically separated faculty and scientists who are working to-gether. Given the archival abilities of the technology, it is curious why more such research has not been conducted using this rich resource.

Listservs. While UARC could be considered an example of a formal communication style, a listserv would probably fall at the other end of the informal/formal continuum. A listserv is essentially a group of people using e-mail who have joined together to discuss issues of common concern. If one assumes that informal communication plays an important role in establishing and maintaining communication networks, the use of a listserv provides an ideal way for colleagues in distant parts of the world to keep in touch.

Over 15,000 individual public listservs exist, ranging in membership from just a few individuals to over 10,000 participants (Catalist, 1997). One Web site focusing on general education, K-12 education, education technology, and education reform provides specific links to about 275 listservs (EdWeb, 1997). Still another site lists over 1,100 education listservs <www.tile.net/tile/listserv/education.html>.

Briefly identified here are three different academic listservs, all operating internationally.

- *DEOS*—The Distance Education Online Symposium (DEOS) listserv was begun by the American Center for the Study of Distance Educa-tion at Penn State University. It is one of the largest international higher education listservs, with over 2,800 members from the United States and 60 other countries. U.S. representatives make up 74 percent of the total membership, with the countries next closest in terms of number of members being Canada with 8 percent and Australia with 3 percent. (R. Isnor, personal communication, Febru-ary 3, 1997)

- *WWWEDU*—This list was established and is currently moderated by an individual at the Corporation for Public Broadcasting. The list is targeted toward educators at all levels who are using or who are interested in using the World Wide Web for educational purposes. Current membership stands at 1,630 from 37 different countries. The majority of members are from the United States. (A. Carvin, personal communication, February 21, 1997)

- *LCTL*—The Less-Commonly-Taught-Languages listserv is part of the LCTL Project in the National Language Resource Center at the University of Minnesota. The focus of the list is discussions regarding any language except English, French, German, or Spanish. It actually serves as an umbrella group overseeing five more specific listservs concentrating on Celtic, Dutch, Hindi, Nordic, and Polish. The general listserv was begun on December 18, 1995, and currently serves 224 members from 24 different countries. Just as in the previous examples, U.S. participants comprise the majority of the membership, in this case over 79 percent. (LCTL-T, personal communication, February 23, 1997)

These three examples illustrate not only the differences in size common among listservs but also the fact that U.S. participants tend to dominate the membership to a substantial degree. This should be expected, since all these lists began recently in the U.S. In spite of the relatively small numbers of foreign participants, the figures nevertheless indicate a broad representation of many countries around the globe.

Another fact common to all three is that they use a moderator to manage the list and to screen messages from participants before broadcasting them to the rest of the list. The result is a more structured communication environment than is typical in an unmoderated list. In spite of this organizational structure, the listservs would still be described as informal communication, with few if any particular goals or tasks and few constraints on topics that can be raised by the members.

As these examples and those listed in Table 12-1 show, a wide range of contexts exists in which faculty are using electronic technologies to communicate and collaborate over substantial distances.

RESTRAINTS ON THE USE OF ELECTRONIC NETWORKS FOR INTERNATIONAL COLLABORATION

In spite of considerable hype over the spread of emerging technologies to every corner of the globe, reality paints a more sobering picture of a complicated system of communication significantly affected by a variety of limitations. The following discussion identifies some of the factors that may be restricting collaboration and communication among international faculty.

Political Factors

With its ability to spread data across borders and oceans instantly, the Internet poses unique challenges to communities and societies that have been able in the past to preserve certain standards and restrict "offensive" materials. The relatively unlimited freedom of the information superhighways is increasingly being restricted by conscious efforts to regular the new electronic networks.

Many countries have attempted to limit access to the Internet and the World Wide Web. In Burma, military leaders have forbidden unauthorized ownership of computers with networking capabilities; those who use a computer to send or receive information relating to the economy, national culture, or state security may be sent to prison for 7 to 15 years (Internet Suppression, personal communication, 1996). The European Commission has recommended a voluntary code of conduct and the use of labeling and filtering systems to restrict the spread of "offensive" materials ("European Commission," 1996). In the United Kingdom, on August 9, 1996, the Charing Cross Police Station contacted all UK Internet Service Providers to demand that newsfeeds be censored (M. Hutty, personal communication, August 18, 1996). Cuba has announced that access to the Internet and similar networks will be limited according to "defense and national security" interests. Most Cubans do not have the hard currency to pay foreign companies for access, and are usually not allowed telephones with direct dialing abroad ("Cuba approves," 1996). In South Korea, attempts to contact North Korea on the Internet are forbidden (Koreans, personal communication, 1996). In Vietnam, the government controls the single Internet provider (Walt, 1996). In India, the only international gateway is through the state-owned telephone company, VSML, which is legally obligated to block objectionable materials (Walt, 1996). In Germany, Internet providers who allow access to a Dutch site that hosts a German left-wing magazine must pay heavy fines (R. Horwitz, personal communication, September 18, 1996).

China has been particularly noted for its attempts to restrict access to the Internet. On January 23, 1996, the government began implementing a series of measures to control the development of the Internet in China (Sautede, 1996). The new Internet regulations required domestic organizations and individuals to register with the police, and emphasized that users were "forbidden to produce, retrieve, duplicate, or spread information that may hinder public order" (Faison, 1996). At the end of August 1996, the government announced that it was blocking access to sites, including the following five categories: (1) English-language sites sponsored by news organizations such as the *Wall Street Journal*, the *Washington Post*, and CNN; (2) Chinese-language sites with news from Taiwan; (3) sites sponsored by Hong Kong newspapers and anti-Beijing China-watching publications; (4) overseas dissident sites, such as those on Tibet and Xinjiang's independence movement; and (5) sexually explicit sites, such as *Playboy* and *Penthouse* (Chen, 1996). In January 1997, China restored access to many of the sites listed in the first category, but maintained the restrictions on the other four ("China loosens restraints," 1997).

The majority of users in China appear to be concentrated within the nation's educational and research institutions. An important question that has yet to be answered is whether government restrictions on access are hindering the ability of China's educators and researchers to further the country's development goals. According to one report, the restrictions do not appear to have been applied to the academic networks (Chen, 1996).

Unlike China, Singapore can boast a high degree of computer and Internet capabilities. With approximately 150,000 Internet accounts, it can also claim the highest Internet penetration in the region (Seng, 1996). One-third of Singapore homes have a computer, and the government plans to connect every home to a network by the year 2000 (McDonald, 1996). In spite of obvious social, political, and economic differences, Singapore shares many of the concerns of China regarding access to the information superhighway. In early March 1996, Singapore announced its own restrictions on the Internet, imposed with the intention of blocking access to political, religious, and pornographic sites that might incite people in this island-state of three million people. In July, the government announced its guidelines "to safeguard the national interest." The rules require all Internet operators–from main providers to cybercafes–to register with the Singapore Broadcasting Authority (SBA). In addition, organizations putting locally produced political and religious information on Web pages must also register with SBA ("Singapore launches," 1996).

As in China, little evidence exists to indicate the extent to which government controls might be affecting educators and scientific researchers. Some have expressed strong complaints against the official restraints, however. One Singapore educator confided that "there are complaints galore, not only in private, but also in public" (Singapore educator, personal communication, November 6, 1996).

Whatever steps Singapore takes regarding the Internet will undoubtedly be watched closely by other countries in the region, including China. At a September 1996 meeting in Singapore of the Association of Southeast Asian Nations (ASEAN) to discuss both the promotion and the policing of the Internet, no consensus emerged on either the proper limits or the means of enforcing those limits ("Southeast Asia," 1996). All the countries seem to recognize the importance of information access to their development efforts, but they are also genuinely concerned about the social and political ramifications of open access to electronic networks.

Clearly, political restrictions on access to information technologies may affect the ability of faculty to collaborate with colleagues in other countries, but indications are that such restrictions are selective, and apply primarily to information sources that authorities believe threaten the political or social stability of the country involved. Thus, the implication is that censorship might prevent collaboration among specific disciplines. The examples above, seem to show that those areas most likely to participate in collaborative research (i.e., the hard sciences) are probably little affected by governmental censorship, while other areas (e.g., political science), could face serious obstacles in obtaining information from and sharing information with faculty in other countries.

Technical Factors

More "democratic" restrictions, in the sense that all communicators are affected regardless of national characteristics, include structural and physical problems with the technology. These problems include both transmission capabilities and what might be labeled the "readability" nature, or more commonly, the "user-friendliness" of the technologies.

In terms of the former, a serious problem affecting faculty collaboration within and across borders is the issue of bandwidth and the capacity of the existing telephone Internet networks. For example, a Russian medical college in Volgograd (about 1000 km. south of Moscow) is well-equipped with computers and related hardware, but e-mail and Internet access are problematic because of the outdated and limited number of phone lines (C. Iwasiw, personal communication, November 5, 1996). Even in Singapore, which has placed tremendous resources into increasing connections, it can take frustratingly long to download pages from outside the country (I.S. Talib, personal communication, November 6, 1996). When St. Lawrence College in Kingston, Ontario, tried to establish Internet connections with colleges in Kladno in the Czech Republic, compatibility of hardware, software, and phone connections all interfered with attempts at collaboration (R. Rainey, personal communication, November 20, 1996). Although connections in most countries seem to be faster when using a university system, just the opposite is true in South Africa. According to one faculty member, off-campus modems provide better access than the academic UNINET, which links all academic institutions in the country (J. Viljoen, personal communication, January 21, 1997).

Because of the tremendous increase in usage of the Internet over the last few years, the available bandwidth has not been able to keep up with the demand, particularly for those scientists and researchers who in the past have comprised the bulk of faculty collaboration overseas. Paul Woodward, director of the University of Minnesota's Laboratory for Computer Science and Engineering, states that "we'd like to be able to have visualization of this data and point things out to each other as if we were in the same room," but, he laments, there is too much congestion from the proliferating number of sites with fancy sound and color graphics to allow this (Germain, 1996).

This problem with delays caused by traffic on the information superhighway is the primary justification behind the development of Internet II, a growing consortium of universities in the United States that hopes to establish a faster, more dependable, second generation of the Internet to serve the needs of long-distance academic collaboration. Some scientists have already abandoned the "old" Internet and are now communicating through a new vBNS (very high-speed Backbone Network Service) sponsored by the NSF (Germain, 1996).

Two other elements of technical restrictions on access merit comment here. One involves the dependability of the systems themselves. Recent news stories featured the disruptions caused when one commercial online provider, such as America Online, "crashes," with communication links broken for millions of people. A similar event involved the loss in early January 1997 of an AT&T communication satellite. The failure of the satellite, known as Telstar 401, meant that institutions that depended on the satellite for transmitting courses and collaborating with other institutions (such as the National Technological University, which serves 46 dispersed colleges and universities) abruptly had their entire communication systems canceled (Blumenstyk, 1997).

Aside from these large-scale technical limitations, there is also the more personal problem of individual users being able to read and view materials on computer monitors. Few studies have been done on this topic, in spite of frequent complaints about the positioning and resolution of the screens. As one observer commented, "How many of us when reading books hold them up at eye level and at arms length?" (J. Harned, personal communication, January 23, 1997). This convergence of physiology and technology merits further study.

Economic Factors

If one were to choose a single area that illustrates restrictions on access to emerging technologies, the hands-down winner in terms of popular coverage would easily be economic factors. A forthcoming study by the Organization for Economic Cooperation and Development claims that high access costs and not language or culture differences really determine a country's Internet usage ("High access charges," 1997). The reason is obvious–technology is expensive, particularly hardware and infrastructure, and existing gaps in income worldwide imply that the richer the country and the individual, the more likely they are to be able to afford to participate in a global "information society." Stories focusing on the information "haves" and "have-nots" typically detail how economic discrepancies make it difficult for certain segments of society to benefit from the revolution in communications technologies. Simply providing the infrastructure for information technologies can cost billions of dollars, and annual operating costs are likely to be substantial. Even just providing access to the Internet can be prohibitively expensive. In the U.S., it can cost $10,000 a year to provide enough computers and phone lines to give patrons at a small library access to an online card catalog (Smith, 1996).

The economics of computer ownership and access are also clear. A recent study on computer ownership in the U.S. found that 16 percent of homes with annual incomes under $30,000 had a computer, while 37 percent of those with incomes between $30,000 and $50,000 and 72 percent of those with incomes above $50,000 owned a computer (Lewis, 1996).

There is no reason to believe that the same pattern of ownership does not exist in other countries as well. A major difference, though, is that while the costs of the infrastructure and hardware tend to remain relatively stable internationally, levels of income do not. For example, a professor at a Venezuelan university earns in the range of $370-$780 per month (with estimated living expenses of about $450 per month for a family) ("Venezuelan professors," 1997).

No data exist that attempt to evaluate the relationship between per-capita income in a country and access of faculty members to information technologies. Although reports suggest that those most likely to be connected to such technologies are centered in a country's universities and research centers, it would probably not be unlikely to find significant differences in access based solely on economics.

Sociocultural Factors

Researchers have only just begun to examine how an individual's cultural orientation may affect collaboration among individuals in different countries using information technologies. Stephen Ehrmann (1990) suggests that "computer conferencing is an especially friendly medium for foreign-born students and teachers. The ability to 'leap in' is not artificially favored...." (p. 12). Walls (1993), in noting the differences between intercultural communication (when the participants are aware of the expectations of those from different cultures) and cross-cultural communication (where at least one of the parties is unaware of or disregards differences in expectations), asserts the need for electronic communicators to practice intercultural communication.

Tubbs and Moss (1994) focus on inevitable differences in communication between low-context cultures, such as Germany and the U.S., and high-context cultures, such as many Asian countries. Ishii (1993) similarly discusses how such considerations apply when examining interactions between Japanese and Americans. Noting that CMC offers both "public" areas, such as bulletin boards, and "private" areas, such as person-to-person e-mail, Ishii predicts that Japanese might prefer the use of e-mail to facilitate behind-the-scenes negotiations and discussions, while Americans might prefer the more public debating and decision-making characteristics of bulletin boards and chat rooms. Brown and Duguid (1995) also suggest that distinctive communication styles arise out of cultural differences: "What's brisk and to the point to an American or amiably assertive to an Italian can be quite offensive to British or Japanese contributors, with their distinct and culturally specific notions of politeness, deference, and self-deprecation" (p. 22).

Van Ryckeghen (1996) contends that computer technology is not culturally neutral. "Computer technology assumes a particular (national) world view and an individualized approach based on values such as efficiency, rapidity, and functional rationality" (p. 153). As an example, she notes that the importance in Africa of communalism, oral traditions, and hierarchy are certain to affect attitudes toward and the use of computers.

Gender roles also must be considered when looking at the cultural implications of collaboration. For instance, one informant in Russia comments that Russian society tends to discourage women from participating in the Internet. "Although almost all women work in Russia, they are not equal to men, are rarely the boss, and expend much effort trying to make men look good. Therefore, it is not acceptable for women to know more than men.... So, for female nurses to know about technology and to have access to a wealth of information via the Internet would be pretty distressing to many people (C. Iwasiw, personal communication, November 8, 1996).

The convergence of issues of intercultural communication and collaboration via emerging information technologies presents a fascinating and important area that is just beginning to be explored.

Linguistic Factors

Another filter of particular importance for international communication is language, or to be more precise, different languages. As recently as 100 years ago, German was the international language of science and technology, French of culture, and English of trade. Today, English is used for all three (Quarterman, 1993). Not surprisingly, discussions in the United States seldom even mention the issue of language in electronic communication. Outside the U.S., however, the role of language in communicating over electronic networks has been discussed extensively. Several important issues are involved here. Suppose, for example, that a non-English-speaking scientist in Hong Kong wishes to collaborate on a project with non-English-speaking colleagues in Taiwan. Until 1996, that workhorse of electronic communication, e-mail, could not have been used because the technical specifications of the medium could not handle Chinese characters. Because of the way that the programming and codes were developed for the Internet (at American research universities), only phonetic characters could be transmitted. Even today, although it has become possible to use graphic script (such as that used in Chinese, Thai, Arabic, etc.) on the World Wide Web, it is still extremely difficult, and in some systems impossible, to transmit pictographic symbols over e-mail.

The result has been to reinforce the supremacy of English as the international language of communication. One Belgian academic writes, "The Internet has to have a common language. Whether we like it or not, that has become English." (T. Gore, personal communication, July 8, 1996). The use of English has become so widespread that it is really the only logical choice for a common international language. English is the official or joint official language of over 75 countries; even Algeria recently dumped French in favor of English as a second language in schools. Eighty percent of the world's information on computers is in English; even more important for this chapter is the fact that two-thirds of the world's scientists read English (The Globe and Mail, 1996).

There are two related issues here—the use of non-English languages for electronic communication, and the use of English by non-native-English speakers. For some, this first issue has sparked virtual linguistic-cultural wars. Alain Caristan, a researcher at France's computer research institute INRIA noted that "For me, the Internet is the theatre for a new colonial war.... Anglophones created the Internet. They're at the heart of its growth. There's a danger it'll stay that way" (Glass, 1996). The first all-French search engine, Lokace, made its debut in February 1996. Pierre Oudart, who oversees the creation of a list of French Net jargon, sees the Internet as an opportunity to unite Francophones around the world. "In geographical space, the French-speaking world is dispersed, but in virtual space, via the Internet, the entire French-speaking world is at your fingertips" (Glass, 1996).

Opportunities for international collaboration present some interesting possibilities in terms of language and culture, giving widely dispersed individuals sharing a common language the ability to work together regardless of traditional constraints of time and space. In fact, progress is being made in the advancement of Internet technology that will strengthen the ability of the medium to handle multiple languages. A March 1996 online announcement promoted a Norwegian translator for Windows, described as a "word-for-word translator with grammatical descriptions" (L. Tompkins, personal communication, March 19, 1996). In November 1996, the European Union sponsored an international conference specifically on the topic of developing multilingual support for the Internet (Character set technology, personal communication, October 9, 1996). In spite of some unsubstantiated claims that the Internet will eliminate non-English-languages around the globe (Spennemann, et al., 1996; Treanor, 1996), most reports point to the opposite result—the preservation of languages even when serving a small community.

A slightly different problem arises when considering the use of English by non-native-English speakers. For some, the technology presents distinct advantages. The Belgian educator Gore notes that the use of e-mail is preferable to the telephone for international communication in English because the asynchronous nature of e-mail allows the sender to check the grammar and vocabulary before sending a message (T. Gore, personal communication, July 8, 1996). Another educator claims that hypermedia enables Pacific Rim individuals to overcome English-language barriers (Jensen, 1993). Ishii (1993) contends that e-mail's "asynchronous feature provides great benefits to non-native speakers" (p. 150).

These comments, as well as the earlier discussion of "culture," suggest that the type of collaboration and communication used over international electronic networks may favor certain types of media over others, depending on the language and culture of the participants.

Skill Training Factors

One final factor that needs to be mentioned is the issue of technological training for those participants in international collaborative efforts. Commonly neglected in most discussions, sufficient training to use the technology undoubtedly plays a major role in determining the extent to which faculty and students are able and willing to participate in the vast menu of communication options available through such technologies as the Internet and the Web. In spite of increased financial support for hardware and software in many regions of the world, the support often stops there. At one community college in the U.S., "Professors would stare blankly at the machines that were placed in their offices, not sure how to turn them on, let alone certain how to use the mouse or send a document to the printer" (C. Kilian, personal communication, December 22, 1996). Although computers have become features in most American and European colleges and universities, the competence of the faculty to exploit the capabilities of the technology varies widely within and between countries. For countries where computers and similar technologies are just beginning to make substantial impacts, the issue of training is just as important, if not more so.

Fortunately, steps are now being taken to provide faculty with training in the new technologies. In the U.S., corporations such as Time Warner have begun developing training materials and offering workshops to assist teachers in becoming familiar with computers and the Internet ("Time Warner," 1997). Institutions such as the University of Texas at El Paso provide faculty members with release time to learn how to use technology (Pachecho, 1996/1997). AsianNet launched a massive teaching program in Beijing in October 1996 to help train people in the use of the Internet and related technologies ("AsianNet launch teaching program," 1996). The Internet Society has sponsored Network Technology Workshops specifically targeted at assisting countries just developing their communication networks; past workshops have been held in the U.S., Canada, and the Czech Republic, and the 1997 summer workshop was held in Malaysia (The Internet Society, personal communication, January 30, 1997).

RECOMMENDATIONS FOR THE USE OF ELECTRONIC TECHNOLOGIES IN INTERNATIONAL EDUCATION

The material presented thus far presents a picture of a rapidly expanding technology, little researched and little understood, that embodies within its complex systems potential for access to resources and international collaboration never before possible. Students from universities around the world, not to mention students in the privacy of their own rooms, can participate in the same class and communicate with others both synchronously and asynchronously. Assignments can be shared electronically, edited easily, and sent to distant tutors for correction and feedback. Language learners can listen and watch authentic materials transmitted from overseas. Institutions with small enrollments in specialized courses can share a single instructor teaching from a distant site. Researchers with limited resources can share in access to data and experiments conducted on sophisticated, expensive equipment. Educators interested in professional development have access not only to tremendous resources in their fields but also to respected colleagues on listservs focusing on their specific concerns.

For faculty and administrators being urged to internationalize their curricula and their institutions, technology provides a valuable tool to supplement the more traditional approaches of faculty/student exchange and curricular infusion. Although the possible uses of the technologies will depend greatly on the degree and quality of access, the following suggestions are recommended for those involved in strategic planning:

- Identify one individual to serve as an overall coordinator of campuswide efforts. The position should be of sufficient status to reflect an institutional commitment to international efforts.
- Encourage faculty participation through the use of incentives such as release time.
- Develop partnerships with overseas institutions and private organizations.
- Encourage the creation of an advisory committee involving faculty from a variety of disciplines.
- Provide training for faculty to acquaint them with the capabilities of the technologies.
- Make decisions on the appropriateness of a particular technological approach after you have either seen it in action yourself or, preferably, have experienced it yourself. Many faculty who have never taught outside traditional classroom settings remain critical of electronically mediated education, believing it a poor substitute for the "real" learning possible in face-to-face settings. Rather than adopt an inno-

vation "in spite of" faculty resistance, it makes much better sense to give faculty, and administrators, the opportunity to make a realistic appraisal of the potential of the technologies through a "hands-on" (or "eyes-on") experience. Of course, this should be supplemented by legitimate research.

- Always keep in mind that technology should be selected based upon its appropriateness in helping you accomplish specific educational goals. The curriculum should lead the technology, not the other way around. In many cases, this may mean a combination of different media.

- Expect change and acceptance to be slow. Although technology may be changing rapidly, institutions of higher education seldom reflect such a tradition of progression.

- Finally, recognize that some of the traditional approaches to internationalization may need to be rethought as the emerging technologies present new opportunities for international interaction. Although virtually none of the examples cited in this chapter was begun with the intention of internationalizing a curriculum or a campus, the very nature of the technology resulted in a high degree of interaction and learning as faculty and students from different countries collaborated on group projects.

REFERENCES

AARNet. <Online: http://www.aarnet.edu/au/avcc/aarnet/index.html>.

AsianNet launch teaching program for new internet users. (1996, November 18). *CINET-L Newsletter*, Issue No. 75.

AT&T worldnet benefits from AOL logjam. (1997, January 23). *The Wall Street Journal*, p. B6.

Baldwin, R.G. and Austin, A.E. (1995, Winter). Toward greater understanding of faculty research collaboration. *The Review of Higher Education*, 19 (2), 45-70.

Bikson, T.K. and Eveland, J.D. (1990). The interplay of work group structure and computer support. In J. Galegher, R.E. Kraut, and C. Egido (Eds.), *Intellectual teamwork: Social and technological foundations of cooperative work*, (pp. 245-90). Hillsdale, NJ: Lawrence Erlbaum Associates.

Blumenstyk, G. (1997, January 20). Distance-learning programs hampered by sudden failure of key satellite. *The Chronicle of Higher Education*, Academe Today.

Brown, J.S. and Duguid, P. (1995, July 26). Universities in the digital age. Xerox PARC, Palo Alto Research Paper.

Carvin, A. Personal communication, February 21, 1997.

Catalist. (1997). A catalog of LISTSERV lists of 12,599 public lists. <Online: http://www.lsoft.com/lists/listref.html>.

Character Set Technology. Personal communication, October 9, 1996.

Chen, K. (1996, September 5). China bans Internet access to as many as 100 web sites. *The Wall Street Journal*, Interactive Edition.

China loosens restraints on Internet access. (1997, January 16). *The Wall Street Journal*, p. B4.

Clotfelter, C.T. (1996). *Buying the best*. Princeton, NJ: Princeton University Press.

COMET. <Online: http://www.comet.ucar.edu/npi/vdcfrep.html>.

Couch, C.J. (1996). *Information technologies and social orders*. New York: Aldine De Gruyten.

Cuba approves limited Internet access. (1996, June 21). *Reuters*. <Online: http://www.yahoo.com/headlines/960621/compute/stories/cuba_1.html>.

CUPS. <Online: http://www.ph.surrey.ac.uk:80/cti/catalog/cups.htm>.

Daniel, S.J. (1997, July/August). Why universities need technology strategies. *Change*, pp. 11-17.

Davies, M. Personal communication, September 20, 1997.

DeLoughry, T.J. (1996, November 22). Campus computer use grows at slower pace in 1996. *The Chronicle of Higher Education*, p. A21.

EdWeb. (1997). "E-Mail Discussion Lists and Electronic Journals," <Online: http://edweb,gsn.org/lists.html>.

Ehrmann, S.C. (1990, April). Reaching students, reaching resources: Using technologies to open the college. Annenberg/CPB Project, *Academic Computing*, pp. 10-14, 32-34.

ENIS. <Online: http://www.csc.fi/forum/EAIE/enis.html>.

EuroPACE. <Online: http://www.europace.be/>.

European Commission eyes Internet regulations. (1996, October 17). *BNA Daily Report for Executives*, p. A4.

Faison, S. (1996, February 5). China issues rules to control Internet. *The New York Times*.

Finholt, T.A. (1997, February 11). Collaborative life: Observations of science via the Internet. Presentation at the University of Michigan, School of Information.

Gagne, R.M. (Ed.). (1987). *Instructional technology: Foundations*. Hillsdale, NJ: Lawrence Erlbaum Associates.

GATE. <Online: http://www.edugate.org/vision.html>.

Germain, E. (1996, August 2). Fast lanes on the Internet. *Science*, 273 (5275), 585-88.

Glass, P. (1996, March 11). Francophones fight dominance of English language on the Internet. *The New York Times*, Cybertimes.

The Globe and Mail (1996, October 9). Canadian newspaper, <Online: www.globeandmail.ca/>.

Gore, T. Personal communication, July 8, 1996.

The Gravity Society. <Online: http://www.gravity.org/>.

Green, K. (1996, March/April). The coming ubiquity of information technology. *Change*, pp. 24-28.

Harned, J. Personal communication, January 23, 1997.

High access charges = lower net use. (1997, March 14). *Wall Street Journal*, Interactive Edition.

Horwitz, R. Personal communication, September 18, 1996.

Hutty, M. Personal communication, August 18, 1996.

I*EARN. <Online: http://www.chch.planet.org.nz/iearn.html>.

The Internet Society. Personal communication, January 30, 1997.

Internet Suppression. Personal communication, 1996.

Internet's popularity leaping in Latin America. (1996, June 27). *Reuters*. <Online: http://www.yahoo.com/headlinees/960627/compute/stories/latam_1.html>.

Ishii, H. (1993). Cross-cultural communication and CSCW. In L.M. Harasim (Ed.), *Global networks*. Cambridge, MA: MIT Press.

Isnor, R. Personal communication, February 3, 1997.

Iwasiew, C. Personal communication, November 5, 1996.

————. Personal communication, November 8, 1996.

JAMES. <Online: http://www.labs.bt.com/profsoc/james/>.

Jensen, R.E. (1993, July/August). The technology of the future is already here. *Academe*, p. 10.

Kilian C. Personal communication, December 22, 1996.

Koreans. Personal communication, 1996.

Krauss, R.M. and Fussell, S. R. (1990). Mutual knowledge and communicative effectiveness. In J. Galegher, R.E. Kraut, and C. Egido (Eds.), *Intellectual teamwork: Social and technological foundations of cooperative work*, (pp. 111-45). Hillsdale, NJ: Lawrence Erlbaum Associates.

LCTL-T. Personal communication, February 23, 1997.

Lewis, P. (1996, April). Universal access to the Internet: Can we narrow the knowledge gap? <Online: http://grove.ufl.edu:80/~pflewis/mmc6402.html#EN1>

The List. (1997). <Online: http://thelist.iworld.com/>.

Mansell, R. and Silverstone, R. (Eds.). (1996). *Communication by design*. Oxford: Oxford University Press.

Marvin, C. (1988). *When old technologies were new*. New York: Oxford University Press.

Mason, R. (1993). Computer conferencing and the new Europe. In L. Harasim (Ed.), *Global networks*, (pp. 199-220). Cambridge, MA: MIT Press.

McDonald, J. (1996, March 12). Singapore Internet users unhappy with loss of refuge in land of rules. *The New York Times*, Cybertimes.

McGrath, J.E. (1990). Time Matters in groups. In J. Galegher, R.E. Kraut, and C. Egido (Eds.), *Intellectual teamwork: Social and technological foundations of cooperative work*, (pp. 23-61). Hillsdale, NJ: Lawrence Erlbaum Associates.

Miech, E.J., Nave, B., and Mosteller, F. (1995, December 4). *A review of computer-assisted language learning in U.S. colleges and universities*. Cambridge, MA: Center for the Evaluation of the Program on Initiatives for Children of the American Academy of Arts and Sciences.

Negroponte, N. (1995). *Being digital*. New York: Alfred A. Knopf.

Net gains. (1997, January 28). *Investor's Business Daily*.

Net use growing around globe. (1996). *Reuters*. <Online: http://www.yahoo.com/headlines/960628/compute/stories/china_1.html>.

Our love affair with e-mail. (1997, January 15). *Investor's Business Daily*, p. A6.

Pachecho, A. (1996/1997, Winter). Teacher interns: A new breed of educators. *Edutopia*, 4 (2), 6-7.

Quarterman, J.S. (1993). A global matrix of minds. In L.M. Harasim (Ed.), *Global networks*. Cambridge, MA: MIT Press.

Rainey, R. Personal communication, November 20, 1996.

Richards, C. Personal communication, April 15, 1996.

Rojo, A. (1995). *Participation in scholarly electronic forums*. Unpublished doctoral dissertation. University of Toronto. <Online: http://www.oise.on.ca/~arojo/chap1.html>.

Sautede. E. (1996, March/April). The Internet between the constable and the gamekeeper. *China Perspective*, 4, 6-8.

Seng, Y.A. (1996, November 6). You are never alone out there on the Net. *The Strait Times Interactive*.

Singapore educator. Personal communication, November 6, 1996.

Singapore launches curbs on Internet content. (1996, June). *Reuters* <Online: www.online.reuters.com/online/online.html>.

Smith, D. (1996, July 5). Librarians see public access to Internet as growing challenge. *The New York Times*, Cybertimes.

Southeast Asia mulls self-policing of Internet. (1996, September 3). *Reuters* <Online: www.online.reuters.com/online/online.html>.

Spennemann, D.H.R. et al. (1996, February 1). The electronic colonization of the Pacific. *CMC Magazine*.

Sproul, L. and Kiesler, S. (1993). Computers, networks, and work. In L.M. Harasim (Ed.), *Global networks*. Cambridge, MA: MIT Press.

Talib, I. S. Personal communication, November 6, 1996.

TERENA. <Online: http://www.earn.net/index.html>.

Thompkins, L. Personal communication, March 19, 1996.

Time Warner offers Internet coaching in the classroom. (1997, January 8,). *BNA Daily Report for Executives*, A19.

Treanor, P. (1996). Educational inequality against Europe. <Online: http://web.inter.nl.net/users/Paul.Treanor/int.edu.html>.

Tubbs, S.L. and Moss, S. (1994). *Human communication*. 7th ed. New York: McGraw-Hill.

Van Rycheghen, D. (1996). Computers and culture: Cases from Kenya. In E.M. Roche and M.J. Blaine, (Eds.) *Information technology, development, and policy*, (pp. 153-70). Brookfield, VT: Avebury.

Venezuelan professors join doctors in national strike for higher pay. (1997, January 20). *The Chronicle of Higher Education*, Academe Today.

Viljoen, J. Personal communication, January 21, 1997.

Volkwyn, R. (1996, October 4). Internet bio-ed project. <Online: http://www.botany.uwc.ac.za/sci_ed/>.

Walls, J. (1993). Global networking for local development. In L.M. Harasim (Ed.), *Global networks*. Cambridge, MA: MIT Press.

Walt, V. (1996, May 4). The Internet meets the thought police. *The Wall Street Journal*, Online edition.

Worldwide course on economic development. <Online: http://id-www.ucsb.edu/IC/IAUP/Report.html>.

PART 3

· · · · · · · · · · · ·

Evidence, Evaluation, and Outcomes of Internationalization

CHAPTER 12

Internationalization through the Lens of Evaluation

by Susan Lewis English

A potentially empowering way to view internationalization is through the lens of evaluation. Evaluation can be empowering because, while adding to our general knowledge base, it provides a basis for reflective and informed decision-making. Because knowledge and theories are tested in a real setting, evaluative information can be further used to justify decisions, to garner support, to solicit resource allocation, and to share information with colleagues for collaborative problem-solving. In this chapter, I will suggest reasons why the internationalization of colleges and universities should be guided by evaluation and how evaluators can provide an important link between research and practice.

There are perhaps as many types and purposes of evaluation as there are projects to be evaluated. For this reason, it would be futile to attempt a comprehensive description of all types of evaluation. Nor, according to Worthen and Sanders (1987), would it be fruitful to try to combine all types of evaluation into one streamlined model, considering that evaluation is a fairly young field that is still in a developmental and expansionist stage. Instead, let us look briefly at four general types of evaluation that have been used to study internationalization in higher education and that may hold particular promise for understanding and guiding the future consideration of policy issues: (1) outcomes assessment, (2) needs assessment, (3) process evaluation, and (4) program review.

As we consider each type of evaluation, we will briefly examine the existing research literature for relevant topics. Then, for insight into some of the issues of current interest, we will turn to *A Research Agenda for the Internationalization of Higher Education in the United States*, published in 1995 by the Association of International Education Administrators (AIEA). The "Research Topics and Priorities" section of the *Agenda* will serve as a jumping-off point for future evaluation studies that could be designed. But first, let us consider why evaluation might be a useful tool in this endeavor.

WHY EVALUATE?

Evaluation fills a niche somewhere between educational research and practice. By bringing a broad knowledge base into the decision-making process in real settings, theory can be translated into practice. At the same time, practices that are established on the basis of sound research become academically defensible. While researchers generally start with an idea or hypothesis and then seek a venue where they can test their idea, evaluation begins with a specific group of people or an entity, such as a course, department, or institution. This group or entity, referred to as the object of the evaluation, is then measured against a certain standard or is considered in light of certain desired qualities.

Evaluation is also distinctive from some kinds of research in the way it handles point of view. Evaluators acknowledge that their work is value-based—as the term evaluation implies. The evaluator approaches the object of evaluation in terms of what is desirable from one or more specific points of view. A comprehensive evaluation uses as broad an information base as possible to present information from a variety of viewpoints. This is accomplished by gathering and analyzing information from a wide range of stakeholders. In the field of global education, for example, a stakeholder can be defined as any person or entity to whom internationalization matters. Having assessed the situation from different viewpoints, the evaluator uses this assessment to render judgments and make recommendations from yet another point of view—from the evaluator's own vantage point as an outside observer.

Practitioners, for their part, can use evaluation to make decisions about real-world problems within the realm of their responsibility. Ideally, practitioners in international education attempt to make the best possible decisions based on the information that is available to them at the time. In an institution that has adopted globalization as a mission, faculty may face such decisions as how to internationalize the courses they currently teach. Administrators may be challenged to prepare students for an increasingly global world within the framework of existing academic or accreditation standards. In such cases, practitioners can use the information revealed through evaluation as a basis for informed decision-making.

Evaluation can be particularly useful to practitioners when it is used formatively to guide planning and policy. Strategic planning in particular can be a natural outgrowth of an evaluation that not only looks at the institution itself but also scans the external environment in which the institution is situated in space and time. The recommendations that emerge from such an evaluation can be used to design interventions for change—whether to improve certain sectors, help certain groups, save money, or accomplish any other stated goal. The recommendations might suggest a process for planned change or a cycle for continuous improvement.

Evaluation also can provide useful information to policymakers striving to implement policies and procedures that will benefit a broad range of stake-holders. How can we meet professional or government standards? How favorably does our program compare with other programs or other parts of the institution? What kind of data will support our claims, arguments, and re-quests for funding of our activities? These are the kinds of questions facing policymakers.

OUTCOMES ASSESSMENT

The achievement of stated goals and objectives or *outcomes* has become increasingly important in education in recent decades, as opposed to the enumeration of *input* measures designed to achieve these goals. Looking at internationalization through the lens of outcomes assessment, such outcomes as the foreign language proficiency of college graduates or their intentions to pursue international careers become the focus, rather than the number of credits earned in foreign language courses or months spent abroad during college.

In its simplest form, an assessment of outcomes is like a single snapshot, providing a picture of a single end-point in time, such as the end of a program, a fiscal year, or a decade. A more informative method of outcomes assessment compares two points in time, like a set of photographs that depict a program before and after a particular intervention. This type of assessment might show where an institution is now compared to where it was a month, year, or 10 years ago, to produce a measure of change in specific elements over time. If many points in time are compared along one measure, the data could be used to graph and analyze events such as the number of students enrolled in foreign language classes at a particular institution over a 20-year period.

Adding a value judgment to the outcomes assessment, we might examine where an institution is now compared to where we expected it would be. In this case, expectation can be measured by looking at documents or asking informants for a retrospective judgment; or with careful planning and follow-through in a longitudinal study, similar questions might have been posed five years before. In either case, the result can take the form of a gap analysis that shows the degree to which the institution has met, exceeded, or fallen short of expectations.

A yet more powerful type of outcomes assessment attempts to explain why, given a starting position and all our efforts, we reached a particular end-point. This method seeks answers to the question of attribution—to what can we attribute our present status? One established method for this type of outcomes assessment is the I-E-O model developed over several decades by Alexander Astin for assessing college student outcomes (Astin, 1991). The I-E-O model looks at all possible explanations for why students achieved particular *outcomes* (O) relative to institutional programs, policies, and *environments* (E) accounting for the entry characteristics of the students before they entered the educational program, called *inputs* (I). Such a model relies on statistical analysis to estimate the influence of particular interventions, relative to inputs and environments, on desired outcomes. Let us turn now to past research that is relevant to this type of evaluation.

Outcomes Research

The research literature on internationalization reveals past attempts to define and measure desired outcomes of internationalization and also to identify predictors of those outcomes. In considering student outcomes of international learning experiences, for example, Barrows et al. (1981) found little relationship between college courses and college students' knowledge of world history, geography, and politics. Later studies that investigated global knowledge as outcomes of a wider range of curricular and co-curricular experiences of an international nature did reveal connections, but only for certain types of students in specific settings (Hembroff et al., 1989 and 1990; Malanchuk et al., 1993; Torney-Purta, 1994; Woyach,1988). Most notably, women showed significantly lower scores than men on these tests of global knowledge.

The outcomes of overseas study and travel have been extensively researched, particularly in terms of impacts on students (e.g., Bachner et al., 1993; Carlson et al., 1990 and 1991; Freed, 1995; Hansel, 1986; Hansel and Grove, 1984 and 1986; Koester, 1985 and 1987; Laubscher, 1994; Opper, Teichler, and Carlson, 1990; Useem and Useem, 1955; Uyeki, 1993). Taken as a whole, these studies show that overseas immersion experiences clearly have impacts, but that different types of overseas experiences impact different types of students in different ways. Recent qualitative studies have only begun to reveal the nature of these differences.

In the United States, foreign language offerings and internationalized curricula have been extensively documented, both for liberal arts colleges and for professional schools like business and engineering (e.g., Barber et al., 1990; Burn, 1991; Cavusgil, 1993; Corbett, 1994; English, 1996; Fixman, 1989;

Groennings and Wiley, 1990; Harrop, 1991; Janes, 1991; Johnston and Edelstein, 1993; Klasek, 1992; Kobrin, 1984; Lambert, 1989 and 1994; Mestenhauser et al., 1988; Moore and Morfit, 1993; Pickert and Turlington, 1992; Rugman and Stanburg, 1992; Showalter, 1989). However, a strong connection between international course-taking and desired outcomes remains to be made.

Measures of internationalization at the institutional level have been created, notably the International Dimension Index (IDI) (Afonso, 1990). At the personal level, researchers have measured the components of successful intercultural communication and, in some cases, considered them as outcomes of attitudinal and behavioral predictors (Chen, 1987; Elmer, 1986; Ruben, 1976; Ruben and Kealey, 1979). Others have studied more generally the components of a global perspective or global competence (English, 1996; Hanvey, 1976; Hett, 1993; Lambert, 1994; Tonkin and Edwards, 1981).

In the research literature, the search for viable outcomes is mirrored by the search for predictors of desirable outcomes. These outcomes include both personal qualities and learning experiences. Some researchers have looked for attitudinal and behavioral predictors of intercultural effectiveness (Dinges, 1983, in Landis and Brislin, 1983; Olebe, 1988; Sell, 1983; Wiseman, 1989). Others have looked at contact with people from other countries, whether direct or indirect through the media, as predictors of attitudes toward foreign peoples and cultures (Isaacs, 1958; Paige, 1983, in Landis and Brislin, 1983; Stephan and Stephan, 1989 and 1992; Tims and Miller, 1986).

Such studies exemplify the kinds of outcomes and predictors that have been explored in the internationalization research literature in the past several decades. Together, they suggest various types of knowledge, attitudes, and competence that individuals might develop, and the personal inputs and institutional environments that could prepare people for an increasingly global world. They also document the kinds of educational and developmental experiences, such as study of foreign languages, study abroad, and cross-cultural interaction, that may be predictors or stepping stones to these goals. Let us turn below to some current issues that might be explored using various types of outcomes assessment.

Current Issues in Outcomes Research

The AIEA 1995 *Research Agenda* calls for investigation into a number of outcomes of internationalization as well as predictors of desirable outcomes. Most broadly, it calls for research on the outcomes of the internationalization of higher education, including (section III-2) the impacts on

- K-12 education, the teaching profession generally, schools of education, the public and private school setting

- local, state, and national officials
- U.S. science and technology programs, including foreign scholars and students involved in U.S. science programs
- universities and the university administration

The AIEA *Agenda* raises questions more specifically about the outcomes of overseas experience for students and faculty (section II-3). It asks about the impact of

- overseas immersion vis-à-vis K-12 instruction and general education requirements on career choices, including job placement
- faculty mobility as it affects involvement in international programs
- international students, in the years after their return to their home country, on faculty, students, and U.S. education

The AIEA *Research Agenda* asks for more information about the predictors of a particular faculty outcome—the factors that enhance the maintenance of foreign language proficiency—seeking successful and cost-effective ways to avoid language attrition or loss, possibly through the use of modern communications technology (section III-4).

- What have been the most successful and cost-effective ways to maintain faculty area and language skills once such skills have been attained?
- Do modern communications technologies offer relatively unused, potentially effective opportunities?

In addition to asking questions about outcomes of internationalization and their predictors, the AIEA *Research Agenda* devotes some space to exploring what outcomes might be desirable. It asks broadly, "What will be the need of citizens for international knowledge and language" (section I-2) and, more specifically, what will be the predictable need

for specialists in foreign area knowledge, languages, international substantive fields in government, higher education, the private sector and non-governmental organizations at various levels? (section I-1)

It asks further which outcomes are desirable in the eyes of which stakeholders:

What do various "publics"—business, state and national governments, employers, community leaders—expect graduates of universities to know about the world, about this nation's international relations and interests, and about other cultures? (section I-3)

Let us now discuss this part of the AIEA *Research Agenda* in light of past research and through the lens of the kinds of outcomes assessment studies that might be undertaken.

Discussion

The AIEA *Research Agenda* asks important questions about multiple outcomes and about educational needs for a global future. To study the outcomes of the many efforts to internationalize colleges and universities, future evaluation studies might begin by establishing a criterion or outcome measure. At the individual level, the criterion could be a measure of student achievement, such as foreign language proficiency, global knowledge, intercultural competence, or global competence. At the institutional level, it could be a measure such as Harari's (1992) Structural Approaches to Internationalize Curriculum, Afonso's (1990) International Dimension Index (IDI), or Ellingboe's (1996) Six-Stage Attitudinal Assessment Toward Internationalization or her Nine Internationalization Resistance Factors. The second task would be to identify the efforts toward internationalization that are of interest. At the individual level, these might include student experiences like study abroad or living with a roommate from another culture. At the institutional level, data could be gathered on characteristics of an internationalized curriculum or the presence of international students on campus.

The third task would be to establish a relationship between the criterion and efforts to internationalize. This task deserves thoughtful consideration. In designing studies on outcomes of internationalization, evaluators would be wise to consider models, such as Astin's I-E-O model, that consider the broad context of all possible predictors. To claim that any outcome is the result of a particular intervention, the evaluator will look not only at the interventions to be evaluated but also at all possible contributing factors in the environment, both on campus and beyond. In this way, the effect of certain predictors can be shown relative to the predictive value of other possible factors. Further, the evaluator needs to consider the inputs that existed prior to any interventions. What pre-college experiences may have influenced students' motivation or ability for international learning and development? What qualities, policies, or aspects of the institutional climate predate the current movement to internationalize? Only by looking at the relationship between predictors and outcomes in a broad context can the evaluator attribute change to particular learning experiences or to institutional policy.

For these purposes, qualitative methods might well be combined with quantitative. Recent studies of overseas experience, for example, have used student diaries to track and understand how students spend their free time overseas (Freed, 1995). Experiential education overseas plays a role in student development and student perceptions of the role of out-of-class experiences in education abroad, as described in Laubscher's "Encounters with Difference" (1994). Knowing something about the quality of the overseas experience then provides a basis for evaluating that experience as one possible predictor of quantitative outcomes, such as increases in foreign language proficiency.

Needs Assessment

Needs assessment is related to outcomes assessment in that it presupposes that we have determined the outcome for which we are striving. The task is to determine what remains to be done to achieve that end. The AIEA *Research Agenda* essentially calls for a needs assessment when it asks what types of global knowledge and foreign language proficiency will be necessary for future professionals in government higher education, the private sector, and nongovernmental organizations.

In assessing needs for the future, we need to consider desired outcomes from the viewpoint of multiple stakeholders. Efforts to identify universal needs of human beings in a global world can be seen in measures of intercultural competence, a global perspective, and, most recently, global competence. Evaluators assessing needs for a global future have a choice—to consider special needs for particular settings or to look for needs common to people in all settings. In fact, we need evaluation studies that consider the needs of constituents for global work and living *both* in specific settings and more broadly for global living.

Such questions are already demanding an answer. What knowledge, skills, and attitudes are required by nurses, doctors, and social workers who attend to crisis situations in international settings? What communicative or sociolinguistic competence is required by a cross-national team of peace monitors, financial traders, trade unionists, engineers, or astronauts? To answer broad questions about universals of global competence, social scientists might borrow ideas from vastly different disciplines.

The brief mention in the AIEA *Research Agenda* of communications technology (section III-4) brings to mind a field yet to be explored in the internationalization literature. What will be the demands and possibilities for global interaction with advances in distance learning and the coming of the virtual university? Such a question challenges evaluators to look at the potential for communications technology as they assess changing needs for the future.

PROCESS EVALUATION

While an outcomes assessment looks at the what and why of change, process evaluation looks at *how* change occurs. A process evaluation might consider change within an institution, such as changes in curricular content, administrative structure, resources, standards, or policy. On the other hand, it might also look at influences coming from outside the institution, whether social, political, or economic in origin. The change that occurs can be planned or unplanned, expected or unexpected.

Before evaluative judgments can be made about processes, it is necessary to know something about the process itself. Therefore, a process evaluation generally begins with a description that might sound like the telling of a story. A thorough process evaluation, however, will go beyond description to understand the full context, including antecedents and impacts.

Often, a process evaluation will use qualitative research methods, starting with open-ended questions that allow for other questions and unexpected themes to emerge. Other times, the data will be quantifiable and subject to statistical analysis. A process evaluation can be complex and untidy, or the results might lend themselves to presentation in a structured format, such as a linear series of steps, a flow chart, or a force-field analysis, with arrows pointing in conflicting directions.

Process Questions of Interest

The AIEA 1995 *Research Agenda* (section II-1) raises a number of questions that "take stock of the extent to which an international dimension now exists in higher education, at universities and at community colleges." The agenda calls for documentation and description of the international dimension to answer the following questions:

- To what extent do the various professions now include an international dimension within their educational programs—degree and non-degree?
- What do current institutional mission statements in various segments of higher education say about global and international commitment?
- Regarding accreditation, what are current international education requirements, both institution-wide and in professional schools, as now stated and practiced?
- What is the current status of international dimension within university core curriculum requirements?

Section II-2 also asks for the following descriptive information about funding policies and procedures to "establish objective understanding of the funding of internationalization as it is now occurring at universities and two year community colleges":

- Including international and external sources, how do universities now fund and support the elements of their internationalization efforts?

- What revenues have been gained by universities as a result of their international education efforts, including services rendered at home and abroad to governments and the private sector, and from what sources?
- How does the fund-leveraging experience in university international education programs compare to parallel experiences in other fields? What are the main elements involved in this leveraging?

By asking how organizational approach affects the type and degree of internationalization, the AIEA 1995 *Research Agenda* (section III-3) also asks about the impact of a process.

- What is the relative effectiveness of various organizational approaches to internationalization under differing traditions and circumstances?

Discussion

The AIEA *Research Agenda* appropriately calls for systematic description of various institutional elements of internationalization—of professional schools, of accreditation requirements, of mission statements, of financial sources of support. While the research literature provides descriptions of past change and change process, more systematic descriptions and databases are clearly needed.

The AIEA *Research Agenda* also raises a timely question about the impact of various institutional approaches to internationalization, such as the consolidation of international activities under the leadership of one central office. How has this process occurred, and what have been the impacts of such organizational change? How has this process affected the allocation of resources for internationalization? How has it affected the ability of colleges and universities to better prepare students for an increasingly global world? Case studies are needed to explore these questions at the institutional level and comparatively across institutions. It can be argued that the AIEA is itself a product of the consolidation of international activities on college campuses. AIEA membership calls for representation of each affiliated campus by one top-level administrator.

The AIEA *Research Agenda* offers several research questions about financial sources for internationalization. International education administrators could make good use of information about possible sources of financial support, and evaluation studies can provide administrators with this kind of information by describing the processes by which international offices acquire, retain, and dispense money. At the same time, more probing policy questions about funding sources might also be asked: What factors can influence financial support within an institution? What information is needed to make what kinds of arguments to which policymakers? What kinds of programs and policies generate funding that can be channeled back into international programs?

Change process at the individual level should not be neglected. The AIEA study asks questions about the predictors of language loss by faculty (section III-4). Language learning, maintenance, and attrition are processes that occur over a period of time. Evaluators need to work together with foreign-language educators and applied linguists to set up evaluation studies that examine such processes. The process of acculturation, currently under study by J.M. Bennett and M.J. Bennett at their institute in Oregon, needs further examination, and we need more research on the relationship of intercultural to multicultural processes.

PROGRAM REVIEW

A fourth type of evaluation, program review, has no analog in the research literature because the results are generally not published. The primary function of a program review is to answer questions about the quality or effectiveness of a particular program. The program under review can range from small, local, short-term projects to major projects affecting people over a wide geographic area and addressing long-term concerns. The results can be used summatively at the conclusion of a program to report on past accomplishments. For continuing programs, however, the results can be used formatively—for program renewal and change. Evaluation questions may be imposed by an external stakeholder, such as an accreditation body or a funding source, to mark the conclusion of a budget cycle. On the other hand, a program review can be "goal-free," and can come from within the organization in the form of a self-study. A program review can employ a wide range of methods and techniques to gather and analyze information. These include the methods discussed earlier in this chapter for assessing outcomes and needs and for describing processes and their impacts.

According to Barak and Mets (1995), program review has a number of possible functions. Besides the formative improvement of the program, the results of a program review can be used to communicate the quality of the program both internally and externally. Thus, the review can serve to enhance credibility, market the program, gain support and allocations, and respond to constituents or to state or federal mandates. In a positive sense, generating information through program review can be used to enhance cooperation as it leads to information-sharing between programs and institutions at the local, state, or national levels.

Seeley (1981) summarizes the purpose of program review as developing information for (1) planning, (2) renewal or change, (3) justification, and (4) access to resources. Eaton and Miyares (in Barak and Mets, 1995) emphasize two purposes for review of academic programs: to improve "efficiency" and "productivity." While the industrial-bureaucratic association with such words may be discomforting to educators whose major concern is student learning and development, efficiency and productivity can in a positive sense mean enhancing student learning development in the easiest and most effective way. To achieve this goal, the results of a program review can be most helpful.

The effectiveness of a program review can ultimately be measured by its clearly defined purpose and the extent to which results are used for this purpose. According to Barak and Sweeney (in Barak and Mets, 1995), reports and recommendations from a program review should be linked to outcomes assessment, strategic planning, and the budget process. To accomplish these things, a program review should begin with realistic expectations and lead to recommendations that are simple and practical enough to actually be implemented. The review should involve key leaders and consider environmental factors, looking at the coherence of the program as part of a broader, integrated system.

Lessons from Title VI

In terms of program review, the AIEA 1995 *Research Agenda* calls for comprehensive studies of major federally funded programs that have supported international learning experiences and internationalization efforts in the United States over the past several decades. These include the National Resource Centers (NRCs) and Centers for International Business Education and Research (CIBERs) established under Title VI of the Higher Education Acts at select campuses across the U.S. The *Research Agenda* suggests four different approaches to review these programs in terms of strengths and weaknesses, costs and benefits, responsiveness to change, and societal impacts.

- What are the strengths and weaknesses experienced in establishing and operating such centers? (section III-1)
- How do costs compare to benefits at individual institutions and nationally? (section III-3)
- In what ways are the Title VI programs responding to changes in the world that have occurred in recent years? (section III-1)
- What has been the impact of these programs on society, including impact on (section III-2): undergraduate and graduate level education, both directly and indirectly; the broader university program; NRC graduates and their students; and the international dimension of institutions *without* NRC grants?

Let us examine each of these research topics for its potential as a stimulus to evaluation. The call for a review of the strengths and weaknesses in establishing national centers might begin with a historical description of how the centers came about. Long interviews with individuals present at the start would allow for retrospective judgments to emerge about the establishment process. From these interviews, issues and questions might emerge that could be further investigated through examination of historical documents. From these interviews and documents, lessons could be learned that would have implications for current and future programs with similar goals. From this historical information, data could be used to construct models that would guide future internationalization efforts.

The question of cost-effectiveness calls for another type of evaluation, a cost-benefit analysis. Combining historical data with data about current impacts and outcomes, the evaluator could develop a model relating start-up and operating costs to impacts. Human, temporal, spatial, and financial costs could be examined as predictors of desirable outcomes. For such an analysis, outcomes can include both direct and indirect impacts of the program, such as impacts on graduate and undergraduate programs, on the broader university, on graduates of the programs and their students, and on other institutions. A complex study might trace the competence, aspirations, or career choices of today's undergraduate students to the experience of a professor or mentor whose career was positively affected by a Title VI grant before the student was even born. Similar studies could be conducted for other large-scale programs, like the Fulbright program in the U.S. or the younger ERASMUS or SOCRATES programs of the European Union. The evaluation question need not be limited to *whether* a program was cost-effective or not; it could look rather at kinds of people and purposes for which the program was cost-effective. This evaluation could have implications for the targeting of future expenditures to reach particular or broader groups of people for any range of purposes.

Another question in the AIEA *Research Agenda* asks in what ways the Title VI programs are responding to recent changes in the world (section III-1). The answer to this question might emerge from a review of programs to understand external pressures and internal responses. The learning organization is flexible and able to respond to change; it has a permeable membrane that allows information from the external environment to filter in, (Bolman and Deal, 1991). A large body of existing documentation—program reviews of many NRCs or CIBERs—could be examined for evidence of external pressures and internal responses. Yet another study might look at alternative funding sources, at the future capacity of these programs to adapt to changing needs for these programs, at education and training, and at new technological means of delivering education.

INITIAL STEPS

Suppose a large nonprofit organization wanted to know the extent to which American colleges and universities are preparing students for an increasingly global world. They have requested an evaluation to provide information and make recommendations that will guide the organization in distributing funding for internationalization projects.

To begin the evaluation process, an evaluation team might seek answers to the following questions:

- Who are the stakeholders? To whom does internationalization matter?
- What key evaluation questions shall we investigate?
- What sources of information are available?
- What methods shall we use to gather and analyze information?
- To whom shall we report the information and in what form?
- How will the information be used?

Identifying stakeholders early in the evaluation process will make it possible to collaboratively identify the purpose of the evaluation, develop evaluation questions, and gain access to information. Support for the evaluation and ultimately implementation of its recommendations will depend in part on the ability of the evaluator to involve stakeholders in crucial steps in the process.

In terms of standards for evaluation, the four categories developed at Western Michigan University provide guidelines: (1) utility, (2) feasibility, (3) propriety, and (4) accuracy (Joint Committee, 1981). Among the ethical issues relevant to evaluation are matters of voluntary participation, privacy, confidentiality, and benefit to those involved in the study (English, 1995). The approach where the evaluator works together with clients on self-empowerment and change, called participatory action research, can be particularly effective in sharing the benefits of research with clients.

CONCLUSION

We have seen how evaluation is distinctive from both research and practice, and yet how it can make a contribution to both. While the primary goal of evaluation is not to be generalizable to other times and places, it is possible that the information learned through evaluation can contribute to basic or applied research. Evaluation can, for example, provide an in-depth look at a particular program while preserving the richness of contextual information. Like a research-based case study, evaluation can serve to generate questions for future research. It can lead to the definition of constructs and the building of conceptual models as people discover new ways of thinking about such concepts as internationalization.

A recurrent question in the research literature on internationalization can be stated in the following way: What can colleges and universities do to prepare students for an increasingly global world? If research can show what kinds of institutional strategies prepare which kinds of students for global work and living, then international educators will have data to support arguments for favorable policies and funding of programs at the institutional, state, and national levels. In this way, evaluation can provide important means to gaining support for internationalization. Even in the face of inadequate funding, evaluation can be used to assign priorities and make wise, research-based decisions about the most effective ways currently known to prepare students for an increasingly global world.

REFERENCES

Afonso, J.D. (1990). *The international dimension in American higher education.* Ph.D. dissertation, University of Arizona, Tucson.

Association of International Education Administrators. (1995). *A research agenda for the internationalization of higher education in the United States.* Washington, DC: AIEA.

Astin, A. W. (1991). *Assessment for excellence.* Phoenix: Oryx Press.

Bachner, D. J., Zeutschel, U., and Shannon, D. (1993). Methodological issues in researching the effects of U.S.-German educational youth exchange: A case study. *International Journal of Intercultural Relations,* 17, 41-71.

Barak, R. J. and Mets, L. A. (Eds.). (1995). *Using academic program review.* New Directions for Institutional Research, No. 86. San Francisco: Jossey-Bass Publishers.

Barak, R.J. and Sweeney, J.D. (1995). Academic program review in planning, budgeting, and assessment. In R.J. Barak and L.A. Mets (Eds.), *Using academic program review.* New Directions for Institutional Research, No. 86. San Francisco: Jossey-Bass Publishers.

Barber, E. G., Morgan, R. P., and Darby, W. P. (1990). *Choosing futures: U.S. and foreign student views of graduate engineering education.* New York: Institute of International Education.

Barrows, T. S. et al. (1981). College students' knowledge and beliefs: A survey of global understanding. *The final report of the global understanding project.* New Rochelle, NY: Change Magazine Press.

Bolman, L. G. and Deal, T. E. (1991). *Reframing organizations: Artistry, choice, and leadership.* San Francisco: Jossey-Bass Publishers.

Burn, B. B. (1991). *Integrating study abroad into the undergraduate liberal arts curriculum: Eight institutional case studies.* New York: Greenwood Press.

Burn, B. B., Cerych, L., and Smith, A. (1990). *Study abroad programmes, higher education policy series 11, vol. 1.* London: Jessica Kingsley Publishers.

Carlson, J. S. et al. (1991). *Study abroad: The experience of American undergraduates in Western Europe and the United States.* New York: Council on International Educational Exchange.

Carlson, J. S., Burn, B. B., Useem, J., and Yachimowicz, D. (1990). *Study abroad: The experience of American undergraduates.* Westport, CT: Greenwood Press.

Cavusgil, S. T. (1993). Internationalization of business education: Defining the challenge. In S. T. Cavusgil (Ed.), *Internationalizing business education: Meeting the challenge*. East Lansing: Michigan State University.

Chen, G.-M. (1987). *Dimensions of intercultural communication competence*. Unpublished doctoral dissertation, Kent State University, Ohio.

Corbett, J. (1994). The internationalization of professional education. In C. M. Brody and J. Wallace (Eds.), *Ethical and social issues in professional education*. Albany: State University of New York Press.

Dinges, N. (1983). Intercultural competence. In D. Landis, and R. W. Brislin (Eds.), *Handbook of intercultural training, volume I: Issues in theory and design*. New York: Pergamon Press.

Eaton, G.M. and Miyares, J. (1995). Integrating program review in budgeting, and planning: A systemwide perspective. In R.J. Barak, and L.A. Mets (Eds.). *Using academic program review*. New Directions for Institutional Research, No. 86. San Francisco: Jossey-Bass Publishers.

Ellingboe, B.J. (1997, June). *Evidence of internationalization and recommendations for future campus-wide strategies*. Working Papers on Semester Conversion and Internationalization of the Curriculum. Minneapolis, MN: Institute of International Studies and Program, University of Minnesota. Available at http://edpa.coled.umn.edu/IntEdu/workpaper/coverpag.html.

————. (1996, June). *Divisional strategies on internationalizing curriculum: A comparative five-college case study of deans' and faculty perspectives at the University of Minnesota*. Unpublished Master of Arts thesis. Available through the University of Minnesota Twin Cities Campus Library System, or contact the author at BEllingboe@aol.com.

Elmer, M. I. (1986). *Intercultural effectiveness: Development of an intercultural competency scale*. Unpublished doctoral dissertation, Michigan State University, East Lansing, Michigan.

English, S. L. (1996). *International competence: Professional intentions of college seniors*. Unpublished dissertation, University of Michigan.

————. (1995). *Assessing student outcomes of internationalization*. Working Paper. Washington, DC: NAFSA: Association of International Educators.

Fixman, C.S. (1989). The foreign language needs of U.S.-based corporations. *NFLC Occasional Papers*. Washington, DC: National Foreign Language Center.

Freed, B. (Ed.). (1995). Second language acquisition in a study abroad context. *Studies in Bilingualism, Vol. 9* . Amsterdam: John Benjamins Publishing Co.

Goodwin, C. D. and Nacht, M. (1988). *Abroad and beyond: Patterns in American overseas education*. Cambridge: Cambridge University Press.

Groennings, S. (1990). Higher education, international education, and the academic disciplines. In S. Groennings and D.S. Wiley (Eds.), *Group portrait: Internationalizing the disciplines*. New York: The American Forum.

————. (1987a). The changing need for an international perspective. *International Studies, 13*(3), 64-68.

————. (1987b). *The impact of economic globalization on higher education: A regional project on the global economy and higher education in New England*. Boston: New England Board of Higher Education.

Groennings, S. and Wiley, D.S. (Eds.). (1990). *Group portrait: Internationalizing the disciplines*. New York: American Forum.

Hansel, B. (1986). *The AFS impact study: Final report. Research Report 33.* New York: The AFS Center for the Study of Intercultural Learning.

Hansel, B. and Grove, N. (1986). International student exchange programs—Are the educational benefits real? *NASSP Bulletin, 70*(487), 84-90.

————. (1984). *Why an AFS experience accelerates learning and the growth of competence. Research report 250.* New York: AFS International/Intercultural Programs.

Hanvey, R. G. (1976). *An attainable global perspective.* New York: Center for War/Peace Studies.

Harari, M. (1992). Internationalization of the curriculum. In C.B. Klasek (Ed.), *Bridges to the future: Strategies for internationalizing higher education.* (Chapter 4). Pullman, WA: Washington State University/Secretariat for the Association of International Education Administrators.

Harrop, J. C. (1991). *International education and the college student.* Unpublished doctoral dissertation, University of Virginia, Charlottesville.

Hembroff, L. A., Knott, J. H., and Keefe, M. (1990). *Survey of Michigan State University students' knowledge of international affairs.* East Lansing: Michigan State University: Center for Survey Research.

————. (1989). *Internationalizing education: A longitudinal analysis of efforts at Michigan State University.* East Lansing: Michigan State University, Center for Survey Research.

Hett, E. J. (1993). *Development of an instrument to measure global-mindedness.* Unpublished doctoral dissertation, University of San Diego.

Isaacs, H. R. (1958). *Scratches on our minds.* Armonk, NY: M. E. Sharpe, Inc.

Janes, J. (1991). *Priming the pump: The making of foreign area specialists.* New York: Institute of International Education.

Johnston, J. S., Jr. and Edelstein, R. J. (1993). *Beyond borders: Profiles in international education.* Washington, DC: Association of American Colleges.

Joint Committee on Standards for Educational Evaluation. (1981) *Standards for evaluations of educational programs, projects, and materials.* New York: McGraw-Hill.

Klasek, C. B. (Ed.). (1992). *Bridges to the future: Strategies for internationalizing higher education* . Carbondale, IL: Association of International Education Administrators.

Kobrin, S. J. (1984). International expertise in American business: How to learn to play with the kids on the street. *IIE Research Report, No. 6.* New York: Institute of International Education.

Koester, J. (1987). *A profile of the U.S. student abroad—1984 and 1985.* New York: Council on International Educational Exchange.

————. (1985). *A profile of the U.S. student abroad.* New York: Council on International Educational Exchange.

Lambert, R.D. (Ed.). (1994). *Educational exchange and global competence.* New York: Council on International Educational Exchange.

————. (1989). *International studies and the undergraduate.* Washington, DC: American Council on Education.

Landis, D. and Brislin, R. W. (Eds.). (1983). *Handbook of intercultural training, volume I: Issues in theory and design.* New York: Pergamon Press.

Laubscher, M. R. (1994). Encounters with difference: Student perceptions of role of out-of-class experiences in education abroad. *Contributions to the Study of Education, No. 105.* Westport, CT: Greenwood Press.

Malanchuk, O., Hoelscher, S., Brown, D. R., and Jacobson, H. K. (1993). *Preparing for an international and global world: A survey of undergraduates at the University of Michigan.* Ann Arbor: University of Michigan.

Mestenhauser, J. A., Marty, G., and Steglitz, I. (Eds.). (1988). *Culture, learning, and the disciplines.* Washington, DC: National Association for Foreign Student Affairs.

Moore, S. J. and Morfit, C. A. (1993). *Language and international studies: A Richard Lambert perspective.* Washington, DC: National Foreign Language Center.

Olebe, M. G. (1988). *The influence of background, attitudes and global knowledge on intercultural adaptation: A comparison of college students in two residential settings.* Unpublished doctoral dissertation, University of Minnesota, Minneapolis.

Opper, S., Teichler, U., and Carlson, J. (1990). *Impacts of study abroad programmes on students and graduates, higher education policy, series 11, vol. 2.* London: Jessica Kingsley Publishers.

Paige, R. M. (1983). Cultures in contact: On intercultural relations among American and foreign students in the United States university context. In D. Landis, and R. W. Brislin (Eds.), *Handbook of intercultural training, volume III: Area studies in intercultural training.* New York: Pergamon Press.

Pickert, S. and Turlington, B. (1992). *Internationalizing the undergraduate curriculum: A handbook for campus leaders.* Washington, DC: American Council on Education.

Ruben, B. D. (1989). The study of cross-cultural competence: Traditions and contemporary issues. *International Journal of Intercultural Relations, 13,* 229-40.

———. (1976). Assessing communication competency for intercultural adaptation. *Group and Organization Studies, 1*(3), 334-54.

Ruben, B. D., and Kealey, D. J. (1979). Behavioral assessment of communication competency and the prediction of cross-cultural adaptation. *International Journal of Intercultural Relations, 3,* 15-47.

Rugman, A.M. and Stanburg, W.T. (Eds.). (1992). *Global perspective: Internationalizing management education.* University of British Columiba, Vancouver.

Seeley, J. A. (1981). Program review and evaluation. In N. L. Poulton (Ed.), *Evaluation of management and planning systems.* New Directions for Institutional Research, No. 31. San Francisco: Jossey-Bass.

Sell, D. K. (1983). Research on attitude change in U.S. students who participate in foreign study experiences. *International Journal of Intercultural Relations, 7,* 131-47.

Showalter, S. W. (1989). *The role of service-learning in international education: Proceedings of a wingspread conference.* Goshen, IN: Goshen College.

Stephan, C. W. and Stephan, W. G. (1992). Reducing intercultural anxiety through intercultural contact. *International Journal of Intercultural Relations, 16,* 89-106.

Stephan, W. G. and Stephan, C. W. (1989). Antecedents of intergroup anxiety in Asian-Americans and Hispanic-Americans. *International Journal of Intercultural Relations, 13,* 203-19.

Tims, A. R. and Miller, M. M. (1986). Determinants of attitudes toward foreign countries. *International Journal of Intercultural Relations, 10,* 471-484.

Tonkin, H. and Edwards, J. (1981). *The world in the curriculum: Curricular strategies for the twenty-first century.* New Rochelle, NY: Council on Learning.

Torney-Purta, J. (1994). Assessment and measurement of global competence: A psychologist's view of alternative approaches. In R. D. Lambert (Ed.), *Educational exchange and global competence.* New York: Council on International Educational Exchange.

Useem, J. and Useem, R. H. (1955). *The Western-educated man in India: A study of his social roles and influence.* New York: The Dryden Press.

Uyeki, E. (1993). *As others see us: A comparison of Japanese and American Fullbrighters.* New York: Institute of International Education.

Wiseman, R. L. (1989). Predictors of intercultural communication competence. *International Journal of Intercultural Relations,* 13, 349-70.

Worthen, B. R. and Sanders, J. R. (1987). *Educational evaluation: Alternative approaches and practical guidelines.* New York: Longman.

Woyach, R. B. (1988). *Understanding the global arena: A report on the Ohio State University Global Awareness Survey.* Columbus, OH: Ohio State University.

CHAPTER 13

Divisional Strategies to Internationalize a Campus Portrait

Results, Resistance, and Recommendations from a Case Study at a U.S. University

by Brenda J. Ellingboe

INTRODUCTION

Internationalizing curriculum improves, enhances, and benefits higher education, according to many leading scholars who have written about the urgency to interject comparative and international perspectives into many of the disciplines taught at colleges and universities. A university's approach to internationalizing its own curriculum is complex to diagram, paint, or map because there are many stakeholders involved, multiple colleges and professional schools within its system, and varying degrees of involvement and ways of defining or illustrating the complex, proactive process known as internationalization. Groennings and Wiley (1990) presented evidence of global change within seven disciplines in their anthology—*Group Portrait: Internationalizing the Disciplines*. While their book showcased disciplines, this chapter paints a campus portrait of multiple components of internationalization within five colleges at a large public research university, with multiple stakeholders and various strategies contributing toward campus internationalization of curriculum and personnel.

A campus portrait captures an institution's image according to one artist or photographer at one moment in time. Internationalized campus portrait A may not look the same as internationalized campus portrait B. Two of the main concerns for researchers regarding internationalizing higher education are where the differences lie across the spectrum of higher education (and how they can be measured, explained, or described) and what accounts for the differences.

Curriculum within a higher education institution could be thought of as the complete portfolio of requirements and electives offered by individual co-cultures (colleges, divisions, departments, and units) operating within a larger system (the higher education institution). The curricular portfolio of college says more about its values and priorities with its curricular array of offerings than anything contained in its mission statement or planning documents. The portfolio is a colorful array of paints on the college's palette that entices learners to choose that palette over others for their educational process. Stakeholders decide *what* "elements" comprise a university-level curriculum; these elements represent the "content" of a learner's college portfolio. "The curriculum affects the faculty as much as the faculty influences the curriculum" (Birnbaum, 1988, p. 47). *Educare* (Latin, "to educate") can mean to teach or instruct others, but also infers a process of "drawing out" a person's talents, as opposed to "putting in" instruction.

Internationalization will be defined as the *process* of integrating an international perspective into a college or university system. It is an ongoing, future-oriented, multidimensional, interdisciplinary, leadership-driven vision that involves many stakeholders working to change the internal dynamics of an institution to respond and adapt appropriately to an increasingly diverse, globally focused, ever-changing external environment (Ellingboe, 1996). "To internationalize a curriculum actually means to institutionalize that change within the disciplines; this achieved, the interdisciplinary and multidisciplinary acquire much greater strength" (Groennings, 1990, p. 27). Calling it an academic mega-trend and multifaceted, Groennings (1990) asks academic leaders to discuss the role of the disciplines in the development of international education particularly by focusing on undergraduate education and the disciplines that students study in-depth during the latter two years of their baccalaureate programs.

Internationalization as a process could be described as a colorful ribbon that weaves throughout college cultures, from individual faculty of one discipline to a college's dean's office. Sometimes the ribbon begins in a dean's office and makes its way throughout selected disciplines within a college or professional school, taking different routes to reach various departments, leaving its own pattern for others to follow. As it sews and loops throughout a college's many-tiered, multi-layered, and mega-veined structure, it encounters everything from blockades to wide pathways as it integrates international, cross-cultural, and comparative perspectives within and across collegiate units.

Monumental changes are occurring outside academia on a global political, cultural, economic, social and technological scale. Most U.S. higher education institutions react slowly to external environmental factors, especially to those factors attempting to influence or shape thinking from a monocultural, parochial, singular point of view to a broadly based, future-oriented, internationally focused, interdisciplinary dimension. Changing an entire research university—or even one of its many colleges and professional schools—to internationalize its curriculum, programs, faculty, students, and, most important, its leaders, requires proposing systemwide incentives, fostering intercollegiate cooperation, and making individual commitments. It requires change on three levels of human relations—systemic, group, and individual.

Purpose

This chapter is a summary of a higher education Master of Arts thesis based on an educational case study on the University of Minnesota Twin Cities campus.[1] This multidimensional, multi-variable case study attempted to discover the dimensions of divisional internationalization within the University of Minnesota Twin Cities Campus, compare the attitudes toward internationalizing curriculum within and across five colleges, and allow interviewees to generate their own recommendations for leading campuswide internationalization. By uncovering the various divisional strategies and stakeholders' degrees of involvement, resistance and encouragement (or counter-resistance), factors to internationalization emerged. This chapter is an assessment of four groups of stakeholders' curricular thinking and their divisional strategies or individual approaches to internationalizing five colleges. The four groups include central administration, deans, faculty, and international education practitioners and directors of international units.

Statement of the Problem

The new millennium, a rapidly changing work force influenced by technology and diversity, and several nationally circulating reports have influenced many colleges and universities to take major steps in their strategic planning and budgeting cycles to internationalize their home campus curriculum and provide avenues and incentives for their students and faculty to research and study at foreign campuses. Some of these well-known reports include the Association of International Education Administrators' *Guidelines for International Education at U.S. Colleges and Universities* (1995) and *A Research Agenda*

---

[1]Contact the author for a copy of the Master of Arts thesis entitled "Divisional Strategies on Internationalizing the Curriculum: A Comparative Five-College Case Study of Deans' and Faculty Perspectives at the University of Minnesota" at BEllingboe@aol.com or elli0049@tc.umn.edu; it is also available through the University of Minnesota Library System (LUMINA). Access a 49-page working paper entitled "Evidence of Internationalization and Recommendations for Future Campus-wide Strategies" at <http://edpa.coled.umn.edu/IntEdu/workpaper/coverpag.html >, a 10-page executive summary of the M.A. thesis at <http://edpa.coled.umn.edu/IntEdu/exesum.html >, and a 21-page listing of books and journals on internationalization compiled by Brenda J. Ellingboe at <http://edpa.coled.umn.edu/IntEdu/iz.html>.

for the Internationalization of Higher Education in the United States (1995); the American Council on Education's *Educating Americans for a World in Flux: Ten Ground Rules for Internationalizing Higher Education* (1995); the Council for International Educational Exchange's *Educating for Global Competence* (1988); and the President's Commission on Foreign Languages and International Studies Report *Strength Through Wisdom—A Critique of U.S. Capability* (1979).

Internationalizing courses, disciplines, and colleges requires major curricular reform efforts that often begin with top leadership integrating international education into every division within a university, starting with a presidential vision for a more internationalized university, and a mission statement signifying its purpose and accompanied by goals and the appropriate financial, operational, and human resources designed to allow the college, co-curricular units, and sub-units to achieve their goals.

Harari (1992) posed this problem statement to academic leaders and faculty: "With respect to the traditional curriculum itself, the number one problem is probably not *how* to internationalize it as much as it has been the neglect on the part of many institutions in engaging themselves in the process of examining systematically the options before them" (p. 59). Groennings (1990) related a similar problem statement—how institutions approach internationalization differently, in keeping with their mission and resources. "Many approaches have merit, but one element is fundamental: the contribution of the academic disciplines" (p. 27).

One of the challenges of this case study was to determine if there was a commitment to internationalization (at what level(s), by which stakeholder(s), by what approach(es), and with which component(s) in operation). The case study attempted to find and measure the pattern of progress for the University of Minnesota campus. Another important challenge was to discover the divisional directions and strategies for moving internationalization along the continuum (from total resistance to total integration). This led to an attitudinal assessment for launching internationalization as a university priority and to an outcome-based question: Are our college students receiving an international dimension within their disciplines before they graduate? For this particular campus, most internationalization of the student body will have to take place on-campus (both inside the classroom and in the co-curricular units), because so few students (2 percent of the total student body of 37,000) will complete a study abroad program or have an international experience of any kind during their college years. Thus, the palette of curricular options in the collegiate units and the programs offered by the co-curricular units play the major roles in affecting the world views of students during their college years on the University of Minnesota Twin Cities campus.

Tonkin and Edwards (1981) posed this question to college leaders: "If our society's problems have ceased to be locally and nationally based, and have become global, then don't we need a new internationalized curriculum to deal with these new imperatives?" Would this institution be called a leader or a follower in international education efforts? How much evidence exists that this particular university is international in terms of its programs and curriculum and attitudes and interest levels among the leadership of colleges and in central administration in directing the internationalization process?

There are many concerns expressed by internal stakeholders at the University of Minnesota Twin Cities Campus, including the following: Will this university become one of the top five public research universities in the nation? Will it be known internationally for its excellence in teaching, research, and outreach? In addition, will it follow in the steps of other universities that have made the commitment to launch an internationalized vision and have integrated international perspectives into their mission statements, strategic planning processes, institutional priorities, long-term goals, and college-specific strategies?

This chapter presents multiple perspectives and divisional leadership strategies on curricular change and internationalization components according to stakeholders at one university, but strategies to internationalize and lessons learned are meant to be shared with colleagues at other institutions.

RESEARCH PROCESS

A qualitative methodology was designed for this complex task; qualitative research is inductive, descriptive, and interpretive. It concerns itself with *process* (how internationalization is occurring, how curriculum is redesigned, and how organizational change takes place) and *meaning* (why certain disciplines within colleges take various approaches and why some units are so resistant to change). To underscore the complexity of internationalization, several conceptual variables were included in the investigation: the leadership component, strands (or elements) of internationalization presently operating within collegiate units, attitudes toward internationalization, resistance and counter-resistance factors, and recommendations by interviewees.

Context

The University of Minnesota was founded as a preparatory school in 1851, seven years before the territory of Minnesota became a state. Today, the Twin Cities Campus is one of the largest public, land-grant research universities in the United States with 19 colleges and professional schools; 2,828 faculty teaching in more than 250 fields of study; 1,167 executive, administrative, and managerial staff; 13,300 other staff members; and a student enrollment of 37,000 on this metropolitan campus. There are approximately 2,900 international students from 130 countries, plus an additional 1,000 visiting international faculty and scholars. Approximately 600 students register in accredited study abroad programs each year.

The five collegiate units intentionally selected for this case study were the College of Agricultural, Food, and Environmental Sciences; the College of Human Ecology; the College of Education and Human Development; the College of Liberal Arts; and the Curtis Carlson School of Management. These five divisions contained approximately 19,200 students (including 430 international students and 470 students who have studied abroad) and 1,104 faculty members working in 94 disciplines. The fieldwork for this case study took place during winter and spring 1996, when the university was undergoing curricular and systemic changes for the semester calendar curriculum conversion process, debating tenure reform, and beginning the presidential search process.

University of Minnesota personnel have used the term "global leaders" to describe many disciplines and the phrases "a world class university" and "an international center of knowledge" to promote the campus in various admissions brochures and bulletins. However, these phrases need sufficient evidence as proof of institutional validity, accuracy, and reliability of their claims.

Stakeholder Selection

Forty-two individual in-depth, semi-structured interviews took place over a five-month period on campus, after two pilot tests of interviews were conducted. Some stakeholders were selected to be interviewed because of their various responsibilities in leadership of their units. Certain administrators and international unit directors were contacted because of their titles and perceived knowledge of the international dimensions for the units that report directly to them. Deans and associate deans were called upon to learn about their leadership perspectives, personal visions, and future planning efforts for their collegiate units with respect to internationalization. Faculty members, however, were contacted by a modified reputational method from departments within the five colleges to achieve disciplinary variety across colleges. The breakdown of interviewees by title is as follows: 17 faculty members in 5 colleges, 5 college deans, 2 associate deans, 6 professional staff members and directors of international units serving the entire university, 6 professional staff members and directors with international responsibilities within the 5 colleges, and 6 central administrators (provosts, assistant provosts, vice presidents, and assistant vice presidents).

Research Questions

The two major research questions for this case study were as follows: (1) What evidence exists that internationalization is occurring across five colleges? and

(2) What strategies and recommendations for action do faculty members, deans, and professional staff members suggest to central administrators to internationalize the entire university in the future?

Conceptual Framework

The theoretical framework used to analyze findings came from reviewing four bodies of literature: curriculum, international education, organizational change, and intercultural competence. An adaptation of Keller's strategic planning dimensions and Davies's model in Klasek's (1992) strategies book were used to plot evidence of internationalization across six dimensions of organizational change for college leadership (vision, strategic planning, finance, programs, personnel, and evaluation). Bennett's Model of Intercultural Competence (1993) guided the process of assessing attitudes toward launching an internationalization strategy across a six-stage linear developmental scale, and Harari's (1992) structural approaches for internationalizing curriculum provided many avenues from which curriculum could be compared. After interviews were conducted, matrices were crafted to illustrate the findings by component or variable and by specific collegiate unit. Eight matrices and several charts were constructed to analyze and interpret the data from interviews and documents in an organized, at-a-glance visual format.

DESCRIPTION AND ANALYSIS OF MAJOR FINDINGS

The description and analysis of major findings based on both interview data and document analysis will be summarized in the following sections.

A Rationale for Internationalization

This first section of research results summarizes the rationale for internationalizing the University of Minnesota and individual colleges at the present time as the university makes plans for the future. Interviewees stated that campuswide internationalization would net three levels of benefits (university-wide, collegiate level, and individual).

University Benefits. Declaring internationalization as a priority at the present time would generate national and international recognition and attention. Some believe a university poised for internationalization would generate income from public relations and capital campaigns. Several internationalization components could be highlighted in strategic planning documents, university-wide goals, and speeches by administrators. An internationally focused curriculum would attract researchers, faculty, and students to the university; activating many of the present linkages with universities worldwide would create more avenues for both faculty and student international opportunities, including collaboration on joint research projects. Finally, interviewees reported that increasing university-wide attention to internationalization would encourage a more diverse student body and faculty membership valuing the contribution that international students, scholars, and visiting faculty bring to campus life.

College Benefits. The quality of teaching will be considerably broadened and deepened with the addition of cross-cultural, comparative, and international concentrations within disciplines as well as interdisciplinary thinking, team teaching, and intercollegiate collaboration with other disciplines. Curricular and co-curricular initiatives to internationalize college students may benefit the college years later as alumni advance in their respective careers well-prepared for a rapidly changing workforce that is becoming more internationally connected with advances in technology and the global extensions of many job descriptions. In addition, the competitiveness, academic standing, and reputation of individual colleges may net benefits due to collegewide internationalization of both curriculum and personnel.

Individual Benefits. Individual stakeholders, including administrators, faculty, staff, and students, would benefit from an intentionally internationalized campus. This increased awareness of world cultures and attention to the global perspectives of individual disciplines would represent a value-added dimension to the undergraduate curriculum and the professional/graduate school portfolio. Individuals may also receive an appreciation for the cultural diversity of the United States and an understanding of world cultures, an increased understanding of international issues, a greater emphasis on language learning and cross-cultural competence, and a broadening of world views.

Components of Internationalization

Among many important components or strands of internationalization to analyze for a large public research university are the following six: (1) college leadership; (2) faculty members' international involvement in activities with colleagues, research sites, and institutions worldwide; (3) the curriculum; (4) the availability, affordability, accessibility, and transferability of study abroad programs for students; (5) the presence and integration of international students, scholars, and visiting faculty into campus life; and (6) international co-curricular units (residence halls, conference planning centers, student unions, career centers, cultural immersion and language houses, student activities, student organizations). Internationalization can be painted broadly with a wide brush to include all six components or narrowly with a fine-tip pen to focus on one component in-depth. This case study focused on the curriculum but also discovered the other five components to be integral to fully understanding the process involved in internationalizing curriculum. One of the complexities of this case study was to discover which components were operational in which collegiate units and the reasons for the high degree of evidence in the components within some colleges and the low degree of evidence and numerous resistance found in others. The following components represent what could comprise an internationalized college or university, according to interviewees. These components are not evidence of findings at the University of Minnesota but offer a descriptive listing of what interviewees believed could constitute an internationalized university. They are listed in order of importance, according to interviewees.

Component #1: College Leadership. Evidence of college leadership would include:

- Declaration of internationalization as a priority for the college
- Commitment to internationalization by the dean and associate deans
- Discussion of internationalization by collegewide governance committees
- Evidence of a future vision for the college that includes making international education a priority (and various components of it relating to faculty, students, curriculum, programs, research, funding, linkages, alumni outreach, etc.)
- A mission statement emphasizing the importance of international education
- Strategic planning documents and budgets that include internationalization as a priority with goals, plans, projects, and measurable outcomes that underscore international elements
- Financial commitment from the college dean, vice president of academic affairs, president, and other leaders showing support for internationalization goals, projects, and efforts (including curricular change and faculty and student mobility)
- Collegewide integration of international education in degree programs, core course work, electives, and the availability, affordability, and transferability of study and research abroad experiences for students
- Collegewide initiatives to hire faculty with international interests or experience; to provide opportunities for faculty to do research, teaching, and study at partner universities or maintain college-to-college international linkages; to provide incentives for faculty to internationalize courses and majors; to reward faculty who have international teaching, study, and research experience in the promotion, salary, and tenure reward systems
- Commitment to do evaluations of international education initiatives

Component #2: Faculty Involvement in International Activities. Evidence of faculty involvement would include:

- A favorable attitude toward internationalization and a high degree of personal commitment toward making international education a priority in their own college
- The availability of international courses in every discipline, including internationalized units within core courses and a wide variation of international education elective courses
- A high level of faculty involvement in international research and consulting activities
- A connection with colleagues, organizations, and conferences in a wide variety of countries, including joint research projects, international organization membership, frequent communication in an informal or formal linkage with a foreign university
- A high percentage of faculty who travel abroad for scholarly purposes
- On-campus contact with international students, scholars, and visiting faculty members
- Faculty promotion of study abroad programs for their own advisees and students including being knowledgeable about the international resources of their home university and college

Component #3: An Internationalized Curriculum. Evidence of an internationalized curriculum would include:

- Making available international majors or minors or concentrations in each college or professional school
- Revising core courses in most majors to include international, comparative, or cross-cultural elements of the disciplines
- Creating elective courses and interdisciplinary intercollegiate courses open to all students on international topics, countries or regions, key issues, perspectives, or skills
- Urging discussions within faculty governance committees and individual departments concerning the need for international education in the undergraduate portfolio for the twenty-first century and also the requirements for graduate or professional degrees
- Intra-institutional resources concerning internationalizing curriculum, including Web sites with sample syllabi, faculty development seminars, faculty and teaching assistant orientation workshops
- Faculty reward systems for internationalization, travel grants for faculty travel, and promotion of internationalization of curricula upon return from an international teaching or research experience, and public discussion sessions for faculty upon re-entry to the home campus

Component #4: International Study Opportunities for Students. Evidence of international study opportunities for students would include:

- Study, travel, service, internship, research, or work abroad opportunities for undergraduate and graduate students
- Accessibility of scholarships and travel grants for students
- Availability, affordability, and transferability of study abroad programs in a wide variety of countries to complement course work already completed on-campus
- Study abroad pre-departure and re-entry intercultural communication sessions designed to assist U.S. students with their transition and to integrate international students

Component #5: Integration of International Students and Scholars. Evidence of integration of international students and scholars would include:

- Integration of international students and scholars into campus life, including classroom and extracurricular activities
- International student orientations and receptions for U.S. students and faculty to meet with international colleagues

Component #6: International Co-curricular Units and Activities. Evidence of internationalizing of co-curricular units and activities would include:

- International programming on-campus in cooperation with other collegiate and co-curricular units to include residence halls, student unions, international student organizations, international student service units, study abroad offices, and international travel centers
- Programming might include conferences, fairs, speakers, events, panels, and artistic, musical, and theatrical events of an international nature to broaden the world views of participants and to introduce them to cross-cultural perspectives without leaving campus
- Opportunities for student involvement in on-campus international clubs, activities, events, and organizations to meet other students interested in cross-cultural perspectives
- Co-curricular involvement may also include making internationalization one focus of career development centers, internship placement offices, alumni outreach, and admissions offices
- Greater visibility of study abroad and international student service offices with more public events, fairs, and receptions designed to introduce campus stakeholders to the many opportunities for involvement

Evidence of Internationalization in One College

I took into consideration all the components mentioned above as possible contributors toward internationalization for the five colleges in this case study. One of these colleges scored the highest in its internationalization components, in the lowest number of resistance factors, the highest overall in internationalization interest on a six-stage attitudinal scale, and evidence of intercollegiate cooperation with other colleges in its internationalization components (especially regarding the curriculum and degree programs). It is described below.

The College of Education and Human Development, founded in 1905, is now almost exclusively a graduate school of education after undergoing major organizational change and strategic planning efforts since 1992. It includes 6 departments, 25 research and service centers, 135 faculty members, and 3,300 full-time equivalent degree-seeking students. The internationalization of this particular college has been stimulated by the following factors: the college's active committee on international education; a collegewide international education coordinator; the involvement of many international graduate students and scholars in the college; a comparative and international development education (CIDE) graduate level concentration housed within the Educational Policy and Administration Department; international concentrations within four degree programs in the Work, Community, and Family Education department; international education elective courses held annually; a free-standing international education graduate minor; and high levels of faculty participation in international teaching and research opportunities. Evidence of internationalization in the College of Education and Human Development is listed below.

- *International Majors* such as the concentration within the Department of Educational Policy and Administration, known as the Comparative and International Development Education (CIDE) program, and the international concentration for four degree programs within the Department of Work, Community, and Family Education)
- *International Education Graduate Minor* as a freestanding, university-wide minor open to any graduate or professional student at the university
- *Internationalized Courses* and units within the College
- *International Education One-Credit/One-Month Special Courses* updated annually, concentrating on examining education-related international issues, focusing on specific countries or world regions, and practicing cross-cultural skills; these courses are open to any University of Minnesota student regardless of college of enrollment or graduate/undergraduate status

- *International Involvement among the Faculty* of the college, including ties with researchers in various countries; informal collaboration, communication, and networking with universities worldwide; participation at international conferences; membership in international organizations, boards of directors, and associations; and evidence of teaching, consulting, and research abroad
- *International Linkages with Universities* worldwide and partnerships with universities in many world regions, such as the Kenyatta University USIS grant pairing University of Minnesota faculty with faculty in Kenya
- *International Graduate Students and Scholars* (about 178 annually) who contribute to the college's international direction both within and outside of the classroom, including visiting junior faculty from Russia and other republics of the Commonwealth of Independent States
- *International Visitors* including rectors, chancellors, faculty, and fellows from overseas universities, directors of international organizations, and other administrative staff
- *International Education Committee,* which meets monthly and is collegewide
- *International Education Coordinator,* who coordinates the college's International Education Committee and who works to internationalize all departments and personnel within the college
- *International Education Events, Programs, and Activities,* including an annual reception for international students and scholars sponsored by the dean's office, an annual awards ceremony for recognizing outstanding international alumni of the College, and monthly informal presentations known as the International Pizza and Talk Series
- *Internationalization as a Recognized Criterion* for the semester conversion process (the only college on the Twin Cities campus to make it a priority)
- *Internationalization of the Curriculum Seminar* was a unique faculty/ graduate student course, held Spring Quarter 1996, which led to the production of 11 faculty papers presented at that seminar and to the circulation of these working papers university-wide for discussion among deans and administrators
- *Internationalization* as deemed important to the college by the present and former dean of the college and all six departmental chairs
- *International Education World Wide Web Site* that includes resource listings, survey reports, executive summaries, working papers, present and past course syllabi, minor and degree programs, and upcoming events <http://edpa.coled.umn.edu/IntEdu>.

Resistance Factors

This study's five colleges revealed much intra-institutional variation in terms of stakeholders' attitudes toward international education, evidence of internationalization components, and resistance factors that demonstrated deeply held feelings of resistance to make organizational and curricular changes to internationalize. Nine resistance factors (or sources of resistance to pursuing internationalization) were identified based on interviews with deans and associate deans, faculty, directors of international units, and central administrators. The following categories are based on interviewees' responses to the question: "To what do you attribute this resistance?"

Cognitive Component. Some faculty had not made the cognitive shift to internationalize their curriculum. Those who had international experiences had not connected them with their teaching, and ways of infusing their disciplines with international perspectives were unknown to them. Some are unaware of international opportunities; others are aware but remain focused on their disciplines and defend their purity from being diluted. The best way to persuade them to make the cognitive shift, according to interviewees, is to provide them with international experiences related to their teaching/research interests that are deeper and more culturally relevant than short travel seminars or conferences. Until an individual cognitive shift occurs, resistance will remain.

Incentive Ingredient. Many department chairs and leaders of departmental sub-units do not give their faculty incentives or encouragement to internationalize their courses and do not encourage them to apply for travel grants/fellowships to teach overseas, partake in international faculty development opportunities, or share their international experiences upon return home. There may not be departmental awareness of college-level international education committees or task forces. Deans revealed that some professors will not take part in international teaching and research activities or redesign their courses without incentives, encouragement, or financial assistance.

Financial Factor. Colleges are financially constrained and cannot offer their faculty members financial assistance that would enable them to go overseas for a meaningful period of time to do research, teach, or do consultation work. Some colleges have sufficient funding from large-scale and long-term projects for international activities (such as those funded by private foundations, federal grants, and other sources). Many faculty members in this case study would not go overseas to research, teach, or consult without considerable funding. A few administrators stated that faculty development is solely the responsibility of individual faculty and their departments, and will consequently not allocate any central funds to internationalize the faculty.

Institutional Dilemma. There are institutional roadblocks for junior untenured faculty who may want to go overseas to research, teach, or consult but have been restricted by their own departments' promotion and tenure codes and criteria for performance evaluation. This case revealed that 88 percent of deans/associate deans and 57 percent of faculty interviewed would favor changing the faculty reward system to include participation in international activities as a requirement for promotion and tenure along the professorial ladder. Only 40 percent of central administrators interviewed would change the faculty reward system to include international activities on the grounds that it is difficult to change the faculty promotion and tenure policy university-wide. Some untenured assistant professors admitted that some senior members of their own departments look down upon their participation in international activities. However, in a follow-up probing question to administrators, most agreed that participation in such activities should not be looked upon as negative or constraining, especially for junior faculty. In addition, the institutional dilemma is compounded by the fact that internationalization is not one of the major strategic planning priorities for the university, nor is it mentioned in the university (or most college-specific) mission statements, nor is it a criterion in the recruitment of new faculty.

Disciplinary Direction. Disciplinary walls are often high, hard to scale, and difficult to tear down to create bridges across disciplines in interdisciplinary courses, programs, team-teaching, and faculty collaboration. This is a commonly cited resistance factor operating within the university because many believe in the purity of their own discipline and in the solid specialization of single-disciplinary study to teach, research, and function in that field. To internationalize means, for some, to take out something valuable in the syllabus or reading list from the core content of one discipline, and some revealed that the amount of material is so great and the time limit so stretched that international perspectives could not possibly fit in with the way they currently teach their subjects. Many faculty revealed they believe their disciplines are United States-focused, and knowledge bases are largely constructed from a U.S. American point of view. However, contrary voices in many departments favor interdisciplinary approaches. Such attitudinal, intracollegiate splits were common to this university case study.

Public Perception Syndrome. International educators or multiple specialists may not be understood or accepted by their peers, whether they are in their own department, at other universities, on journal editorial boards, or in professional associations. Conducting research internationally, taking a group of students abroad, or teaching for a year in another university overseas may not be perceived favorably, particularly among administrators, who wonder who will teach those courses while that faculty member is away. Some view it as a luxury or an extra perk. Faculty who cannot be categorized neatly into one box may be viewed as "different." In short, participating in international activities does not always translate well back in one's tenure home.

Future Orientation Fear. There may not be a commitment and a connection between acquiring knowledge of more than one culture or language and preparing graduates to live and work in an increasingly interdependent and globally functioning workplace. Many resist internationalization, fear change, and are more content to be present-oriented and solidly grounded in their own discipline, which may be U.S.-centered. Future-oriented, high-technological changes such as distance learning or teleconferencing with students in other countries is also met with resistance. The future workplace will not center around *one* major, career field, vocation, or job; cultivating knowledge of many disciplines, fields, and ways of thinking will better prepare students for their future careers. Resistance to future orientation has paradoxically not been found as a factor for central administration, which has made some progress in this area by directly making technology a major university priority.

Collaboration Component. Faculty collaboration on joint international research projects often involves making interdisciplinary and intercultural connections. Evidence of resistance to collaborative teaching and research was found operating at the university. Some colleges have proven that multidisciplinary projects crossing international borders and disciplinary boundaries could produce good research experiences. Independent, individualized teaching and research still is the norm in many departments, and this university and others are not set up for this new paradigm. Most job descriptions are individualistic. Collaborations on projects, courses, research interests, and team leadership may be a future trend if faculty are internationally experienced and interculturally competent.

Graduate School Preparation Piece. Although some newly hired faculty members come onboard with international experience or interests, most interviewees stated their graduate school preparation did not adequately address international education. Some have not yet traveled outside the country and may resist cross-cultural or interdisciplinary teaching because it goes against the way they were educated and how they currently view their own profession. Some graduate programs recognize the need for their graduate students to acquire international experiences while they are degree-seeking students; others resist this idea and reserve "academic mobility" only for their undergraduates for short-term study abroad experiences.

Hiring new faculty with international interests or evidence of international activities was supported by 76 percent of faculty interviewed, as compared with 71 percent of deans and associate deans and 80 percent of central administrators. Many believe that new faculty should bring international interests or experience with them upon arrival and that job postings for faculty positions should clearly publicize that. Some deans already include that question on their interview guide during the interview process for new professorial candidates. Some administrators believe it is harder to change a promotion and tenure policy to include international activities for faculty already onboard than it is to create a new policy for hiring new faculty.

Plotting Resistance Factors by College

The following three resistance factors were apparent for all five colleges: financial factor, institutional dilemma, and disciplinary direction. The College of Education and Human Development had the fewest resistance factors with three; the College of Liberal Arts had the most with nine. Each of these factors represents a valid category of obstacles that certain stakeholders said they are confronted with when they try to internationalize their own college.

Measuring Attitudes Toward Internationalization

I classified five colleges of the University of Minnesota along six "stages of international development," an adaptation of Bennett's Developmental Model of Intercultural Competence moving from ethnocentrism to ethnorelativism on a linear spectrum (Bennett, 1993). These six attitudinal stages were designed to assess individual colleges' readiness toward launching an internationalization of the curriculum effort.

- *Stage Six: Total Integration of Internationalization in the Curriculum*
- *Stage Five: Adaptation of Vision/Strategies* (College of Education and Human Development scores here; all International Co-curricular Offices such as international student services, study abroad offices, international education administration also reside here)
- *Stage Four: General Acceptance; Minor Obstacles* (College of Agricultural, Food, and Environmental Sciences and Carlson School of Management score here)
- *Between stages 4 and 3 is a Dividing Line known as the Great Divide Between Attitudes of Curricular and Systemic Change* (Three colleges scored above the line; two colleges plus central administration scored below the line).
- *Stage Three: Minimal Interest/Awareness; Major Obstacles* (Central Administration, College of Liberal Arts, and College of Human Ecology all score here)
- *Stage Two: Total Resistance to Change and International Thinking* (Some faculty are here; pockets of resistance exist within departments and colleges)
- *Stage One: Indifference to Matters International* (Deeper pockets of resistance within departments are present here; some interviewees put some colleagues in this passive and unaware stage)

This overall attitudinal assessment is based upon analyzing interview data and assessing strategic planning documents. It reflects the place where interviewees believe most people's attitudes toward internationalization presently stand. The College of Education and Human Development ranked in the fifth stage, called "adaptation of vision and strategies," for internationalization based on a combination of factors, including faculty interest, international committee accomplishments, college leadership, and evidence of internationalization in course work, research projects, and personnel in the college, including a high number of international graduate students, scholars, and visiting faculty.

The University of Minnesota Twin Cities Campus overall scores in stage three "minimal interest and awareness with major obstacles" concerning university-wide internationalization considering all variables, stakeholders, colleges, and data in this case. (This assessment shows the university system is minimally interested in internationalization but faces major obstacles in making further progress because of the high numbers of resistance factors, lack of interest on the part of central administrators for making it a key strategic planning priority for the overall university, and the absence of an internationalized mission statement and goals). This assessment also shows the university is a follower in international education efforts proposed by a few deans and faculty.

Encouragement Factors

Some interviewees focused more on "encouragement" than "resistance" factors and made recommendations for their college's internationalization process. These counter-resistance factors serve to encourage others to consider making the organizational changes necessary to internationalize the entire University of Minnesota. Encouragement factors include the following:

- Consideration of the student educational process and curricular portfolio
- Recollection of the goal to become one of the top five public research universities in the U.S.
- Preparation for a future workforce that is increasingly internationally connected
- Collaboration with curricular changes already underway with the semester conversion curricular change process
- Recognition of what many collegiate units are already doing in their international education strategies and goals

In addition, interviewees suggested the following six specific ways of overcoming resistance to the internationalization process and organizational change:

- **Promote Faculty International Involvement.** Give faculty members in-depth, cross-cultural experiences so they can teach, research, consult, or do other work related to their interests.
- **Highlight Educational Exchanges.** Strengthen existing and start additional international educational exchanges and cross-cultural opportunities for faculty and students so that the campus becomes more integrated with international personnel.
- **Focus on Fund Raising.** Focus the next capital campaign on the internationalization process for the entire university.
- **Provide Intercultural Encounters for Administrators.** Provide international opportunities for central administrators, deans, and professional staff to visit some of the international research project sites and partnerships with universities worldwide.
- **Gather Student Input.** Involve students in the internationalization process by measuring student demand for international courses, majors, languages, and study abroad programs that may direct a college to initiate programs that coincide with faculty interests in interdisciplinary, issue-oriented, or topical courses.
- **Begin a Campuswide Discussion.** A dialogue with multiple stakeholders may provide more suggestions to campus leaders concerning internationalizing the university, which includes communicating a vision for internationalization and writing a mission statement and strategic planning documents with measurable goals. Faculty and deans could encourage an open discourse of the components of internationalization and discuss the resistance factors holding back colleges from achieving their goals. Deans could ask each unit to make recommendations to eliminate those barriers.

Differing Strategies to Internationalize One University

The approaches to internationalization differ by college and within colleges for many reasons, especially when resistance and encouragement factors are taken into consideration and compared. This case study revealed stakeholders' differences of opinion, varying agendas, and conflicts of interests. Administrators overall were much less interested in initiating, developing, or creating university-wide internationalization than were faculty, deans, and directors of international units; the latter three groups demonstrated far more acceptance of, interest in, and support for internationalization.

This case study did not provide much evidence of "a world class university" in terms of financial support, strategic planning, or leadership. The study also demonstrated that collegiate units differed in their listing of components of internationalization. Some found internationalizing the disciplines to be most important at the present time; others found that providing incentives for their own faculty to do more international research and consulting would benefit students down the road; still others had interests in many internationalization components but lacked a strategy to direct them, to find leadership for them, or sponsorship in terms of strategic planning and budgeting for them.

This study found intra-collegiate and inter-collegiate differences as well as several other important findings concerning the reasons why components, attitudes, and resistance factors vary so widely within and across college units. The descriptions that follow attempt to explain why there are such divergent approaches to internationalization within one university.

Intra-collegiate Differences

These differences occurred within colleges.

- Evidence of intra-departmental attitudinal splits, including a lack of understanding or misinterpretation of what international education is and why some faculty are engaged and others are not and why some departments have people at both ends of the ethnorelativism, ethnocentrism attitudinal scale
- A high degree of intracollegiate variation because of a wide spectrum of individual attitudes towards internationalization
- A wide variation in intracollegiate acceptance because of the international awareness of some departments (complete with positive attitudes toward internationalization and the presence of multiple components of internationalization) and the lack of knowledge about international perspectives in other departments (without much incentive to integrate an international approach to teaching)
- The presence of one international education champion or several persuasive leaders in some departments coupled with their ability to motivate and persuade others to support internationalization efforts
- Where disciplinary purity is the greatest, interdisciplinary cooperation and comparative, global, and cross-cultural perspectives are lacking the most in the curriculum, and those disciplinary walls seem the hardest to scale (i.e., physical sciences, journalism, psychology)
- Evidence suggests that some departments that have most or all the internationalization components can attribute their success to supportive departmental leadership and knowledgeable faculty who have international experience

Inter-collegiate Differences

These differences occurred among colleges.

- The nature of the disciplines in each college or professional school helps explain disciplinary directions, intracollegiate and intradisciplinary attitudinal splits, and the cognitive component
- The composition of stakeholders' attitudes toward internationalization by college
- The presence of an internationalized mission statement or declaration of it as a top college strategic priority by the dean and associate dean
- The inclusion of "international education" in speeches and in collegewide documents, catalogues, and bulletins
- A genuine interest in internationalization backed up by resources to achieve its goals from the dean and associate deans
- The ability of key stakeholders to guide the strategic planning process in each college or professional school
- Faculty socialization within some disciplines toward their disciplines and variation in the public perception resistance factor concerning participation in international activities
- Degree of receptivity for internationalization in administrative organizational lines, committee composition, and reporting structures
- Institutional constraints university-wide seen as influencing individual colleges' abilities to initiate international education efforts independently in a decentralized structure with the presence or absence of international education committees
- Initiatives and incentives by departmental chairpersons for faculty to internationalize their courses
- Degree of interdisciplinary collaboration in teaching, research, outreach, conference attendance, and international travel among faculty colleagues within the same college
- Presence of a champion for international education initiatives and strategic planning within the college

Other Major Findings

Some of the other major findings of this case study included the following:

- Effective organizational communication is viewed as essential among all groups of stakeholders interviewed for the internationalization strategic planning process (both university system-wide and within individual colleges).

- Central administrators are much more resistant to internationalizing the university, to making any new strategic planning priority, and to taking measures to strengthen components of internationalization, than faculty, directors, and deans. Thus, campus internationalization is observable, operational, and evident at the college dean's level. The international ribbon starts in the dean's offices of some colleges or in department channels and moves throughout college units, but does not commence with top administrative leadership for the University of Minnesota.
- Most of the international, comparative, or cross-cultural courses are electives, not required courses within the disciplines. However, concentrations within majors exist in international agriculture, international business, international education, international work, community, family education, and international relations.

The most commonly stated structural approaches for internationalizing disciplines were offering a few international electives, showing evidence of international issue discussions within course units, and using comparative approaches within a discipline.

- Only one of the 19 colleges on the campus has made internationalization a criterion for the semester conversion process (the College of Education and Human Development).
- Three of the five colleges in this case study have written "internationalization" goals in their strategic planning documents (Carlson School of Management; the College of Agricultural, Food, and Environmental Sciences; and the College of Education and Human Development).

APPLICATION AND SYNTHESIS WITH REPORTS AND RESEARCHERS

The ACE Report: Ten Ground Rules for Campus Internationalization

A nationally circulating report published by the American Council on Education (ACE) in 1995 entitled *Educating Americans for a World in Flux* called for a new higher education agenda. The 10 ground rules for internationalizing institutions were written by 40 college and university presidents and define the leadership tasks ahead.

1. Requiring that all graduates demonstrate competence in at least one foreign language
2. Encouraging an understanding of at least one culture

3. Increasing understanding of global systems
4. Revamping curricula to reflect the need for international understanding
5. Expanding international study and internship opportunities for all students
6. Focusing on faculty development and rewards
7. Examining the organizational needs of international education
8. Building consortia to enhance capabilities
9. Cooperating with institutions in other countries
10. Working with local schools and communities.

Central administrators at the University of Minnesota would probably agree that the current curricular portfolio falls short of meeting these 10 ground rules. I found that rule 6, focusing on faculty development and rewards, has much support among interviewees. Many interviewees want to look more positively upon international activities when considering faculty members for promotion and tenure. Some central administrators and two deans are working hard with rule 9, cooperating with institutions in other countries, because partnerships and networks with other institutions present possibilities for educational exchanges and academic mobility for both faculty and students.

Some faculty members individually acknowledged they work on rules 1 (foreign language competence), 2 (understanding of another culture), 3 (understanding of global systems), and 10 (working with local schools and communities) within their classrooms; staff members in several study abroad units work to enhance the international programming opportunities mentioned in rule 5 (expanding international study/internship programs). However, there is not much evidence of faculty agreement on how to accomplish rules 1, 2, and 3 because there has not been a campuswide discussion of how to do these completely and adequately, if competence is indeed the goal. Rules 4 (revamping curricula to reflect the need for international understanding), 7 (examining the organizational needs of international education), and 8 (building consortia to enhance capabilities) are not stated in the central administration's documents or in the task force reports; these rules would require committed faculty committees or a central administrator's directive. However, there is intra-institutional variation on these three. Some evidence exists within colleges concerning working on the organizational needs of international education, redesigning curricula to reflect the need for international understanding, and building consortia with other institutions; these three efforts have generated discussion among international education committees within some colleges and also by some deans in drafting strategic planning documents.

The first five ground rules in the ACE report would directly affect the curriculum; rules 6 through 10 require not only college-level and co-curricular unit cooperation but also top-level, highly committed administrative leadership. In the ACE report, the term "intercultural competence" is inserted as a goal that must be infused with the educational experience. "Without international competence, the nation's standard of living is threatened and its competitive difficulties will increase. Unless today's students develop the competence to function effectively in a global environment, they are unlikely to succeed in the twenty-first century" (American Council on Education, 1995, p. 1).

The presidents who drafted the ACE report stressed student learning outcomes. They believe the U.S. should be producing more knowledgeable graduates who not only know something about the international components of their disciplines, but also have the ability to communicate in at least one other language and have exposure to other peoples, languages, and cultures to understand global systems. They believe in making systemic and curricular changes and revamping curricula to reflect the need for international understanding. They believe that this level of competence (in languages, diverse cultures, and global issues) needs to be provided "not as something extra in the curriculum, but as an integral part of the educational experience" (American Council on Education, 1995, p. 5).

Advice from Other Researchers

Those presidents would concur with Harari (1992) who wrote: "When we refer to the internationalization of liberal education, we are not talking about an additive" (p. 59). Knight (1997) reiterates this point in an article on stakeholders' perspectives on internationalization of higher education in Canada. Though stakeholders attach different meanings and orientations to the concept, Knight's survey found unanimous agreement among three sectors (government, education, and private business) that "the number one reason to internationalize is to prepare graduates who are internationally knowledgeable and interculturally competent" (p. 38). Thus, the sentiment expressed in the literature of the mid-1990s calls on American higher education institutions to organize themselves multidimensionally to produce globally competent citizens.

Tonkin and Edwards (1981) relate two goals for internationalizing curriculum: one emphasizes the quality of the curriculum ("infusing the entire undergraduate curriculum with a sense of the international and global") while the other stresses quantity ("increasing the numbers of programs, courses, and opportunities for the study of international and global affairs") (p.6).

Kanet (1996) explains that "the most obvious way to clarify the goal of internationalization is to describe the expected impact on a college or university of a successful process of globalization: (1) The University will be well placed in an elite community of international universities and research centers; and (2) An expanded commitment to international understanding, awareness, and knowledge will be built into the core of university life and learning" (p. 61).

RECOMMENDATIONS FOR FUTURE CAMPUSWIDE INTERNATIONALIZATION EFFORTS

Interviewees suggested over 140 recommendations for collegiate and university-wide internationalization future planning efforts. Many of these fall into individual, collegiate unit, or systemwide levels of recommendations. Some were specific resource, program, or personnel suggestions; others were more general organizational change efforts. Similarities among almost all interviewees included (1) changing the direction of the university and making international education a stated priority, (2) making faster headway towards internationalization of the curriculum, and (3) encouraging top administrators to become more cognizant of the work being accomplished in departmental and collegiate units. For some colleges, the leadership driving internationalization is coming from deans' offices; for others, it is being led by key faculty members, an international education champion, or a strong international education committee. Recommendations were made by interviewees to the following stakeholders: central administrators, deans and associate deans, directors of international units, faculty members, and professional and administrative staff in collegiate units.

Key Issues for Discussion

During the recommendation part of the interviews, several key issues for discussion arose. The following seven avenues for discussion and possible action are stated for the purpose of supporting a university-wide internationalization agenda; these items were synthesized from interview data after all interviews were completed.

- The role of college and university leaders
- The faculty role in curricular change efforts
- An evaluation of the undergraduate students' curricular portfolio
- An evaluation of the professional and graduate students' curricular portfolio
- The contribution of international students, scholars, and visiting faculty to campus life
- The purpose of planning internationally focused campuswide events, programs, and conferences by co-curricular units

- The availability, affordability, accessibility, and transferability of study abroad programs for students
- The role of internationalization in the campus portrait

Transferable Lessons

Below are some of the potentially transferable "lessons learned" that this case study offers leaders on other campuses.

- Communicate clearly to all units and all stakeholders what internationalization components the university will focus toward, how it will proceed, and what this new priority will mean for the university
- Ask department chairs what resistance factors exist in their units and what it would take to remove those obstacles
- Look for encouragement factors within departments and colleges
- Find stakeholders who are already somewhat interested in building an international education agenda
- Give resistant administrators, deans, and faculty cross-cultural, international experiences related to their interests
- Collaborate through an already existing committee or form an international education committee for each college
- Work with existing international education consortia and linkages with other institutions
- Ask one successful department (or college) to describe how the process of internationalizing curriculum, faculty, and students is taking place and how it results in the college playing such a central role

Recommendations for Central Administrators, Deans, and Faculty

This case study included recommendations made for each of the five colleges plus suggestions for six groups of stakeholders: (central administrators, deans, faculty, the governor and state legislature, employers, and alumni and residents of the state). Some of the most commonly stated recommendations for central administrators are summarized below:

- Communicate the university's international vision to collegiate units to allow deans, department chairs, and faculty to understand where top administrators see international education fitting into the campus portrait
- Write a mission statement including international education, and talk about international education in speeches to various audiences

- Be aware and supportive of faculty initiatives that promote internationalization, including revising the promotion and tenure reward system
- Understand collegiate units' needs to keep strategic planning decentralized and specialized for their particular unit, but also be aware that colleges cannot be expected to attain all internationalization goals without financial resources from central administrators for specific purposes
- Make internationalization a top administrative agenda item for discussion among vice presidents, deans, provosts, and other top administrators

Recommendations for deans included the following:

- Meet with members of the corporate community, alumni, and other external stakeholders to raise awareness of international education, to secure funding for its goals, and to generate support
- Favor multidisciplinarity and intercollegiate cooperation
- Understand the needs, attitudes, opportunities, and obstacles among the faculty
- Become creative and entrepreneurial in launching international goals and raising financial support for them
- Memorize the international evidence (or components of internationalization) within one's own college, and reiterate this in speeches to highlight international opportunities for many different audiences
- Lead a discussion with faculty members concerning the kind of curricular portfolio the college presently has, and do a needs assessment among faculty and students on integrating international, comparative, and cross-cultural perspectives into the curriculum
- Understand the demographics of the student body, including the diverse array of degree programs and their individual needs
- Work on ways of removing the obstacles (resistance factors)
- Be proactive in rewarding faculty for their international activities (through the promotion and tenure system), and support changing the faculty reward system to include international activities as a new criterion for being promoted to full professor

Recommendations for faculty included the following:

- Start with the faculty within individual departments, and discuss internationalization of curriculum and personnel as a possibility at the individual (course), departmental, and collegiate levels
- Help faculty colleagues overcome resistance factors

- Give faculty colleagues some examples of internationalized course units and syllabi
- Recommend that faculty search committees ask questions of prospective candidates about their past international experiences and present international interests
- Communicate to students the importance of gaining an international perspective through course work, study abroad, and intercultural contact with students on-campus and through other means

Eleven Frequently Voiced Recommendations for Enhancing the University of Minnesota's Internationalization Agenda

1. Write a mission statement for internationalization, and clearly communicate it throughout the university
2. Create more undergraduate scholarships for qualified students to study abroad
3. Create faculty fellowships and travel grants for faculty involvement in international activities
4. Allow deans to make funding decisions concerning collegiate internationalization (curriculum, faculty mobility, and student study abroad)
5. Make international teaching, research, consulting, and other activities count in the faculty reward system
6. Favor hiring new faculty members who come on board with a present interest in international education or past experience in international activities
7. Encourage the university foundation to launch the next capital campaign for internationalization of the university
8. Make internationalization a new strategic planning and budgeting priority
9. Encourage more research and study abroad at the graduate and professional student level
10. Communicate with all college units the importance that curricular change opportunities (such as semester calendar conversion) have on internationalizing curriculum
11. Create more networks, linkages, and partnerships with international universities so faculty and students can participate and collaborate as part of a longer term relationship

CONCLUSION

Before concluding this case study, I must list several "next steps" that might comprise a future research agenda. How does a top priority (i.e., to internationalize a college) get communicated throughout a college's complex organizational communication structure to all relevant primary and secondary stake-holders? What role will a mobilized faculty play in convincing a neutral, complacent, or totally resistant central administration to move forward with international education? Is there a significant student demand for an interna-tionalized curriculum and campus?

This case study underscores the complexity of this topic and the varying interests of multiple stakeholders and individual college cultures. It also raises awareness of the consequences of not internationalizing a campus. We face many challenges as we think about internationalization and organizational change at the higher education level. The first challenge is recognizing that the world we live in is becoming increasingly international, and higher educa-tion must respond to that complexity as it prepares graduates to live and work in a global village increasingly connected through communication networks, interpersonal interactions, and global careers. The second challenge is the necessity to individually make a cognitive shift and move beyond the borders and boundaries of disciplines, campuses, states, and nations to educate stu-dents more fully. The third challenge asks administrators to think about some of the recommendations creatively crafted by a wide spectrum of interested and concerned stakeholders. International education above all needs an informed discourse about this complex undertaking, and these recommended strategies could prove to be the launching pad for a campuswide discussion of a major issue.

If faculty and administrators can work together and become proactive to include many components of internationalization in college and university-wide visions and strategies and provide the financial, physical, operational, and human resources to enable colleges to implement their own strategic plans, then those institutions will be much better prepared to meet the demands and challenges of their students. Universities and colleges will be launched into the arena with other internationally focused universities that have met the challenge to prepare their students for the global marketplace as future leaders and twenty-first century globally minded citizens if they incor-porate internationalization into their vision statements, strategic plans, and budgeting cycles.

This study has revealed many reasons to promote international education on a systemwide scale at the University of Minnesota. There is ample evidence of international resourcefulness among faculty members, and there are many programs and linkages in operation that provide cross-cultural experiences. There are examples of international courses in the various college units, although the "international" depth and breadth varies among required and elective courses (as does the approach to, definition of, and components within internationalization). The University of Minnesota lacks a compre-hensive curricular and systemic policy for internationalization as well as a coordinated effort to communicate the importance of internationalization, and some colleges within it lack international visions, mission statements, and strategies. Many of the faculty within these units are unaware of what these internationalization strategies are, which reiterates the need for more effective organizational, internal communication from deans' offices.

The task of threading and weaving a colorful international ribbon throughout the curriculum of all collegiate units still remains. That ribbon could be a well-defined mission statement on international education; it could be an additional priority in the university's strategic plans. Most interviewees in this case had not been motivated by any leadership-driven mission to internationalize, so this ribbon could purposefully be the communication link between central administrators and other college units. It could also signal to many stakeholders that leaders intend to go forward with a vision for internationalizing the University of Minnesota in the twenty-first century, complete with goals, strategies, tactics, and resources that could make the university one of the top five public research universities in the nation.

The task of painting the internationalized campus portrait for the University of Minnesota waits for the appropriate artist, a palette of colors, the correct canvas, proper tools and brushes, adequate light and resources, and just the right amount of artistic inspiration.

REFERENCES

American Council on Education. (1995). *Educating Americans for a world in flux: Ten ground rules for internationalizing higher education.* Washington, DC: ACE. (Booklet).

Association of International Education Administrators. (1995). *Guidelines for international education at U.S. colleges and universities.* Pullman, WA: Washington State University, AIEA Secretariat Office.

Association of International Education Administrators. (1995). *A research agenda for the internationalization of higher education in the United States.* Pullman, WA: Washington State University, AIEA Secretariat Office.

Bennett, M.J. (1993). Towards ethnorelativism: A developmental model of intercultural sensitivity. In R.M. Paige (Ed.), *Education for the intercultural experience* (pp. 21-71). 2nd ed. Yarmouth, ME: Intercultural Press.

Birnbaum, R. (1988). *How colleges work.* San Francisco: Jossey-Bass.

Council for International Educational Exchange. (1988). *Educating for global competence.* New York: CIEE Office.

Ellingboe, B.J. (1996). *Divisional strategies on internationalizing curriculum: A comparative five-college case study of deans' and faculty perspectives at the University of Minnesota.* Unpublished Master's thesis, University of Minnesota. (Available in the University of Minnesota Library System, or contact the author via e-mail at elli0049@tc.umn.edu or BEllingboe@aol.com for a copy of the M.A. Thesis (June 1996). The shorter Working Paper (January 1997) is available at http://edpa.coled.umn.edu/IntEdu/workpaper/coverpage.html.

Groennings, S. (1990). Higher education, international education, and the academic disciplines. In S. Groennings and D. S. Wiley, *Group portrait: Internationalizing the disciplines* (pp. 11-31). New York: The American Forum.

Groennings, S. and Wiley, D.S. (1990). *Group portrait: Internationalizing the disciplines.* New York: The American Forum.

Harari, M. (1992). Internationalization of the curriculum. In C.B. Klasek (Ed.), *Bridges to the future: Strategies for internationalizing higher education,* (pp. 52-79). Pullman, WA: Association of International Education Administrators Secretariat.

Kanet, R.E. (1996, Spring). Internationalization, constrained budgets, and the role of international education consortia. *International Education Forum.* Pullman, WA: Association of International Education Administrators, 16(1), 59-70.

Klasek, C.B. (Ed.). (1992). *Bridges to the future: Strategies for internationalizing higher education.* Pullman, WA: Association of International Education Administrators Secretariat.

Knight, J. (1997). A shared vision? Stakeholders' perspectives on the internationalization of higher education in Canada. *Journal of Studies in International Education,* 1(1), 27-44. New York: Council on International Educational Exchange.

President's Commission on Foreign Languages and International Studies, J.A. Perkins (chairman) (1979). *Strength through wisdom: A critique of U.S. capability.* Washington, DC: U.S. Government Printing Office.

Tonkin, H. and Edwards, J. (1981). *The world in the curriculum: Curricular strategies for the twenty-first century.* New Rochelle, NY: Council on Learning.

INDEX

by Linda Webster